ALSO BY MARJANE SATRAPI

*Persepolis: The Story of a Childhood*
*Persepolis 2: The Story of a Return*

# EMBROIDERIES

# Embroideries

**MARJANE SATRAPI**

PANTHEON BOOKS, NEW YORK

L'Assoc<iation

Pantheon Books and colophon are registered
trademarks of Random House, Inc.

Library of Congress Cataloging-in-Publication Data
Satrapi, Marjane, [date]
Embroideries / Marjane Satrapi.
    p.  cm.
ISBN 0-375-71467-7
I. Title.
PN6747.S245E42 2005    741.5'944–dc22    2004058660

www.pantheonbooks.com
Printed in the United States of America
First American Paperback Edition
11th Printing

# EMBROIDERIES

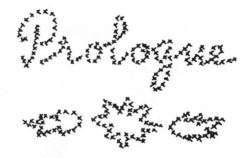

Prologue

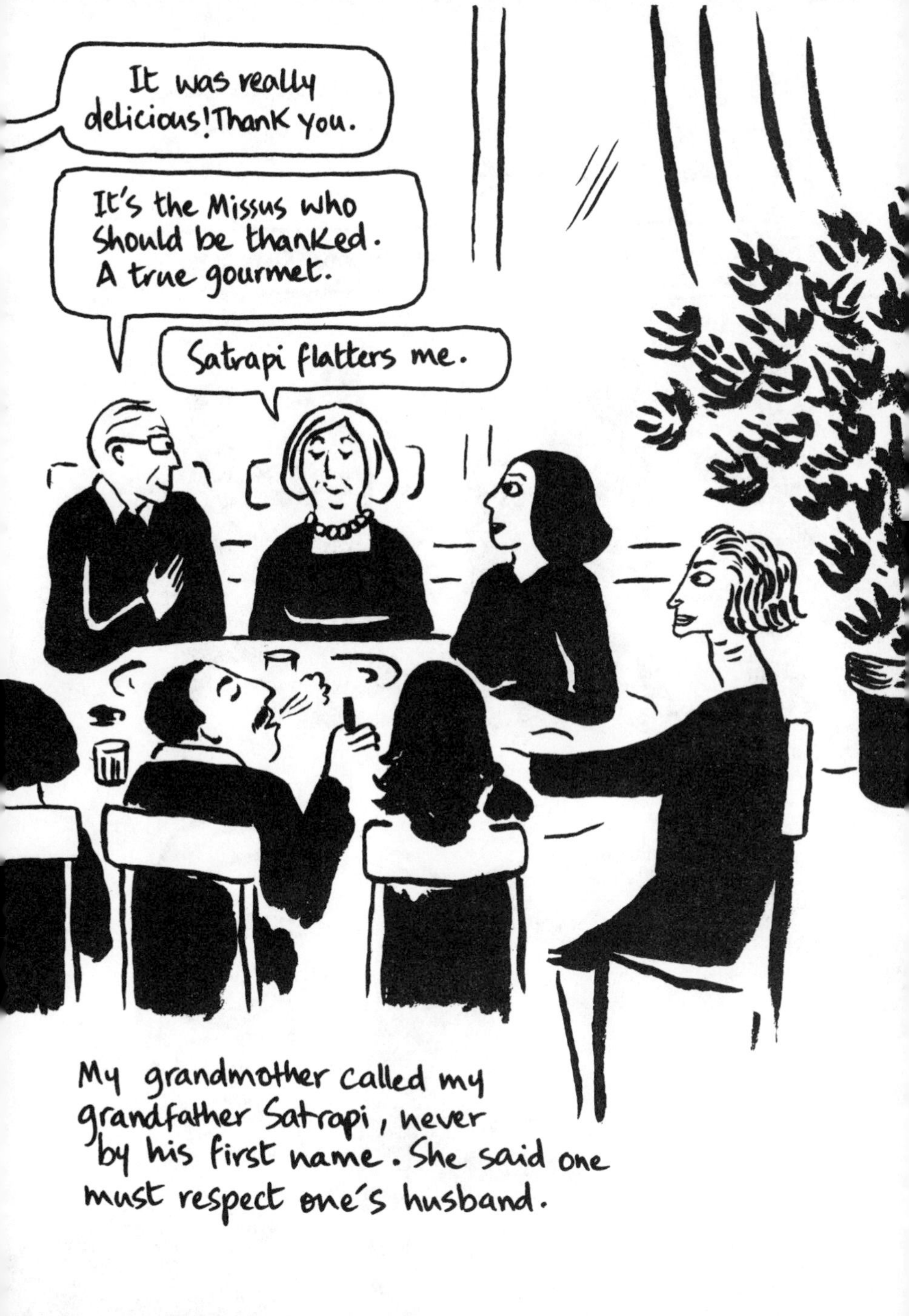
It was really delicious! Thank you.
It's the Missus who should be thanked. A true gourmet.
Satrapi flatters me.
My grandmother called my grandfather Satrapi, never by his first name. She said one must respect one's husband.

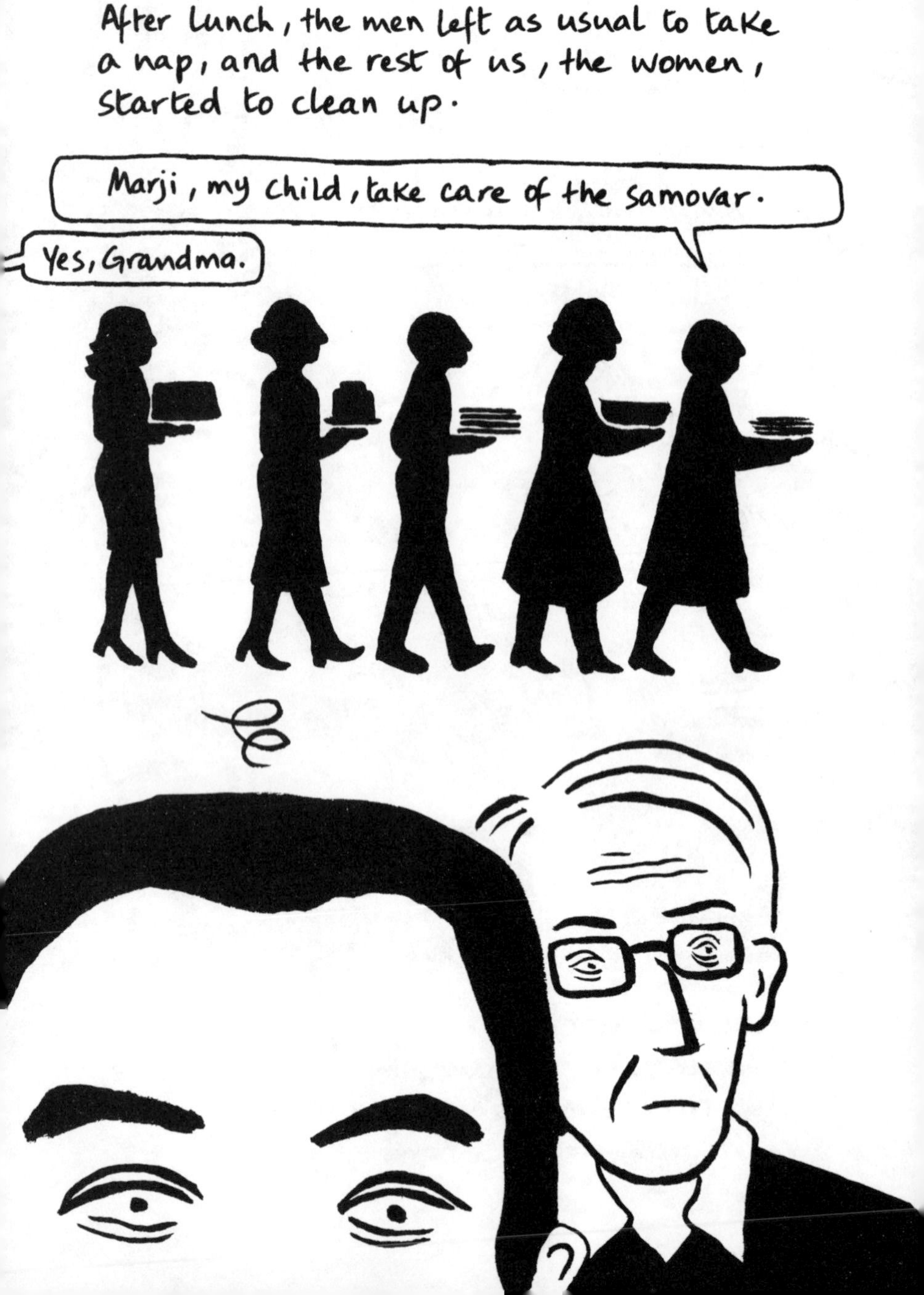
After lunch, the men left as usual to take a nap, and the rest of us, the women, started to clean up.
Marji, my child, take care of the samovar.
Yes, Grandma.

The samovar was my responsibility. I took care of it morning, noon and night. It must be said that the morning samovar didn't play exactly the same role as at other times of the day.

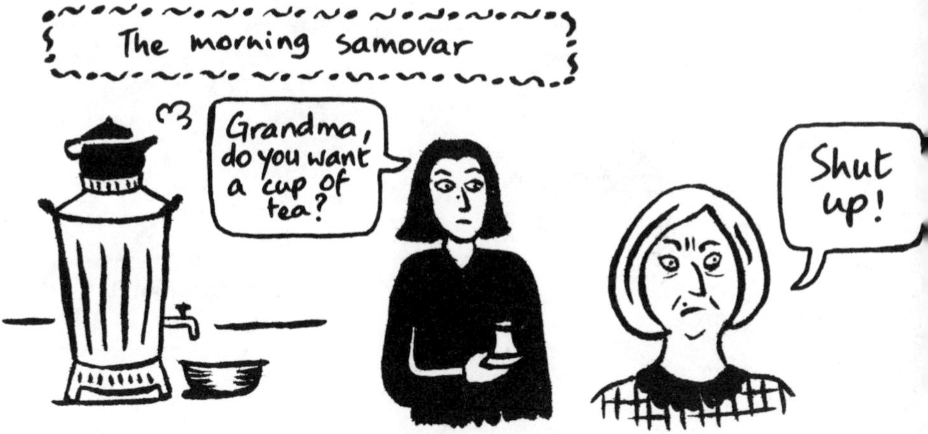
The morning samovar
Grandma, do you want a cup of tea?
Shut up!

My grandma was an opium addict. The doctor had told her to take it to lessen her pain (in any case, that's what she said). And so, on waking up and finding herself in a state of withdrawal, she was often in a very very bad mood, but it never lasted for long. She had only to dissolve a small bit of burnt opium* in her tea to regain her sense of humor and her natural kindness. It was just a matter of waiting.

---

* What is left at the bottom of an opium pipe after it's been smoked.

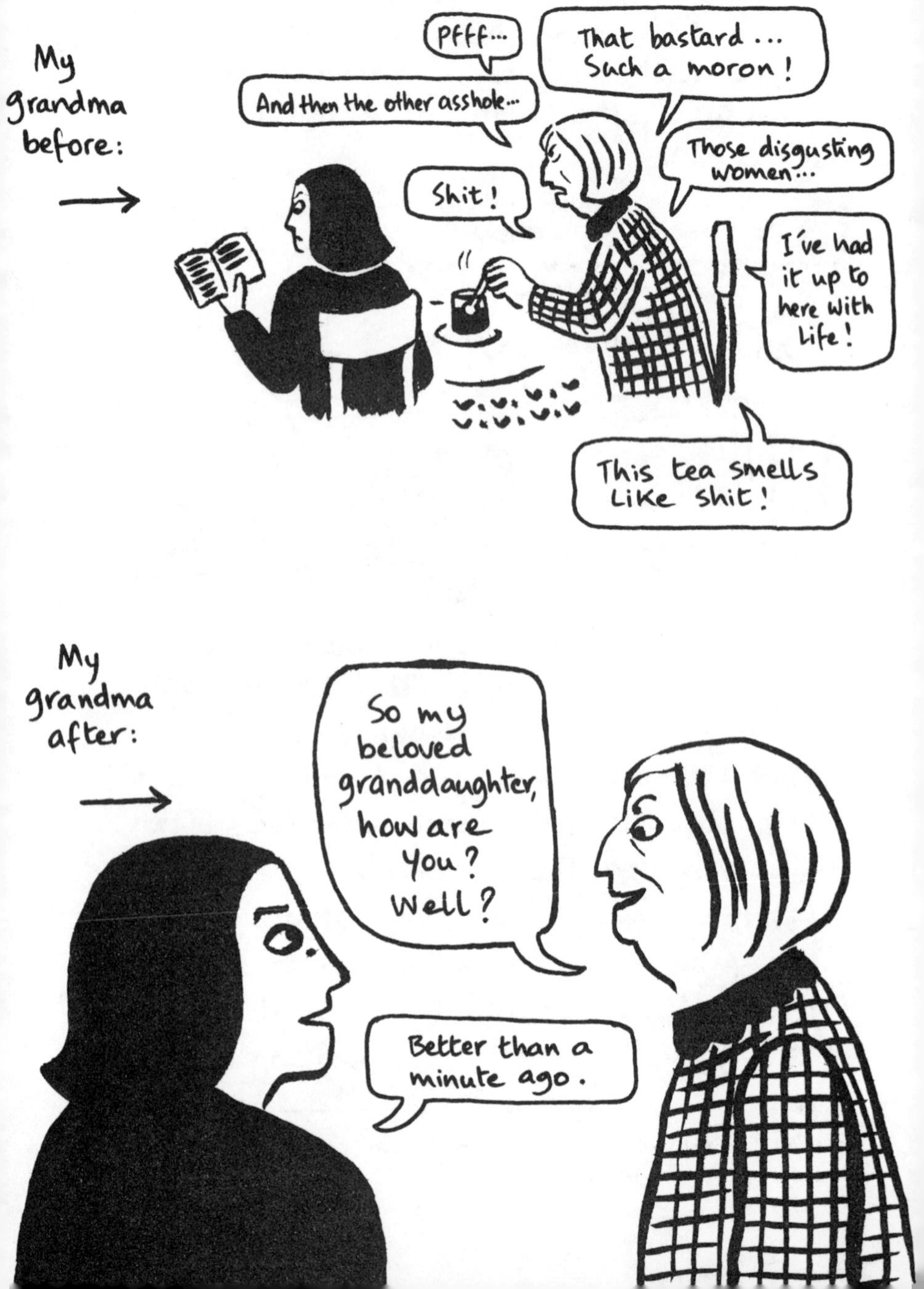

My grandma before:
And then the other asshole...
Pfff...
That bastard... Such a moron!
Shit!
Those disgusting women...
I've had it up to here with life!
This tea smells like shit!
My grandma after:
So my beloved granddaughter, how are you? Well?
Better than a minute ago.

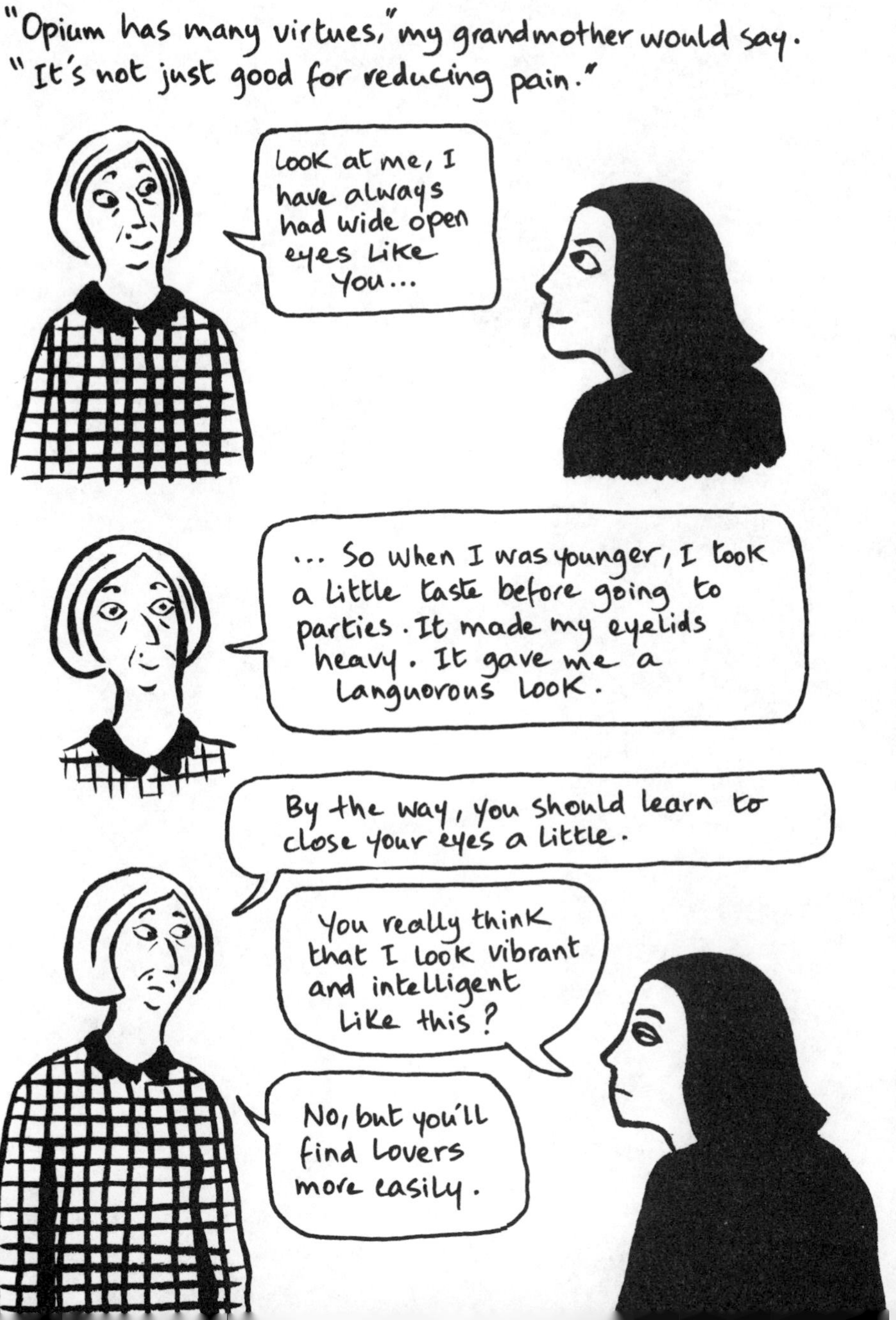
"Opium has many virtues," my grandmother would say. "It's not just good for reducing pain."
Look at me, I have always had wide open eyes like you...
... So when I was younger, I took a little taste before going to parties. It made my eyelids heavy. It gave me a languorous look.
By the way, you should learn to close your eyes a little.
You really think that I look vibrant and intelligent like this?
No, but you'll find lovers more easily.

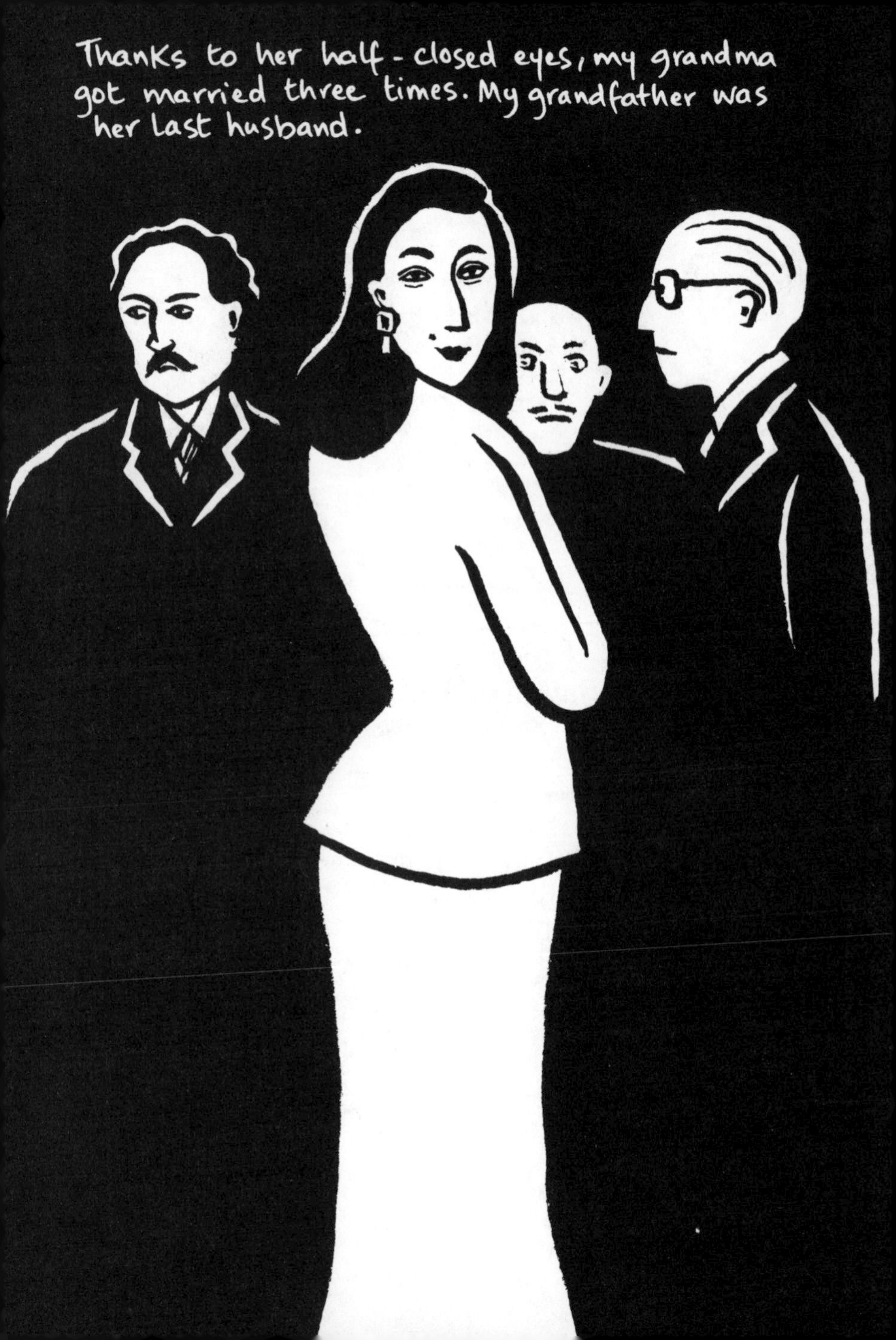
Thanks to her half-closed eyes, my grandma got married three times. My grandfather was her last husband.

## The noon and night samovar

The tea that we prepared at these times had a completely different function.
Everyone gathered around this drink in order to devote themselves to their favorite activity: DISCUSSION.
This discussion had its own purpose:

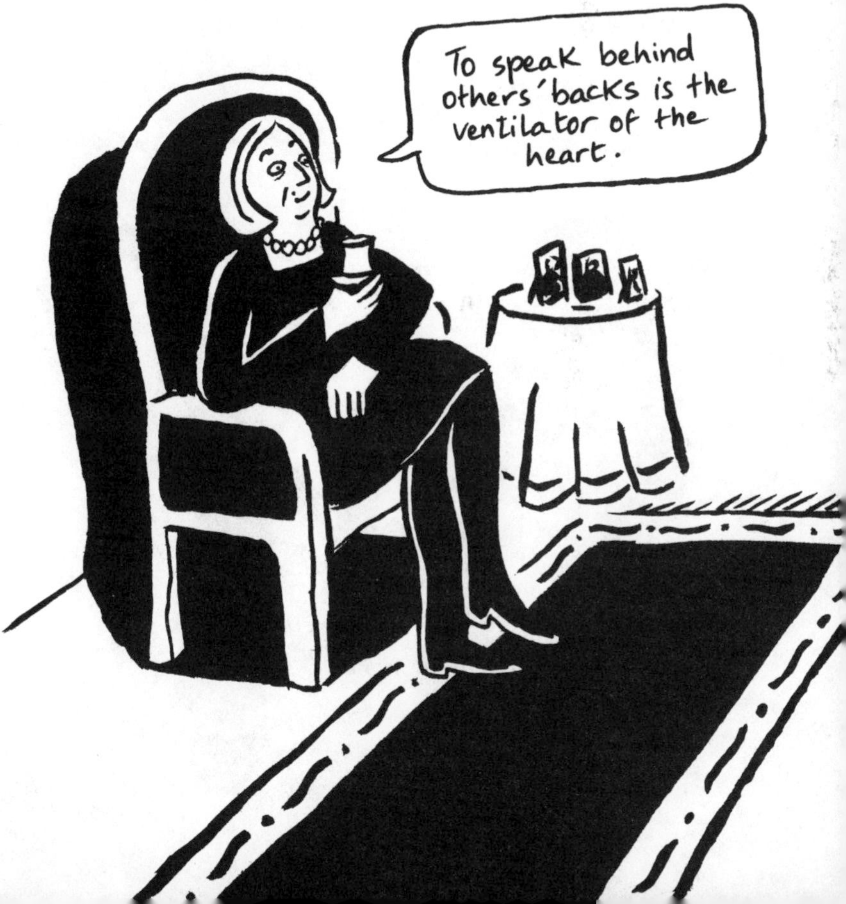
To speak behind others' backs is the ventilator of the heart.

You must allow around three quarters of an hour for the tea to cook and reach its proper strength in a Samovar. (It really is about cooking and not steeping.)

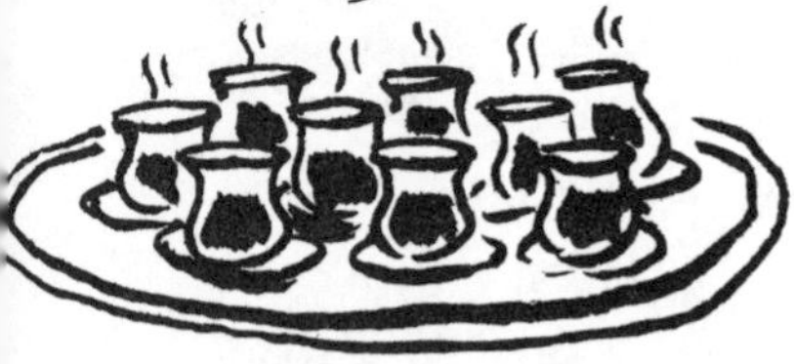

When I finally arrived in the living room with my tray, the others had just finished the dishes.

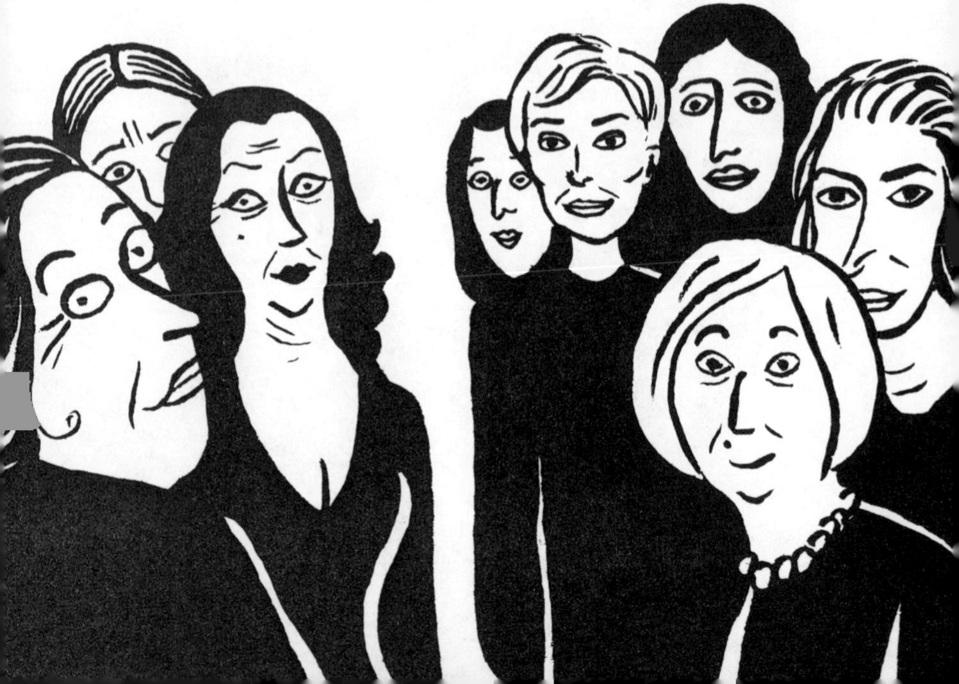
Ah, finally!
Bravo, Marji!
May God keep you!
What timing!
Bravo, my granddaughter! Bravo!
Happiness!
Oh!
Ah!

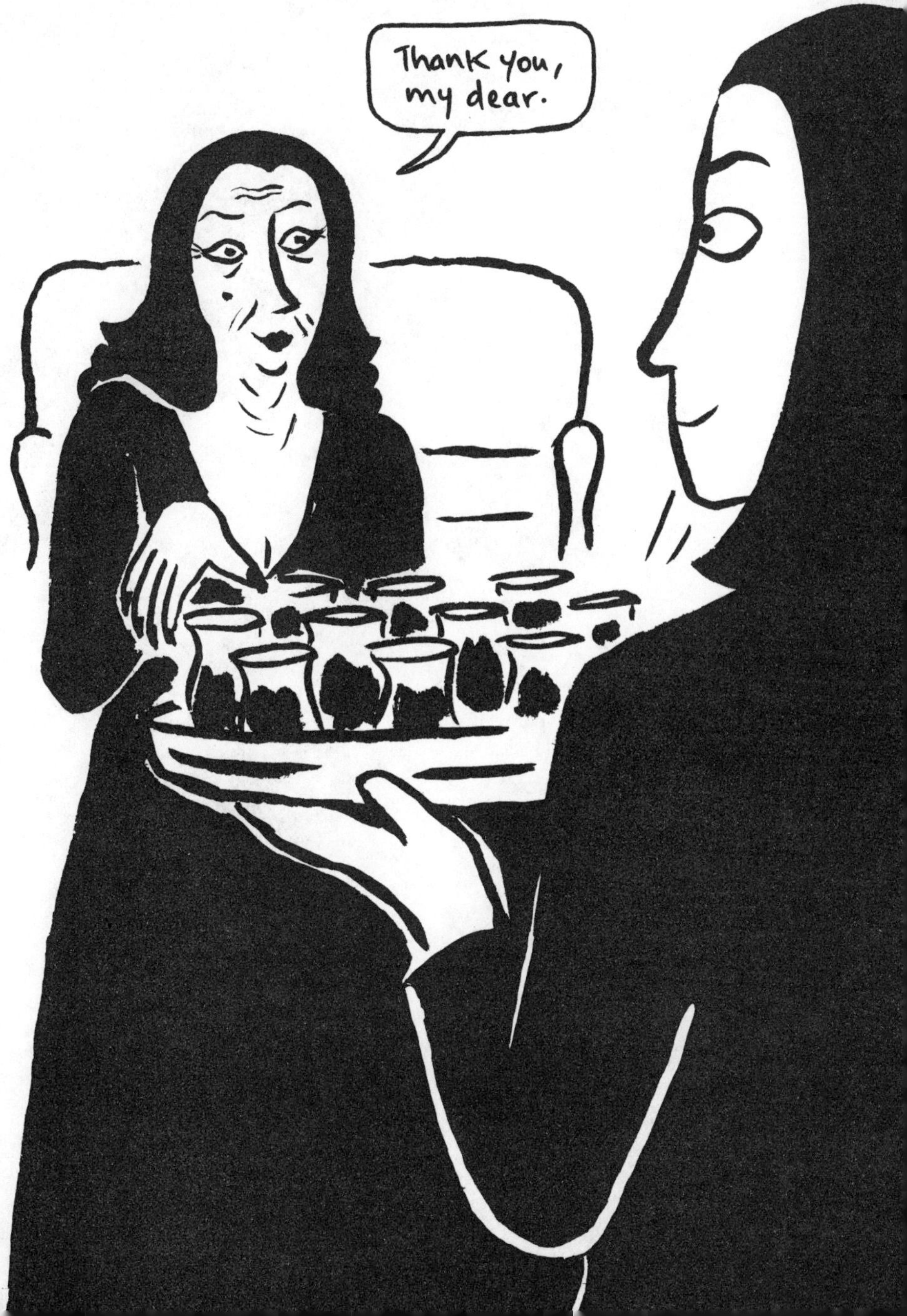
Thank you, my dear.

and in this way we began a long session of ventilation of the heart...

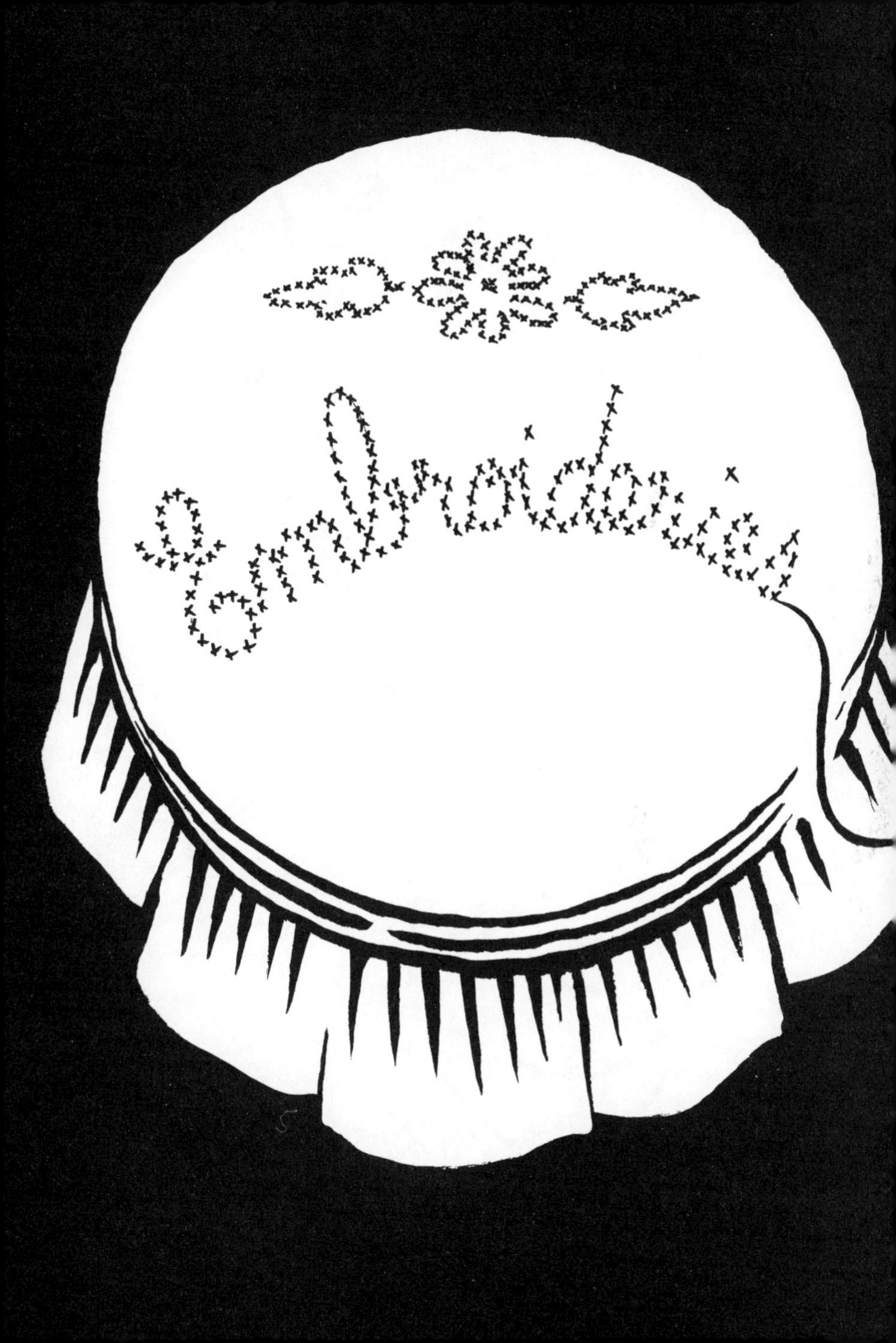
embroideries

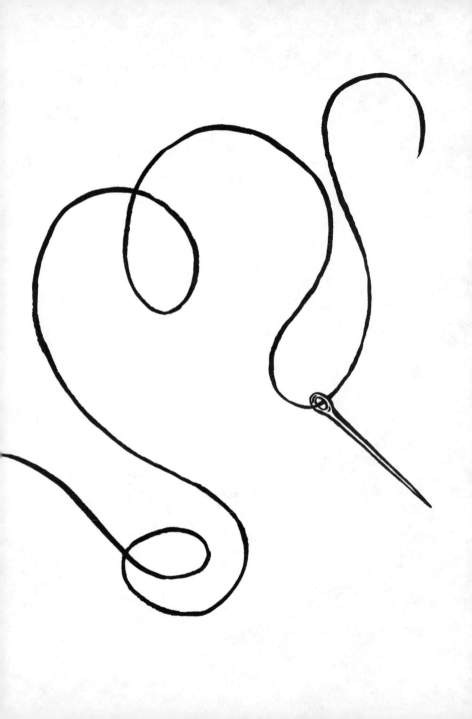

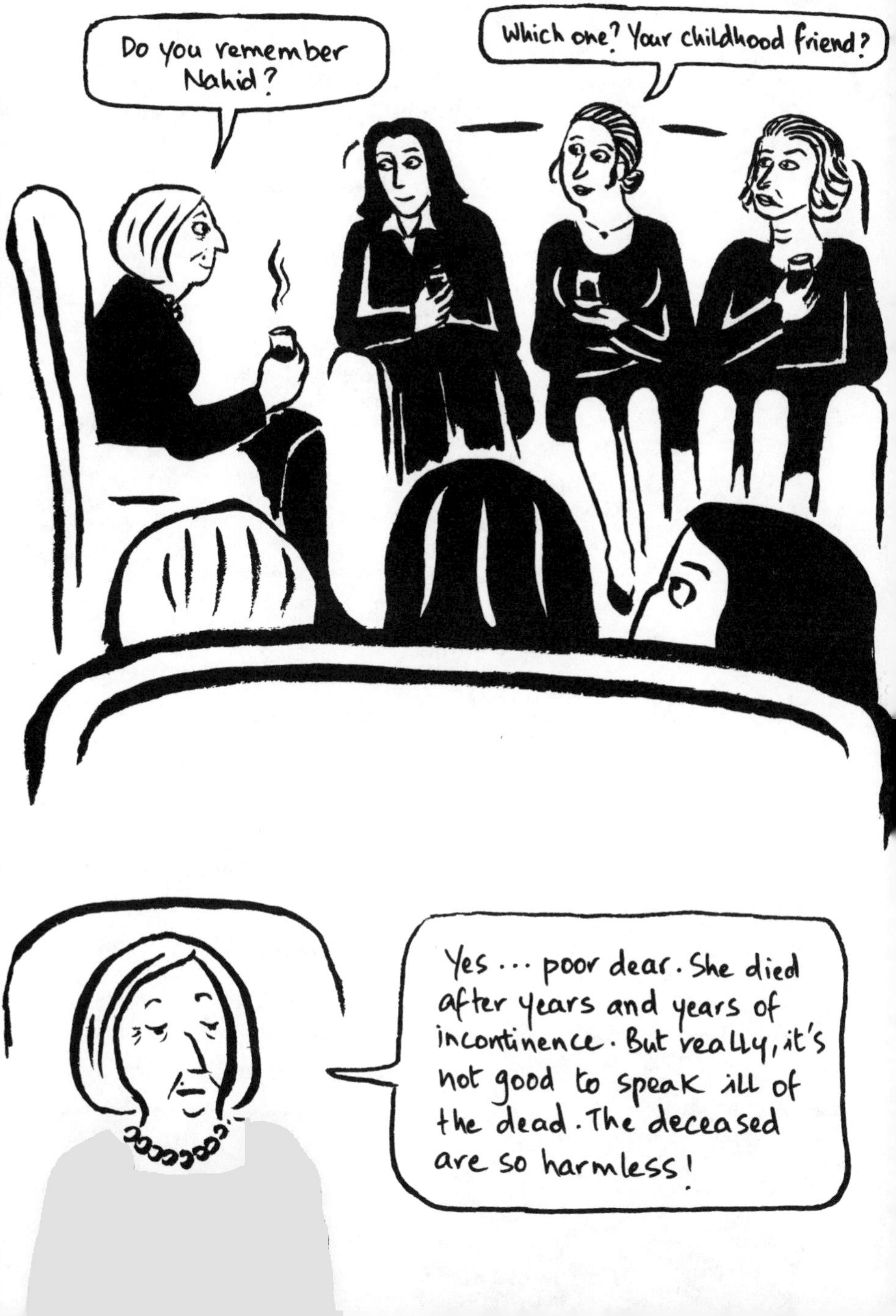
Do you remember Nahid?
Which one? Your childhood friend?
Yes... poor dear. She died after years and years of incontinence. But really, it's not good to speak ill of the dead. The deceased are so harmless!

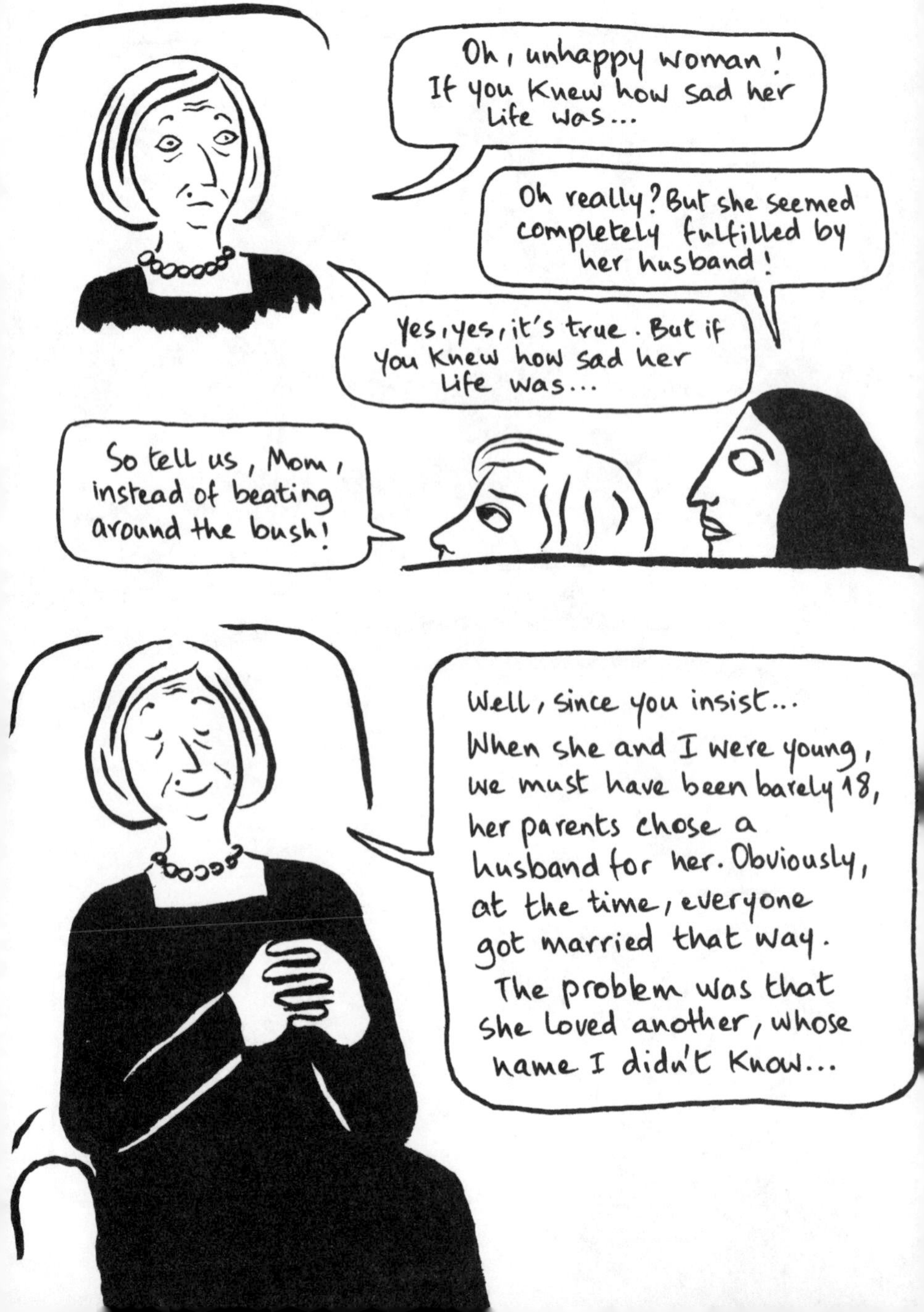
Oh, unhappy woman! If you Knew how sad her Life was...
Oh really? But she seemed completely fulfilled by her husband!
Yes, yes, it's true. But if you Knew how sad her Life was...
So tell us, Mom, instead of beating around the bush!
Well, since you insist... When she and I were young, we must have been barely 18, her parents chose a husband for her. Obviously, at the time, everyone got married that way.
The problem was that she loved another, whose name I didn't Know...

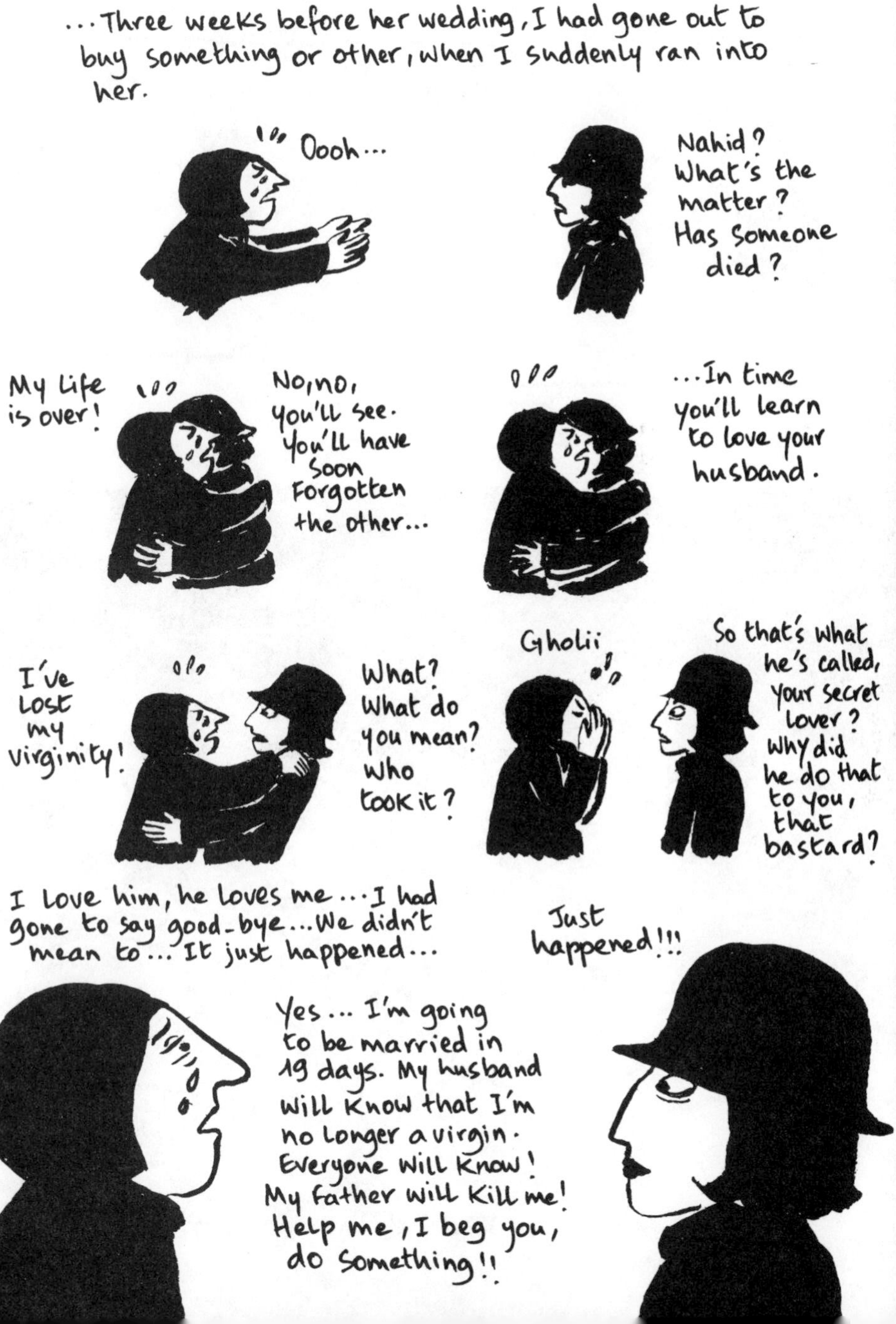
...Three weeks before her wedding, I had gone out to buy something or other, when I suddenly ran into her.
Oooh...
Nahid? What's the matter? Has someone died?
My life is over!
No, no, you'll see. You'll have soon forgotten the other...
...In time you'll learn to love your husband.
I've lost my virginity!
What? What do you mean? Who took it?
Gholi
So that's what he's called, your secret lover? Why did he do that to you, that bastard?
I love him, he loves me... I had gone to say good-bye... We didn't mean to... It just happened...
Just happened!!!
Yes... I'm going to be married in 19 days. My husband will know that I'm no longer a virgin. Everyone will know! My father will kill me! Help me, I beg you, do something!!

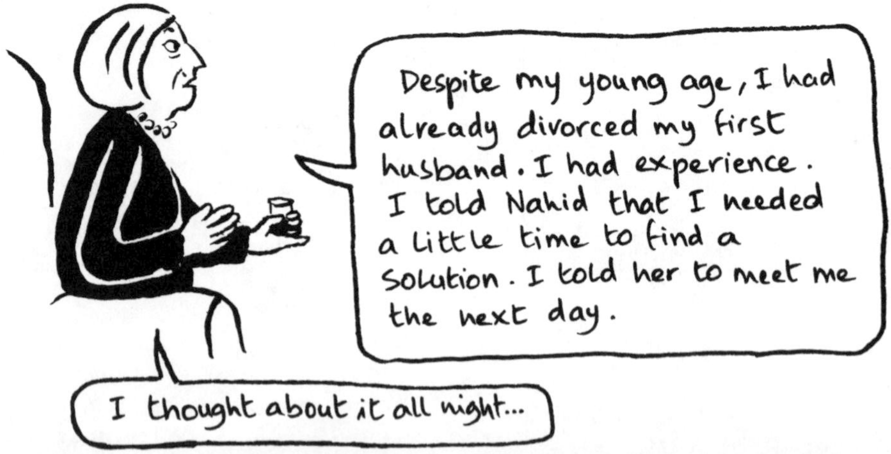
Despite my young age, I had already divorced my first husband. I had experience. I told Nahid that I needed a little time to find a solution. I told her to meet me the next day.
I thought about it all night...

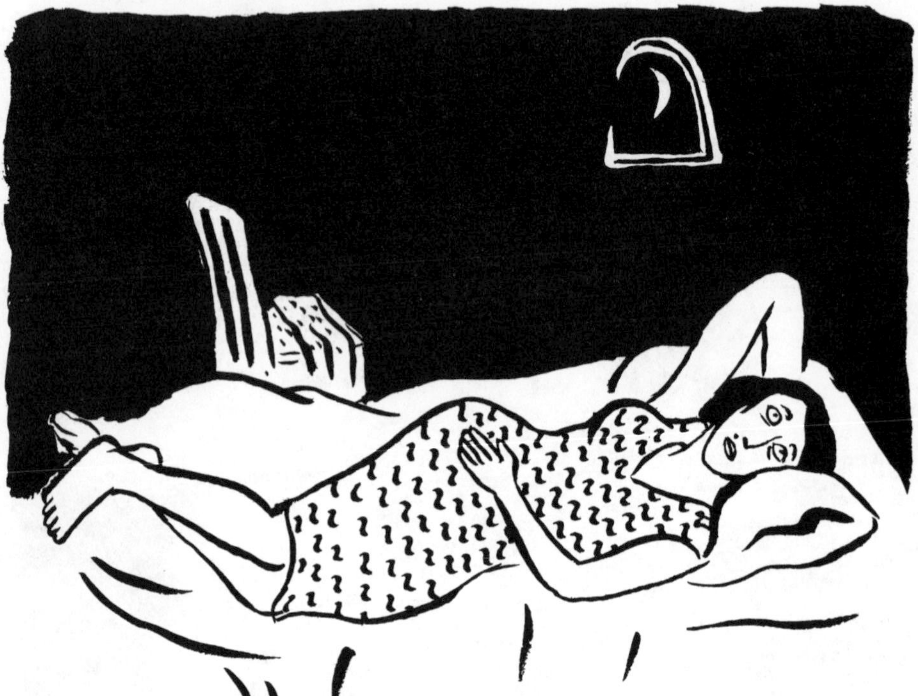
... and in the wee hours of the morning I had the answer.

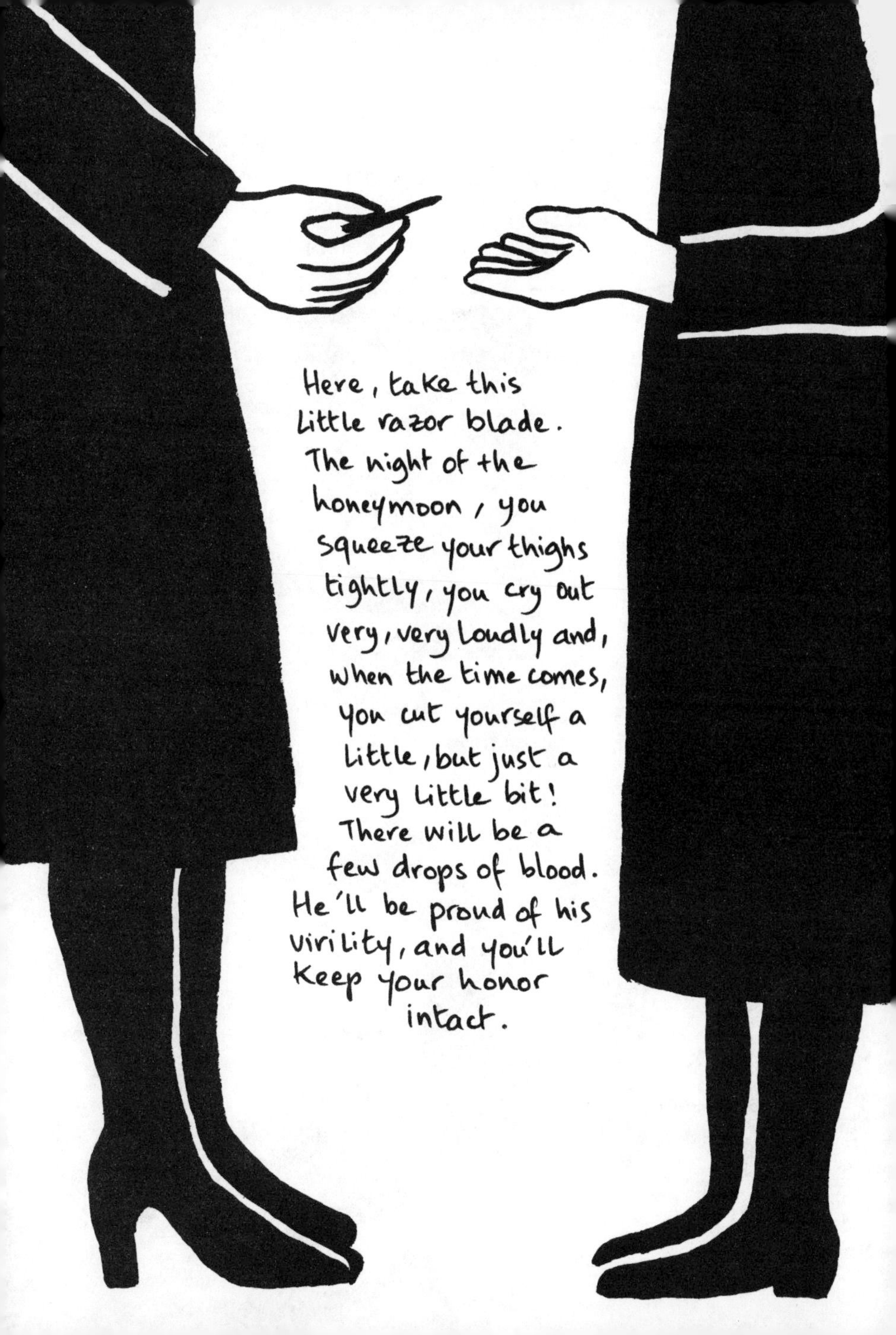
Here, take this little razor blade. The night of the honeymoon, you squeeze your thighs tightly, you cry out very, very loudly and, when the time comes, you cut yourself a little, but just a very little bit! There will be a few drops of blood. He'll be proud of his virility, and you'll keep your honor intact.

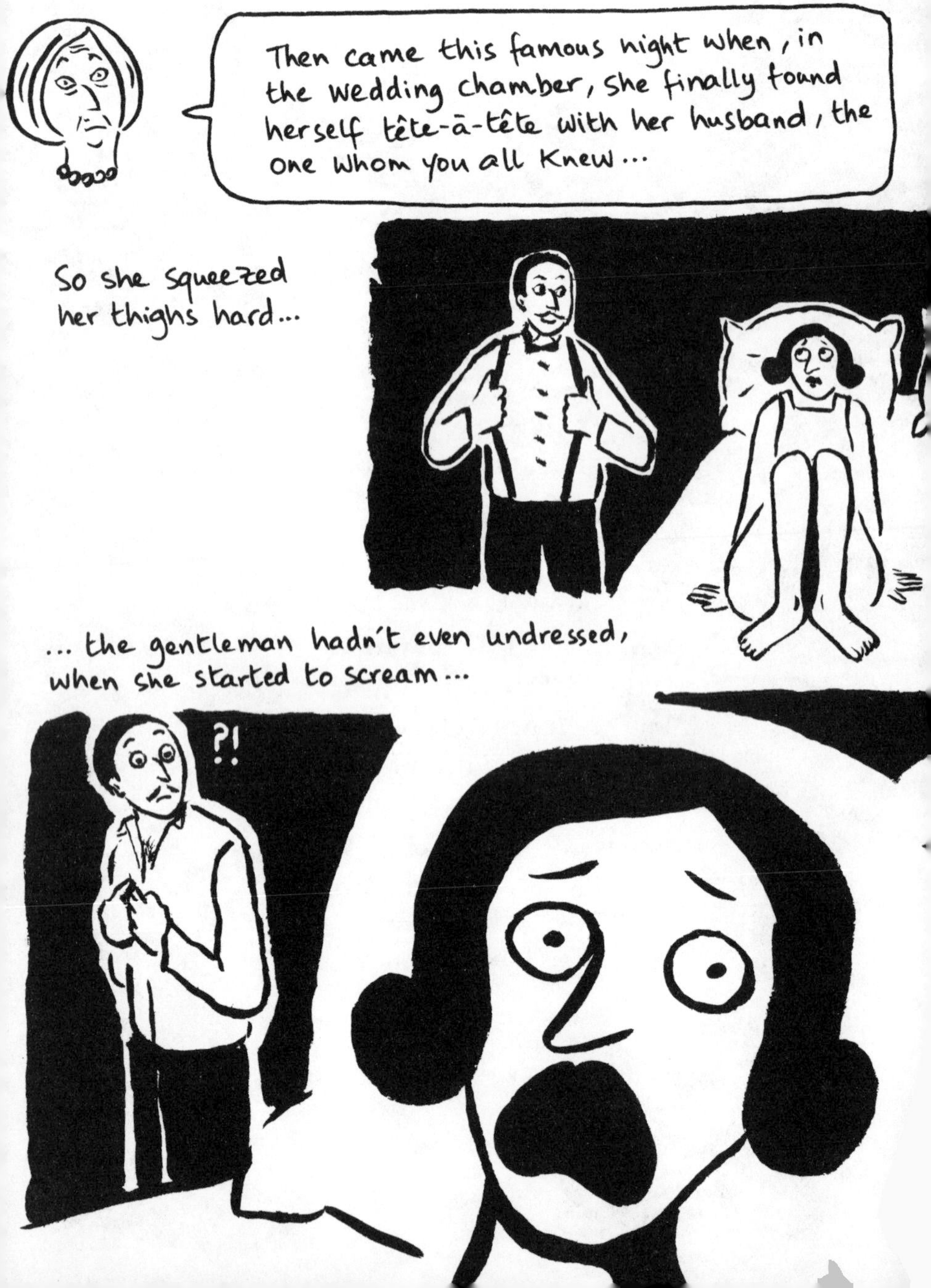
Then came this famous night when, in the wedding chamber, she finally found herself tête-à-tête with her husband, the one whom you all knew...
So she squeezed her thighs hard...
... the gentleman hadn't even undressed, when she started to scream...
?!

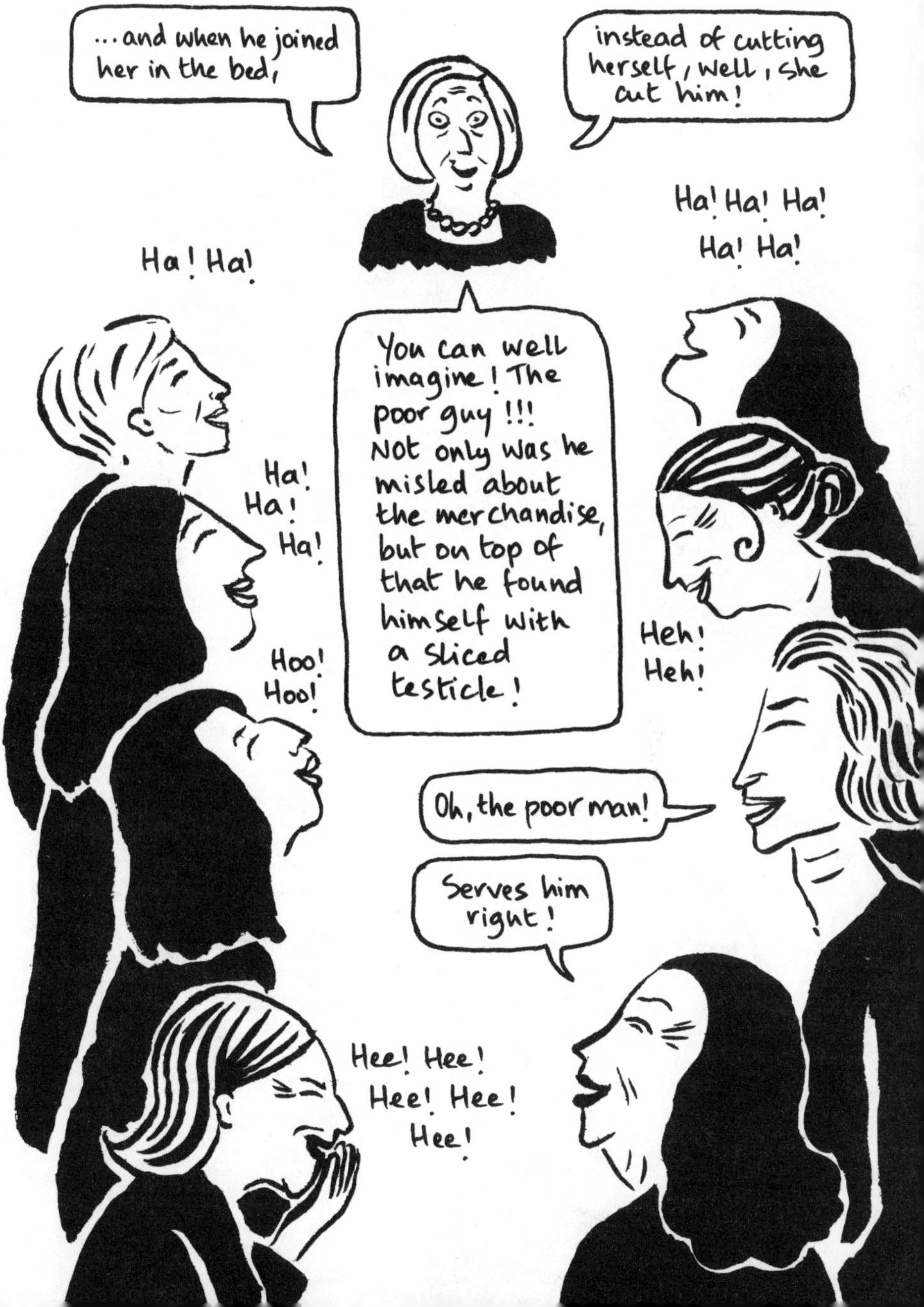
...and when he joined her in the bed,
instead of cutting herself, well, she cut him!
Ha! Ha!
Ha! Ha! Ha! Ha! Ha!
You can well imagine! The poor guy!!! Not only was he misled about the merchandise, but on top of that he found himself with a sliced testicle!
Ha! Ha! Ha!
Hoo! Hoo!
Heh! Heh!
Oh, the poor man!
Serves him right!
Hee! Hee! Hee! Hee! Hee!

They nevertheless lived their whole lives together!
Of course, you know, my child, men's pride is situated in their scrotums. When one finds oneself with a bloody testicle, it is preferable to keep one's mouth shut.
In short, with or without her virginity, she's no longer of this world. One must respect the dead.

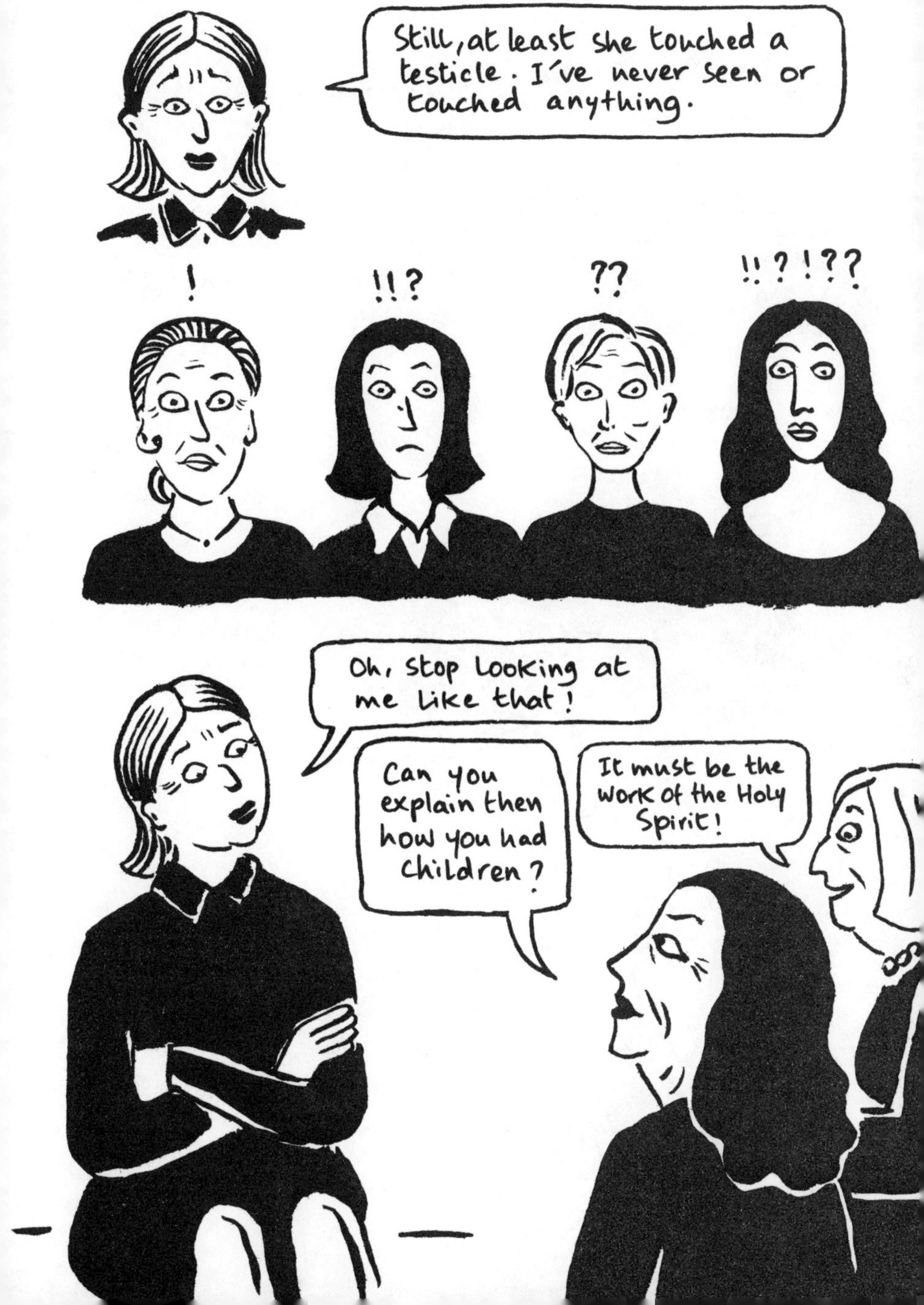
Still, at least she touched a testicle. I've never seen or touched anything.
!
!!?
??
!!?!??
Oh, stop looking at me like that!
Can you explain then how you had children?
It must be the work of the Holy Spirit!

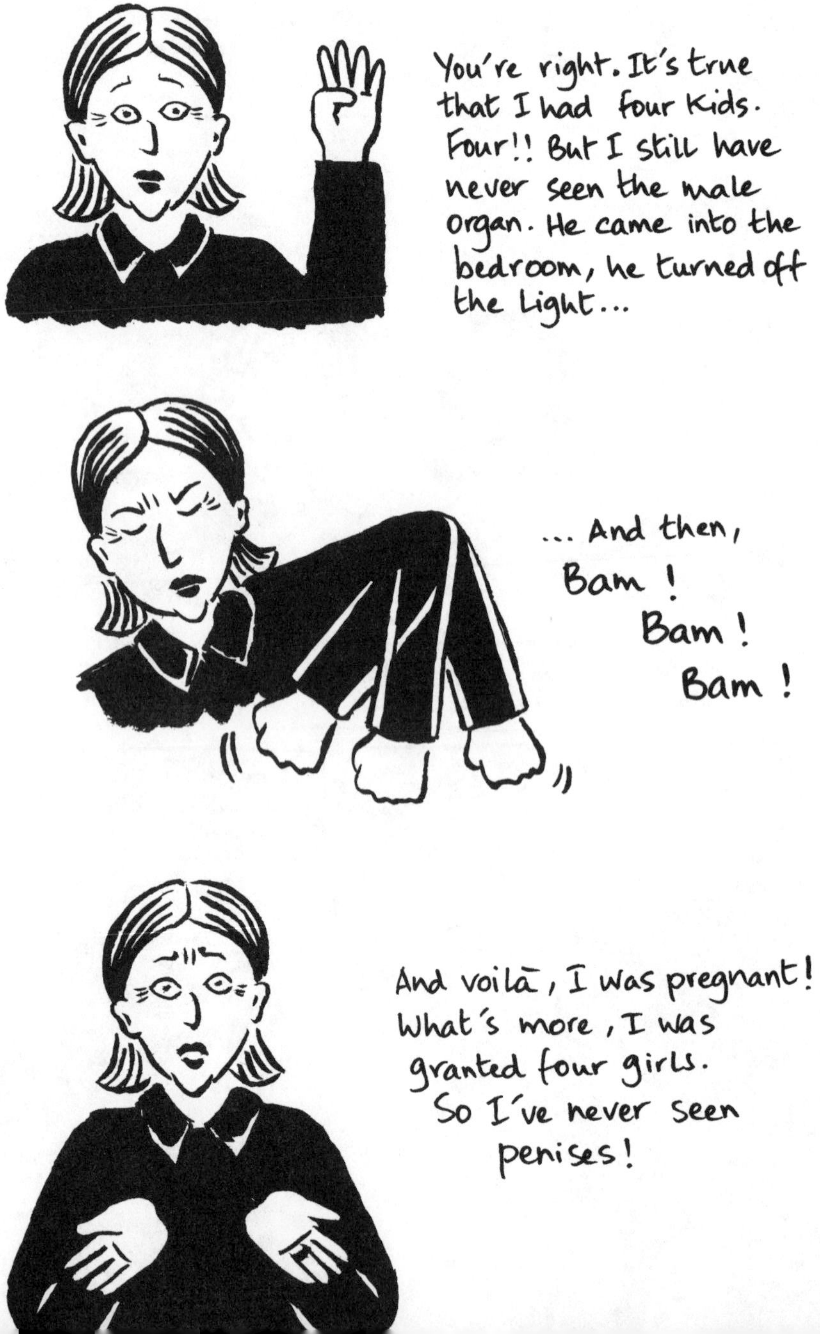
You're right. It's true that I had four kids. Four!! But I still have never seen the male organ. He came into the bedroom, he turned off the light...
...And then,
Bam!
Bam!
Bam!
And voilà, I was pregnant! What's more, I was granted four girls. So I've never seen penises!

Quite honestly, you haven't missed anything.
You're one to talk. May I remind you that you got married three times!
I never really understood how it was possible to marry three times. Just one marriage was enough to make me realize that living with a man was unfeasible!
You must pay close attention when choosing your future husband. Don't marry with your heart but with your brain.

Don't Listen to her! You must marry the one you Love. I had a marriage of convenience. The result? I never Knew what love was, because Love is the opposite of good sense.
Marriage, it's Like roulette: sometimes one wins, often one loses. Even if you're very in Love, it can still go bad.
Yes, but while waiting for it to turn sour, one can experience happiness.
There's no point in getting married!

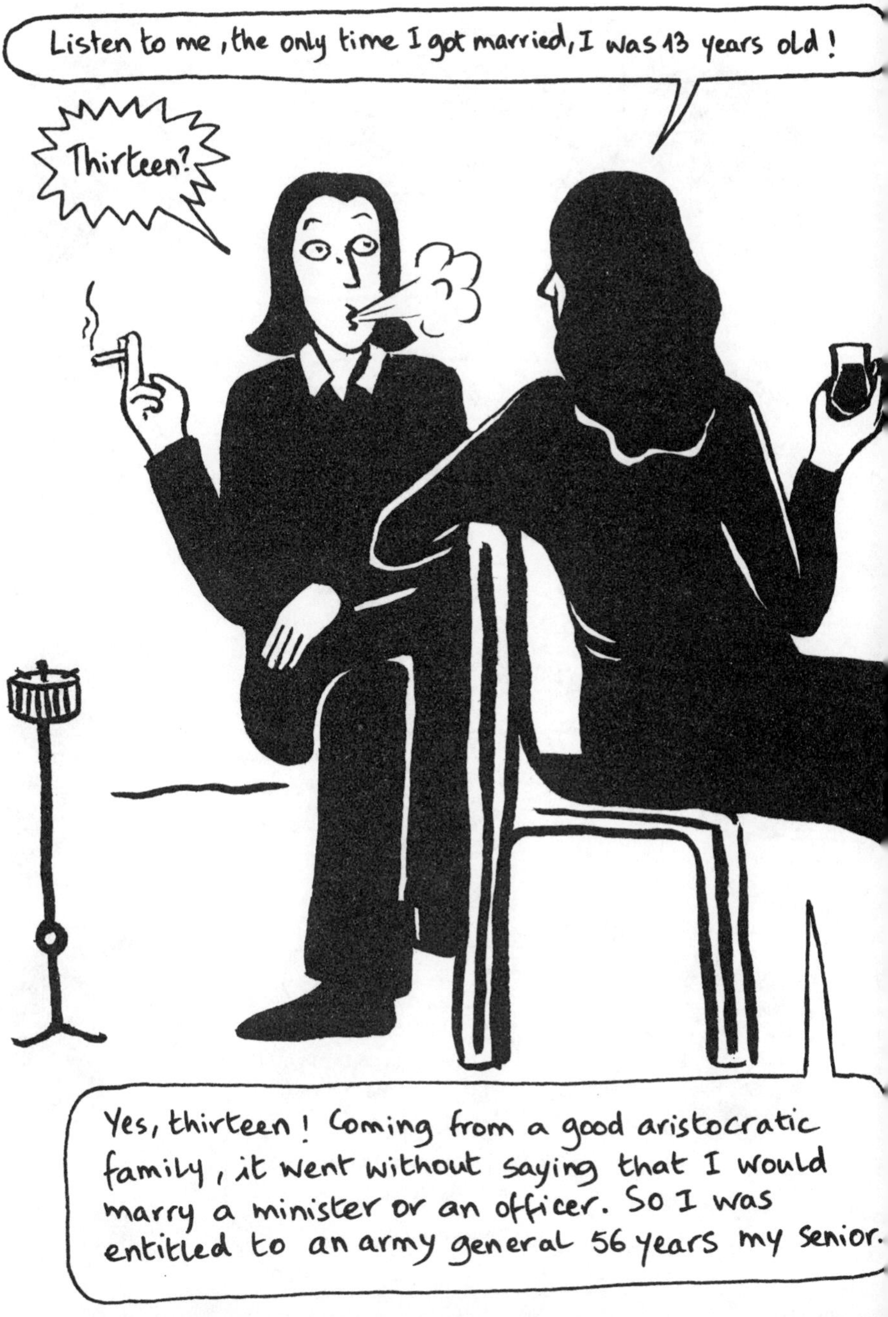
Listen to me, the only time I got married, I was 13 years old!
Thirteen?
Yes, thirteen! Coming from a good aristocratic family, it went without saying that I would marry a minister or an officer. So I was entitled to an army general 56 years my senior.

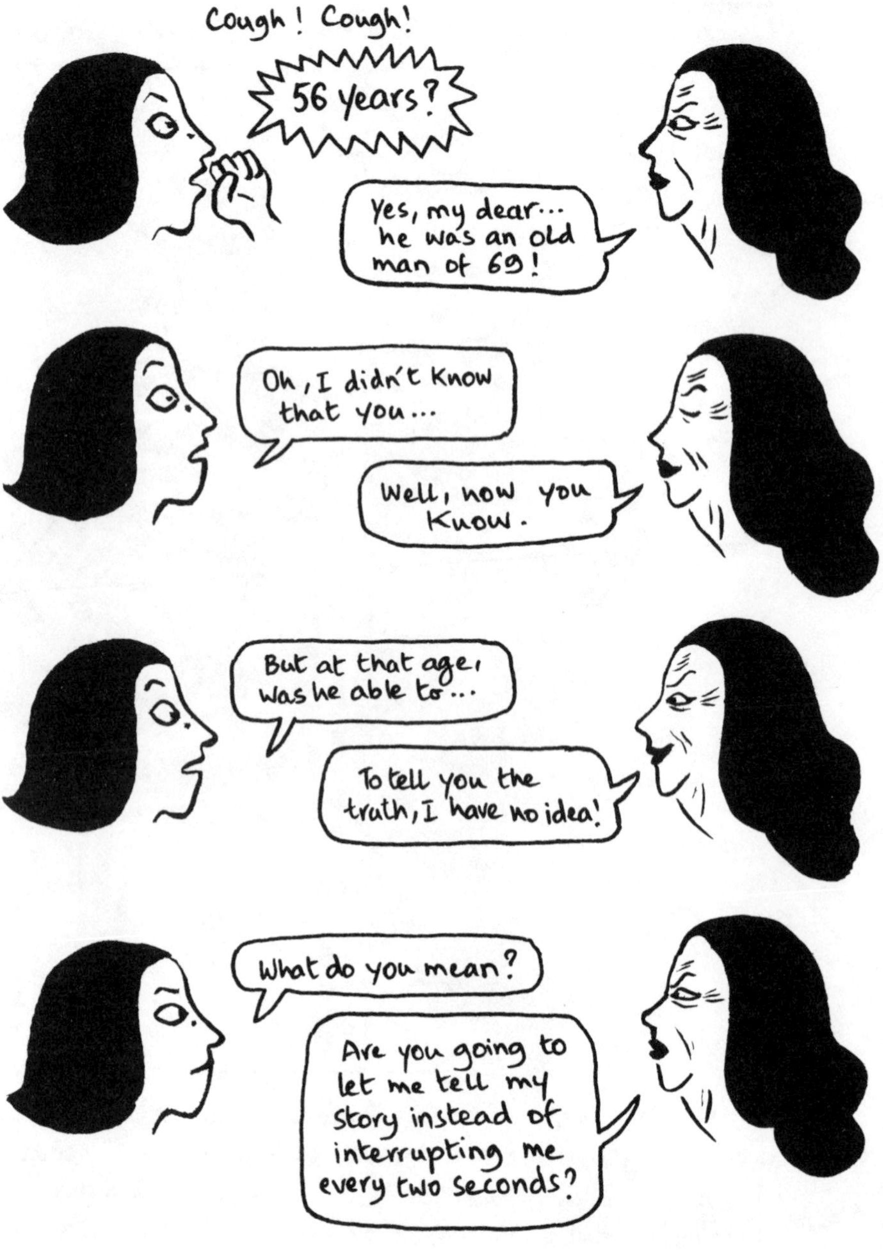
Cough! Cough!
56 years?
Yes, my dear... he was an old man of 69!
Oh, I didn't know that you...
Well, now you know.
But at that age, was he able to...
To tell you the truth, I have no idea!
What do you mean?
Are you going to let me tell my story instead of interrupting me every two seconds?

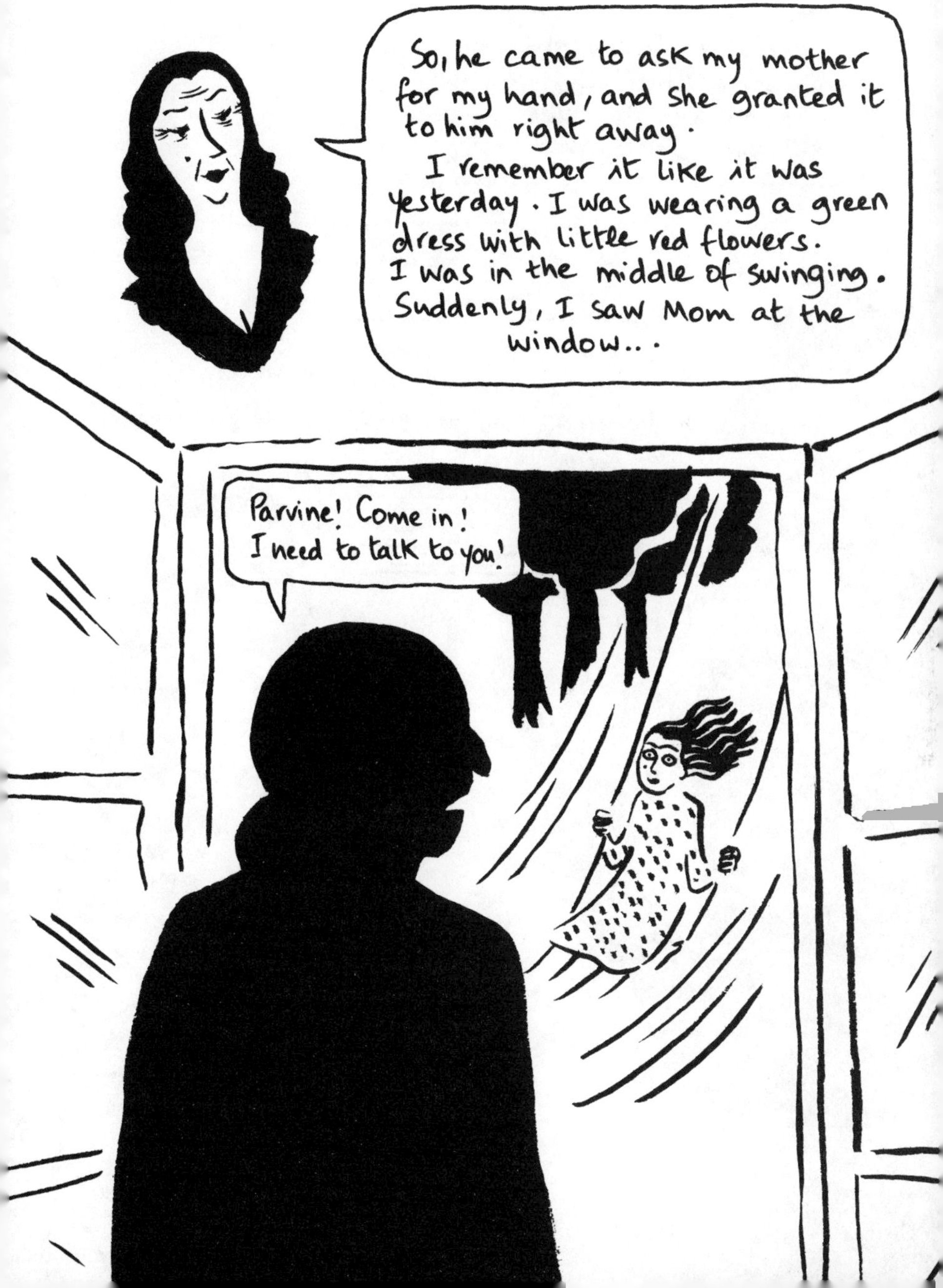

So, he came to ask my mother for my hand, and she granted it to him right away. I remember it like it was yesterday. I was wearing a green dress with little red flowers. I was in the middle of swinging. Suddenly, I saw Mom at the window...
Parvine! Come in! I need to talk to you!

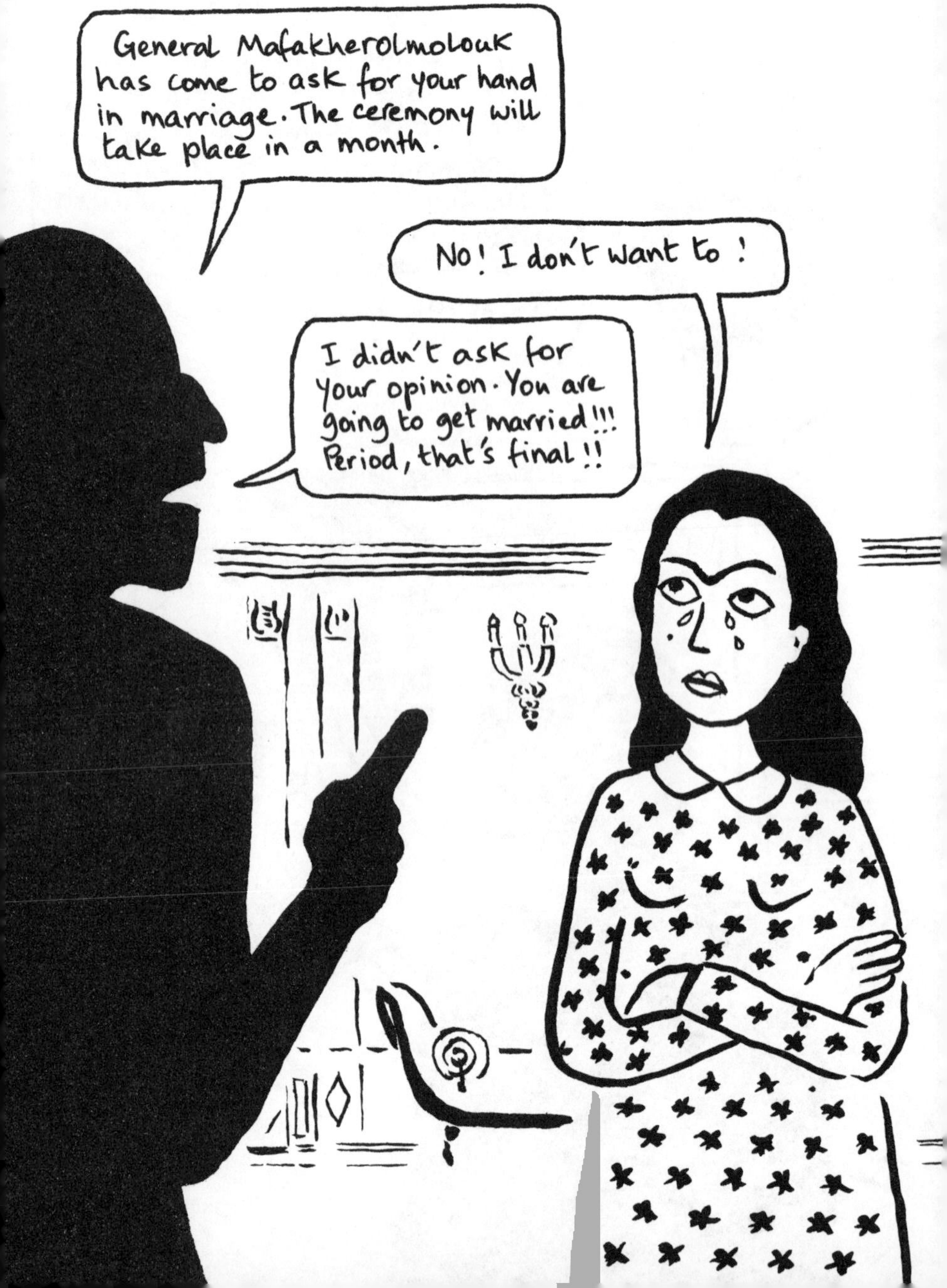
General Mafakherolmolouk has come to ask for your hand in marriage. The ceremony will take place in a month.
No! I don't want to!
I didn't ask for your opinion. You are going to get married!!! Period, that's final!!

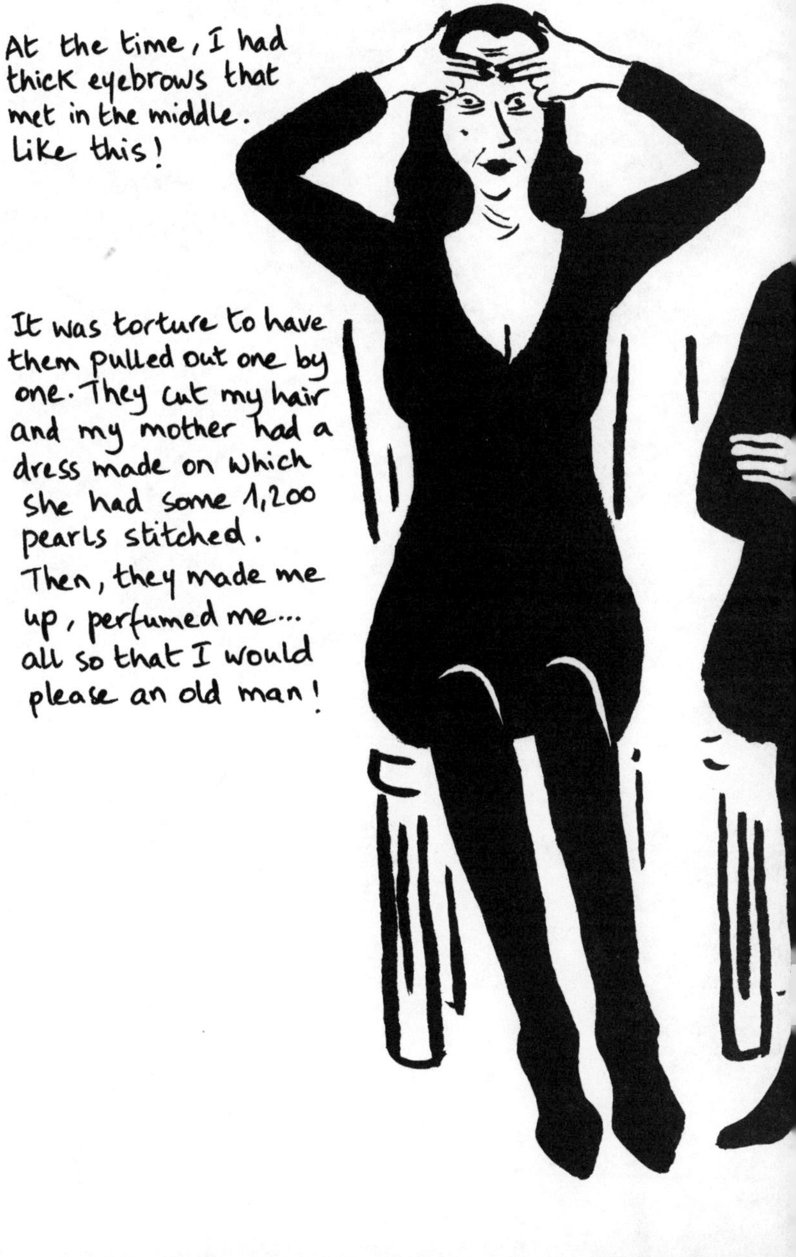
At the time, I had thick eyebrows that met in the middle. Like this!
It was torture to have them pulled out one by one. They cut my hair and my mother had a dress made on which she had some 1,200 pearls stitched. Then, they made me up, perfumed me... all so that I would please an old man!

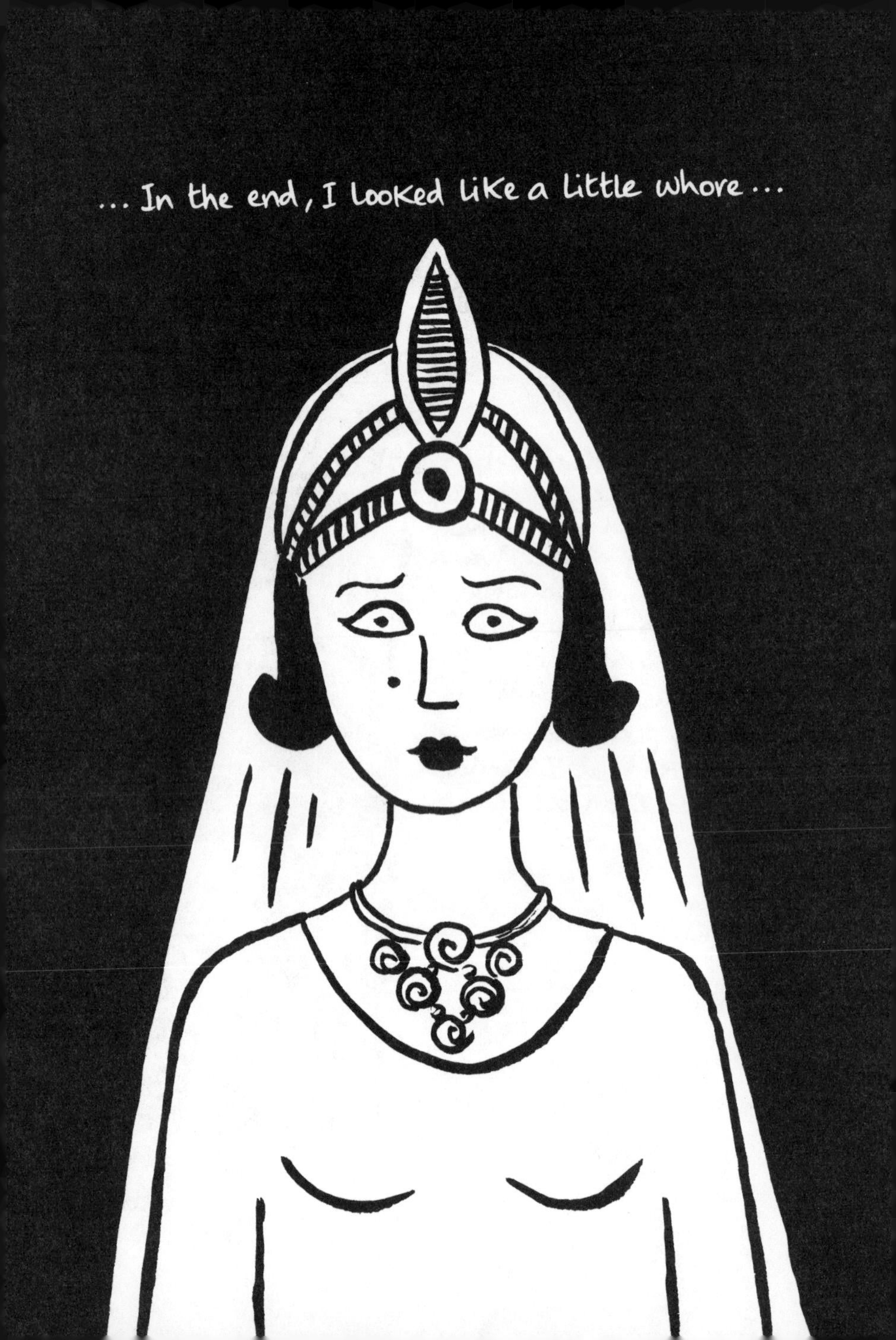
... In the end, I looked like a little whore ...

... I was married as planned. A few hours later, I found myself shut up in the house of the old guy...

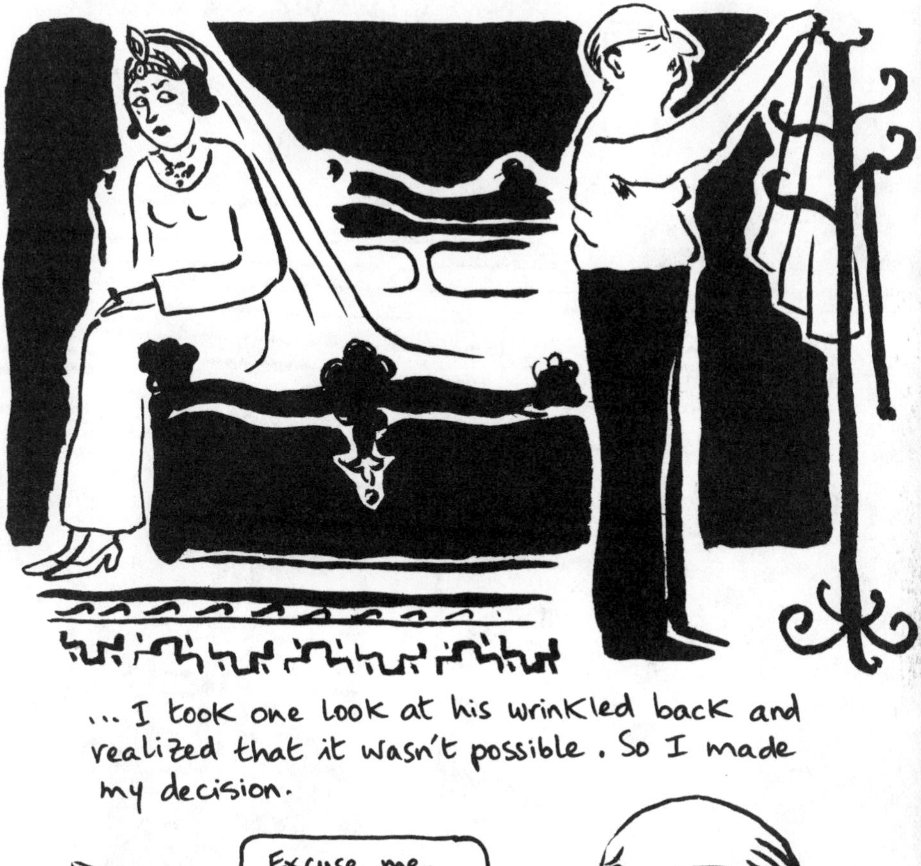

... I took one look at his wrinkled back and realized that it wasn't possible. So I made my decision.

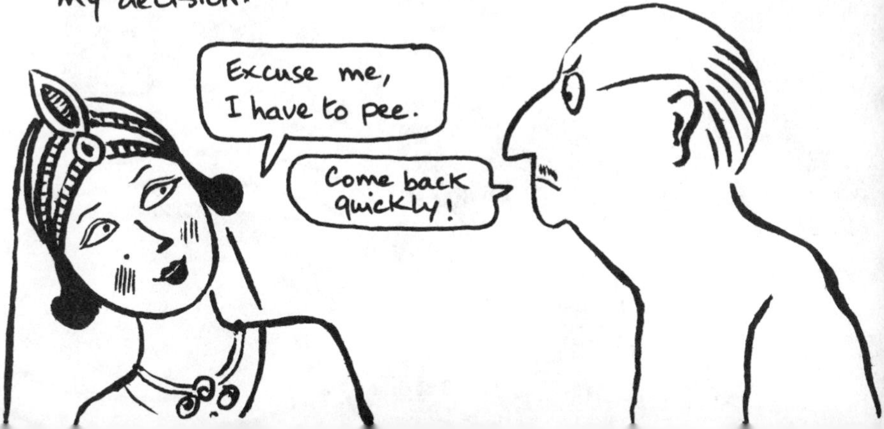
Excuse me, I have to pee.
Come back quickly!

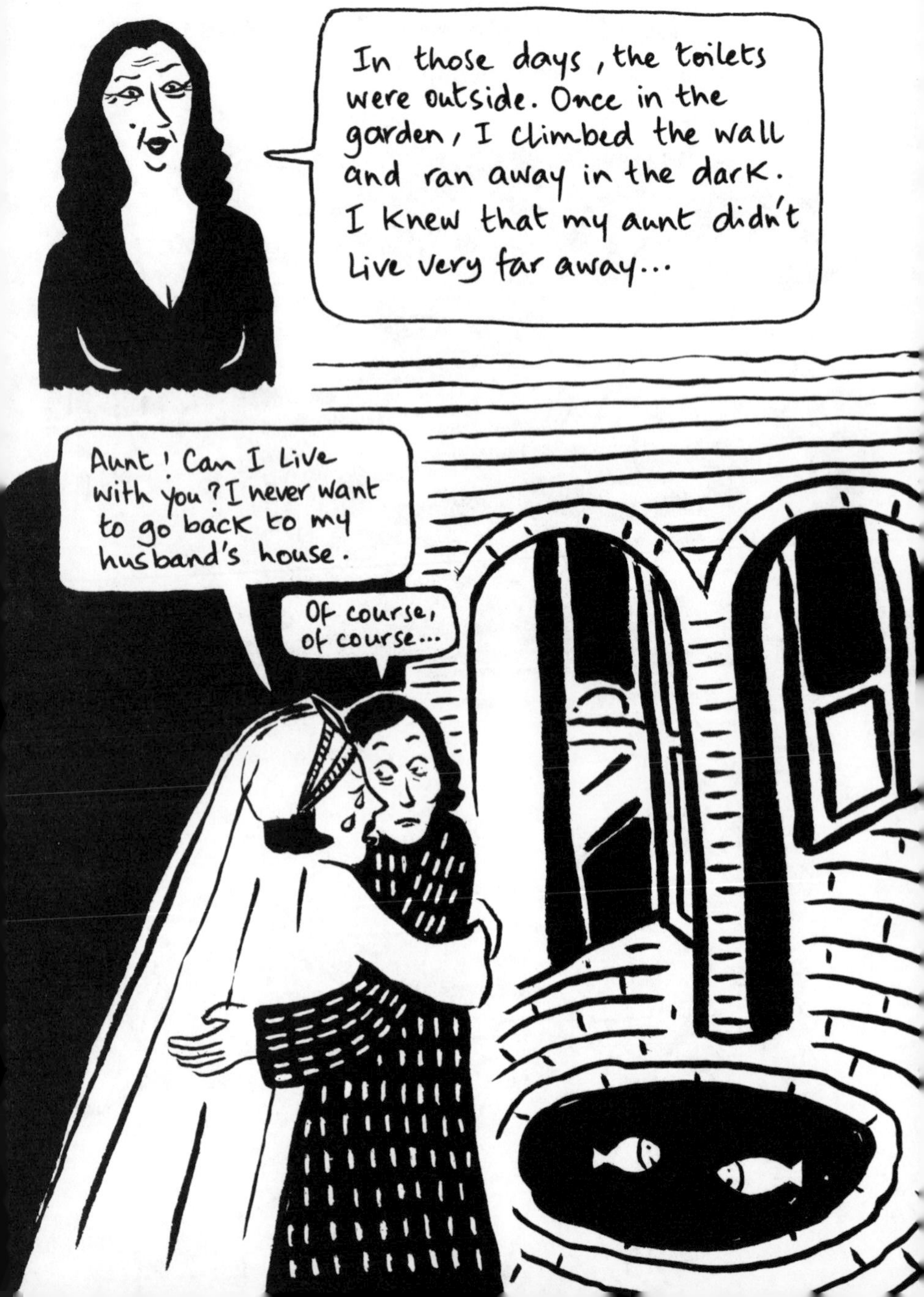
In those days, the toilets were outside. Once in the garden, I climbed the wall and ran away in the dark. I knew that my aunt didn't live very far away...
Aunt! Can I live with you? I never want to go back to my husband's house.
Of course, of course...

... My aunt had much more modern ideas than my parents. And she was a widow, which allowed her to think and to act for herself. So she took me in.
My father, my mother and my brothers tried everything to get me to return to my dear and tender husband. I said, "No!".
But the worst was yet to come. The old guy didn't want a divorce!
I made a thousand prayers for him to die.

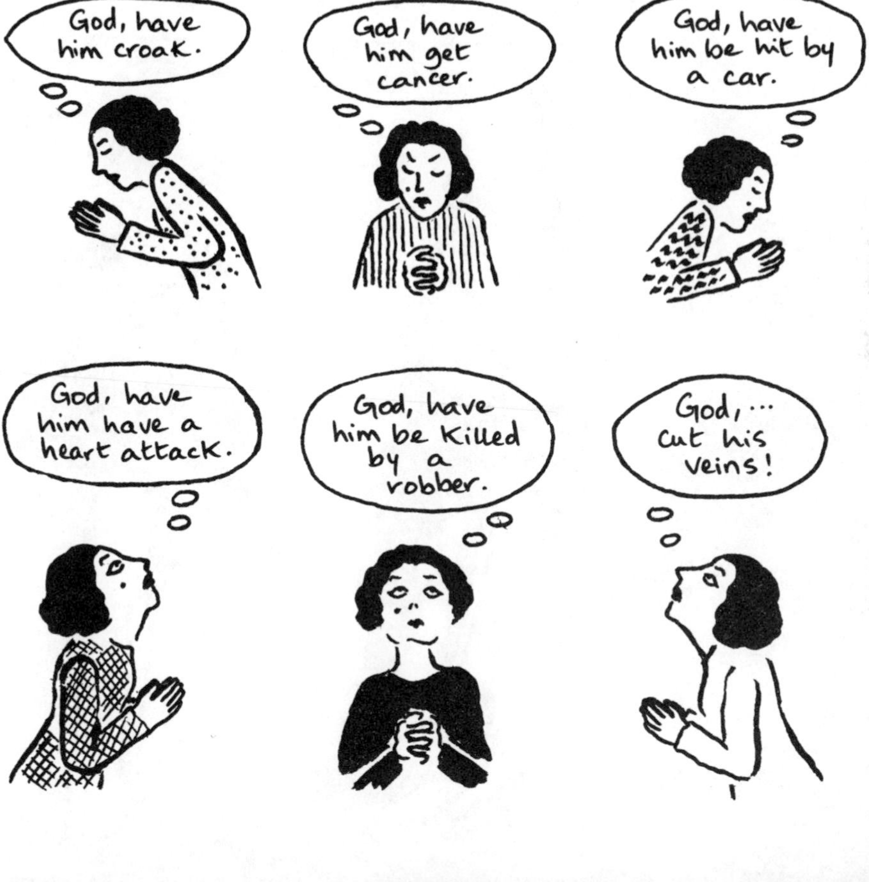

God, have him croak.
God, have him get cancer.
God, have him be hit by a car.
God, have him have a heart attack.
God, have him be killed by a robber.
God, ... cut his veins!

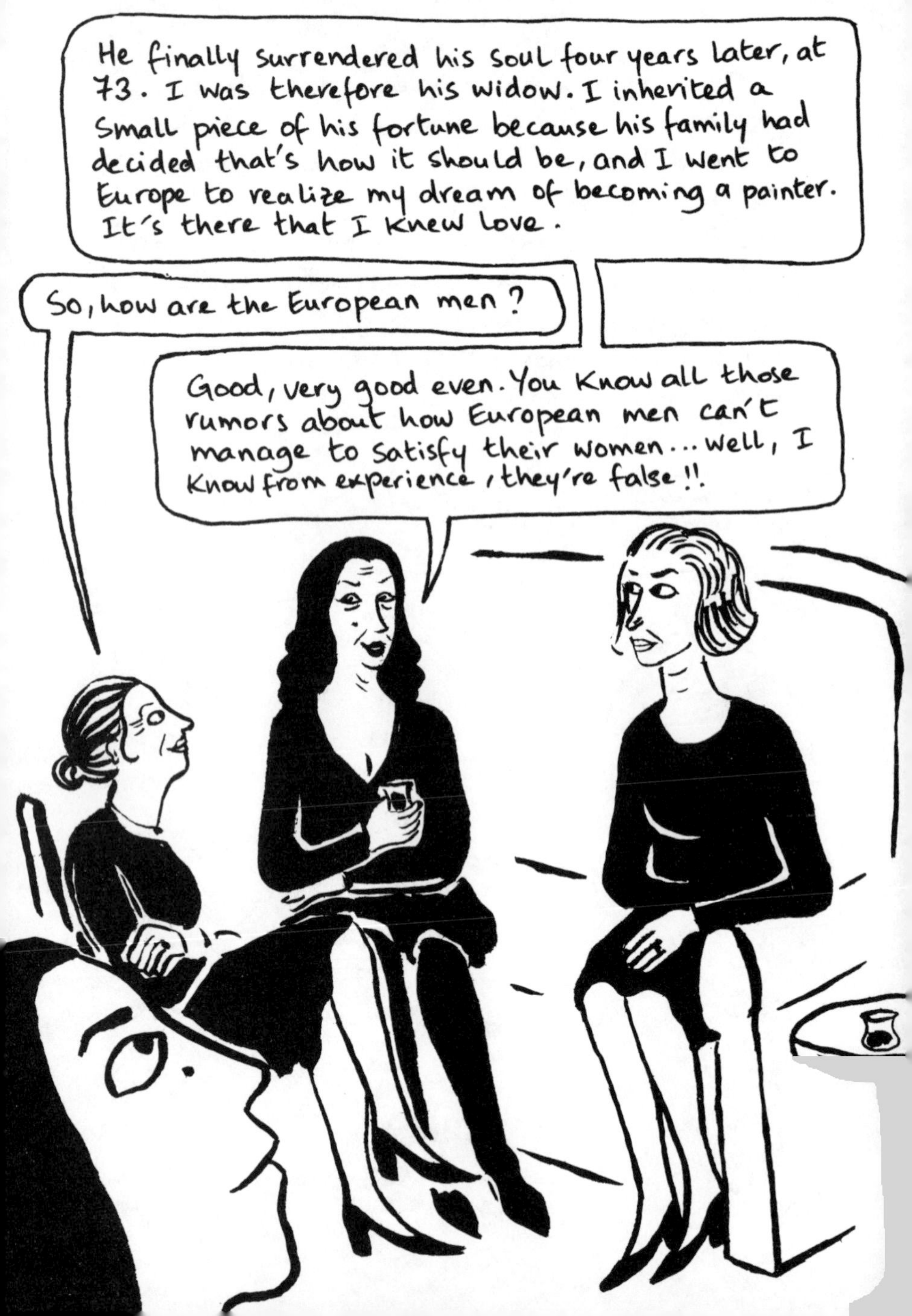
He finally surrendered his soul four years later, at 73. I was therefore his widow. I inherited a small piece of his fortune because his family had decided that's how it should be, and I went to Europe to realize my dream of becoming a painter. It's there that I knew love.
So, how are the European men?
Good, very good even. You know all those rumors about how European men can't manage to satisfy their women... well, I know from experience, they're false!!

It's not disgusting, that little skin that hangs?

The foreskin? No, it's okay. I think that, generally speaking, a dick isn't really photogenic.

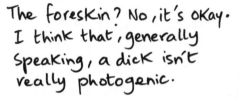

I quite agree.

You agree with what? That a penis is ugly or that a European man knows how to satisfy his woman?
Both!
My first marriage was a love marriage. I married the person who I loved most in the world. His name was Houshang. He was a communist. When the Shah came back to power in '53, they arrested a fair number of people. Houshang was on the list. He had to leave the country...
Amineh, my darling, I must leave for Germany... My life is at risk here.
And what about us?

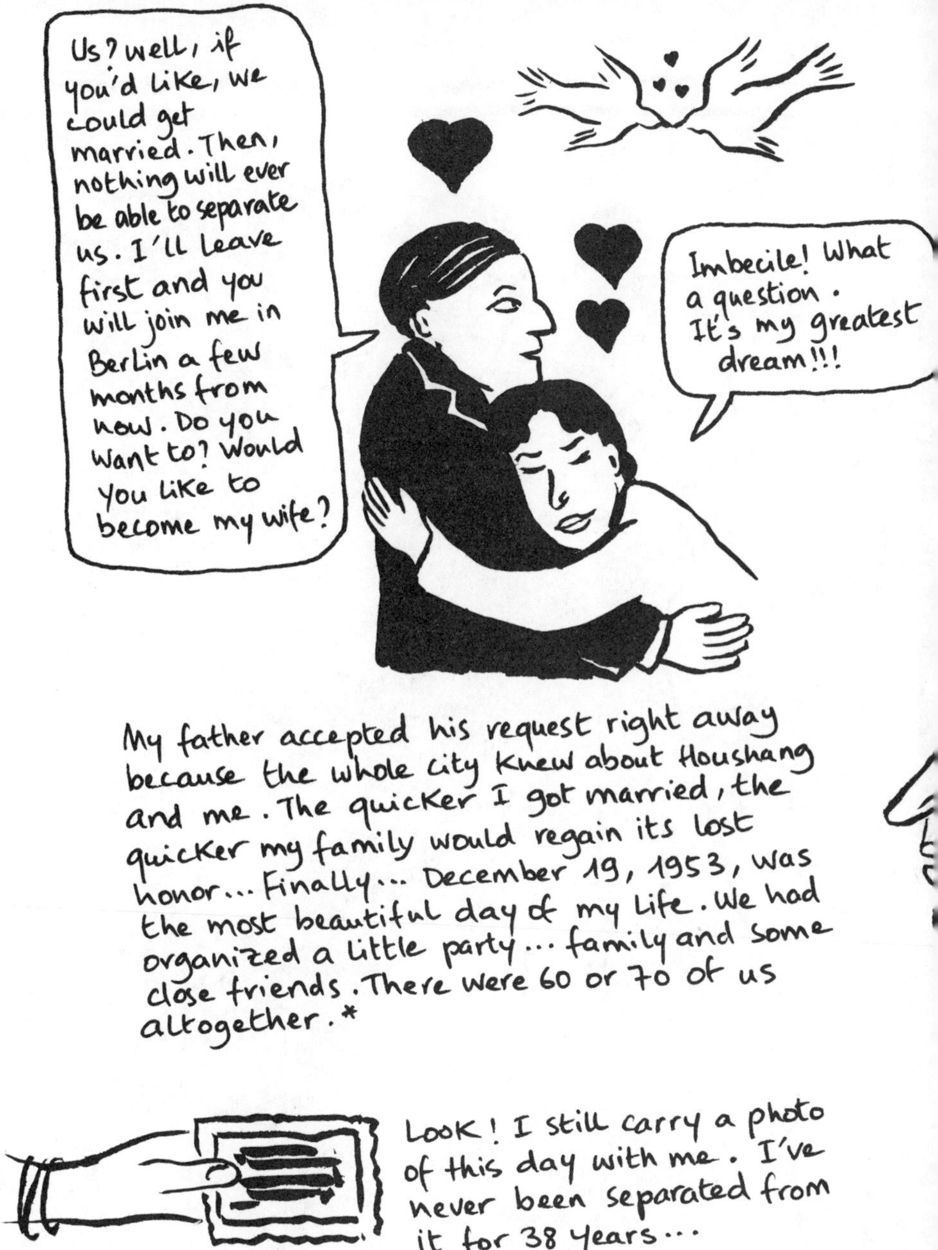

Us? Well, if you'd like, we could get married. Then, nothing will ever be able to separate us. I'll leave first and you will join me in Berlin a few months from now. Do you want to? Would you like to become my wife?
Imbecile! What a question. It's my greatest dream!!!
My father accepted his request right away because the whole city knew about Houshang and me. The quicker I got married, the quicker my family would regain its lost honor... Finally... December 19, 1953, was the most beautiful day of my life. We had organized a little party... family and some close friends. There were 60 or 70 of us altogether.*
Look! I still carry a photo of this day with me. I've never been separated from it for 38 years...


* In Iran, if one has the means, one must invite at least 300 people.

... See how happy my parents look!

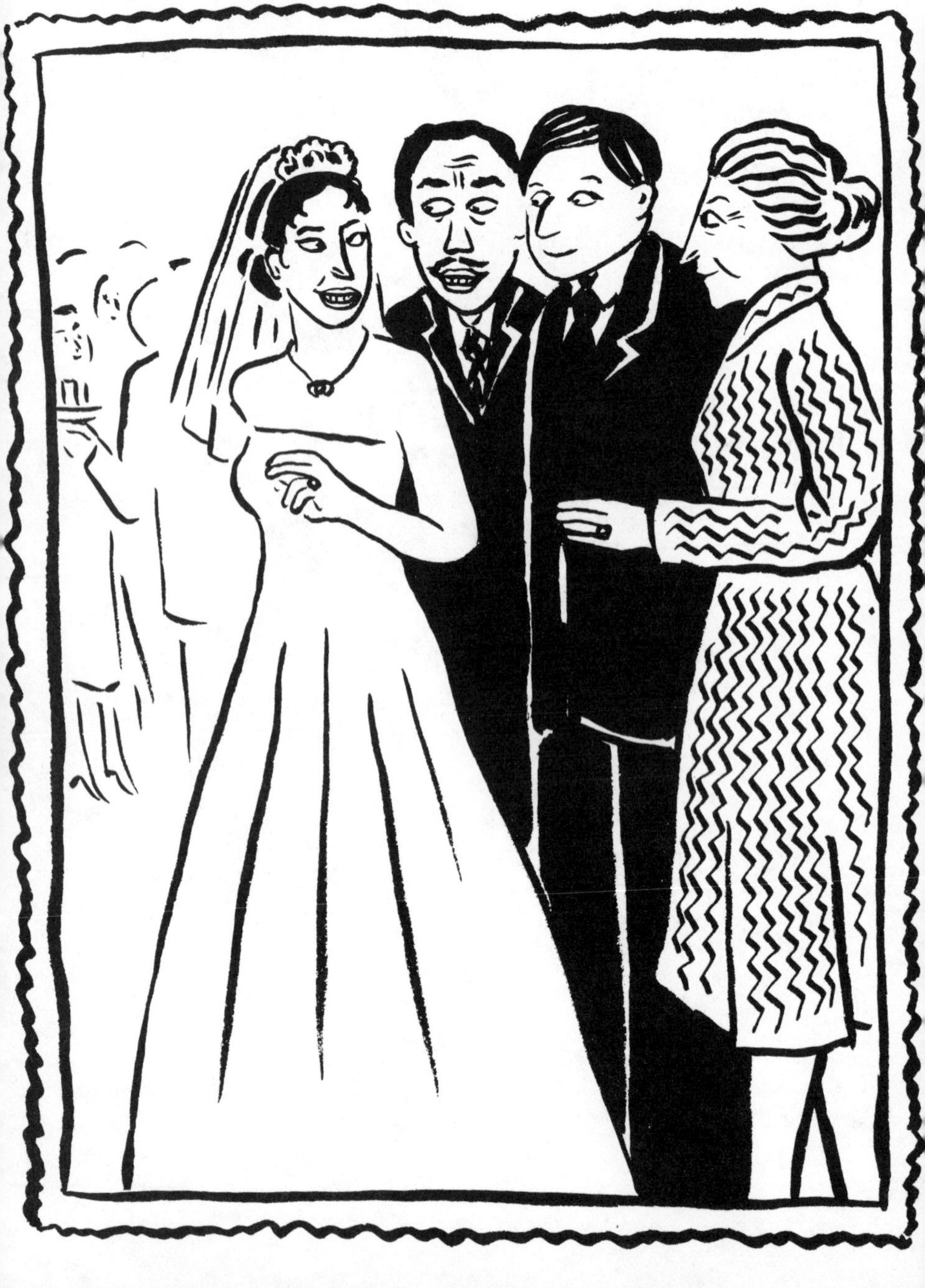

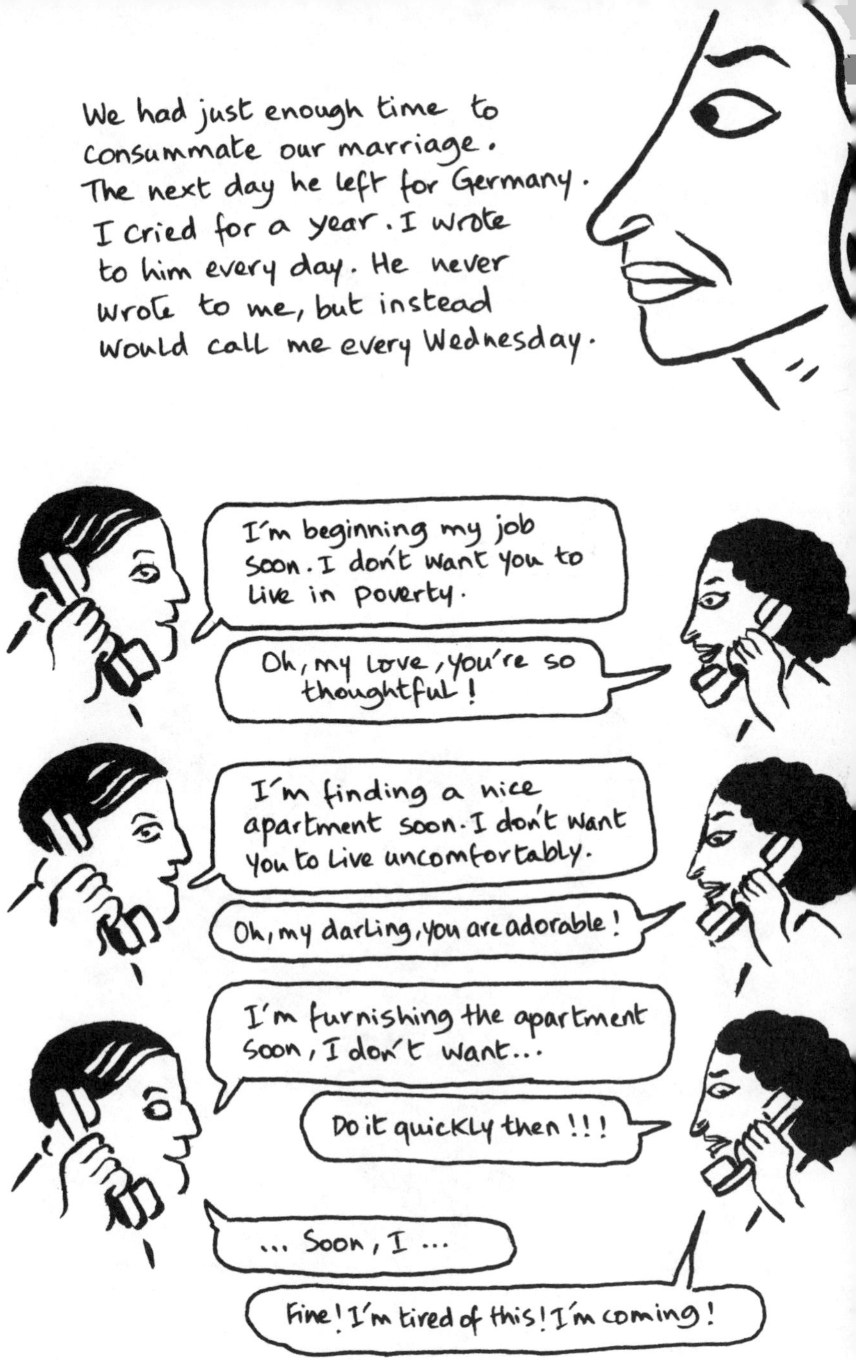
We had just enough time to consummate our marriage. The next day he left for Germany. I cried for a year. I wrote to him every day. He never wrote to me, but instead would call me every Wednesday.
I'm beginning my job soon. I don't want you to live in poverty.
Oh, my love, you're so thoughtful!
I'm finding a nice apartment soon. I don't want you to live uncomfortably.
Oh, my darling, you are adorable!
I'm furnishing the apartment soon, I don't want...
Do it quickly then!!!
... Soon, I ...
Fine! I'm tired of this! I'm coming!

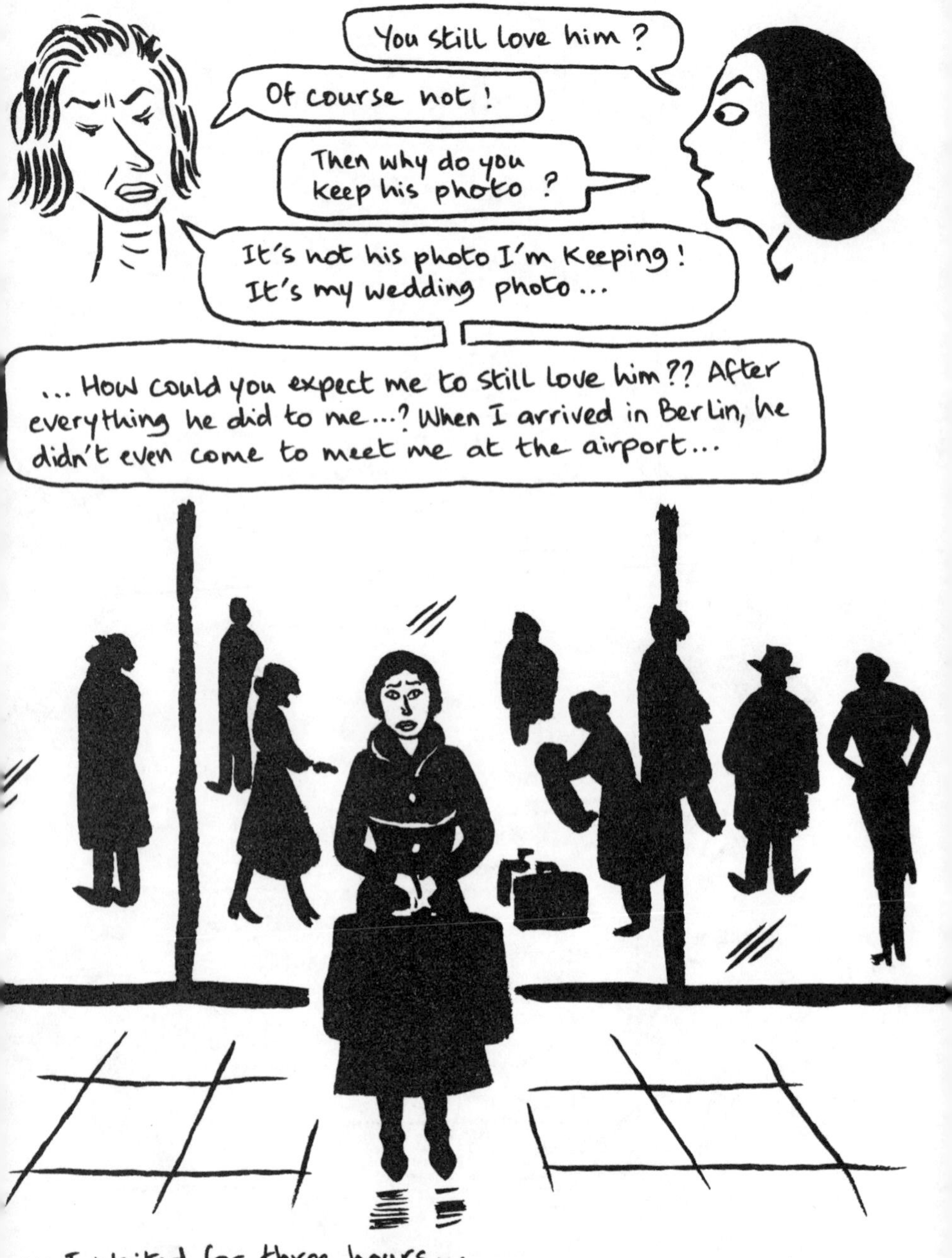
You still love him?
Of course not!
Then why do you keep his photo?
It's not his photo I'm keeping! It's my wedding photo...
... How could you expect me to still love him?? After everything he did to me...? When I arrived in Berlin, he didn't even come to meet me at the airport...
... I waited for three hours...

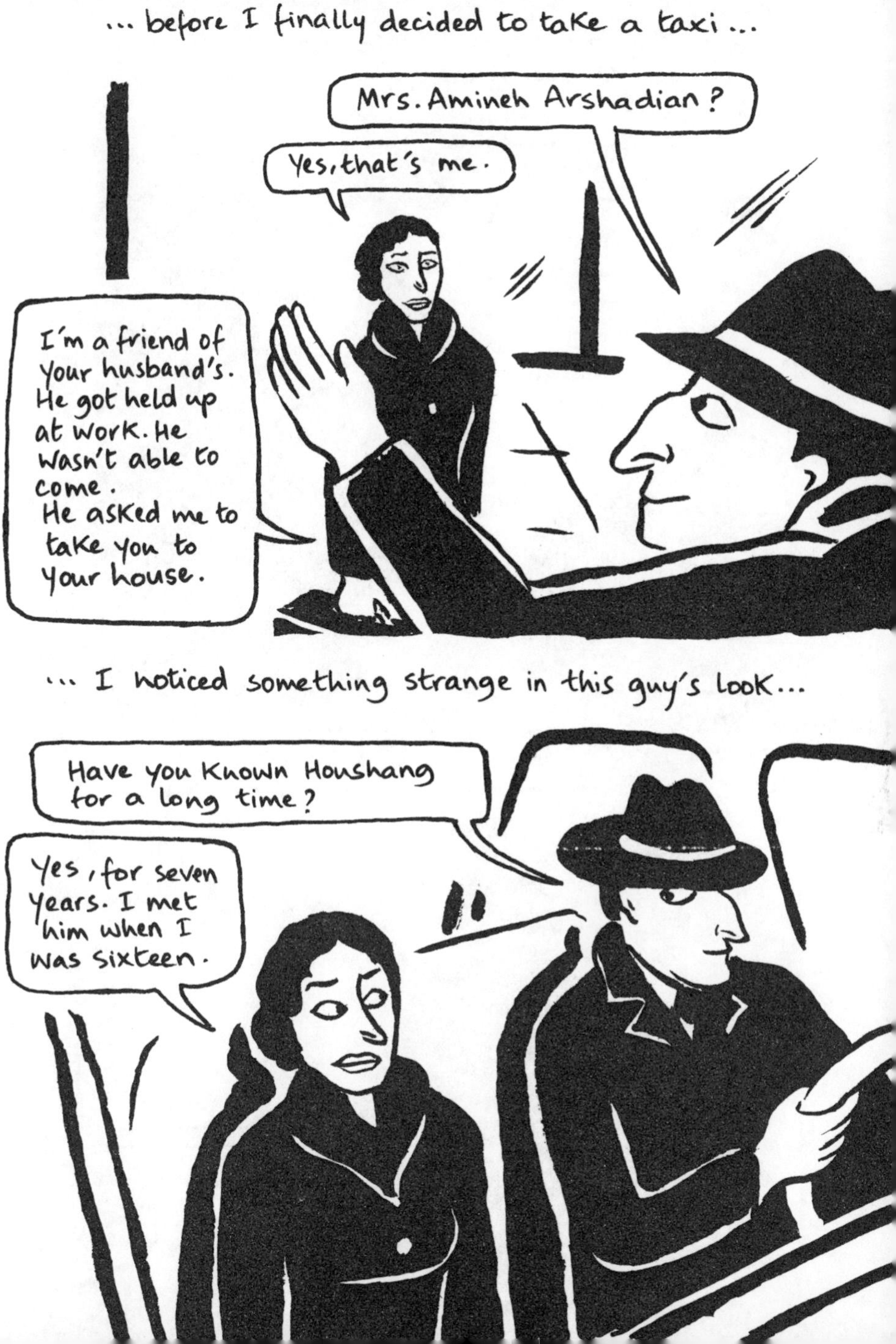
... before I finally decided to take a taxi ...
Mrs. Amineh Arshadian?
Yes, that's me.
I'm a friend of your husband's. He got held up at work. He wasn't able to come. He asked me to take you to your house.
... I noticed something strange in this guy's look...
Have you Known Houshang for a long time?
Yes, for seven years. I met him when I was sixteen.

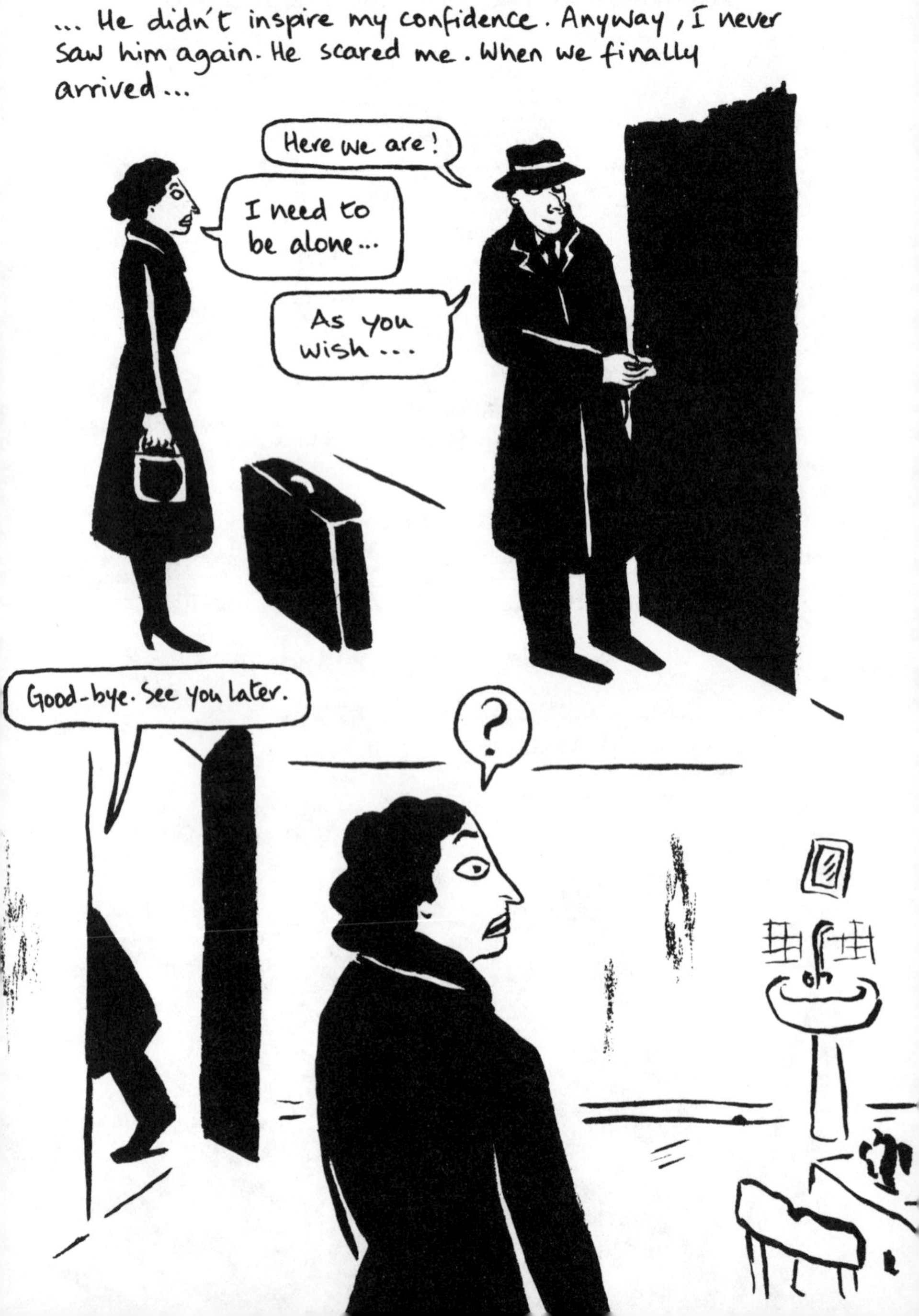
... He didn't inspire my confidence. Anyway, I never saw him again. He scared me. When we finally arrived...
Here we are!
I need to be alone...
As you wish...
Good-bye. See you later.
?

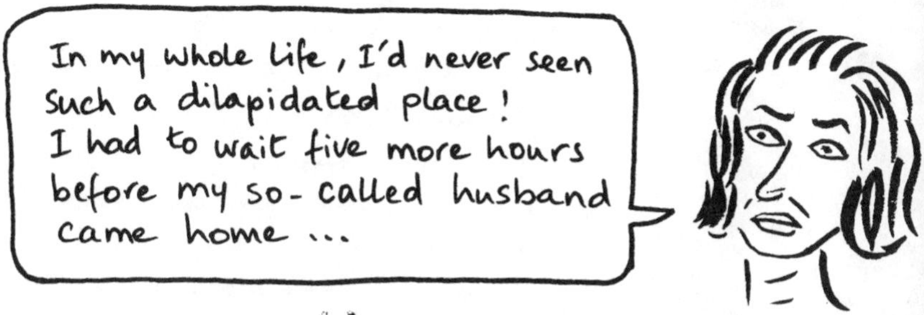
In my whole life, I'd never seen such a dilapidated place! I had to wait five more hours before my so-called husband came home ...

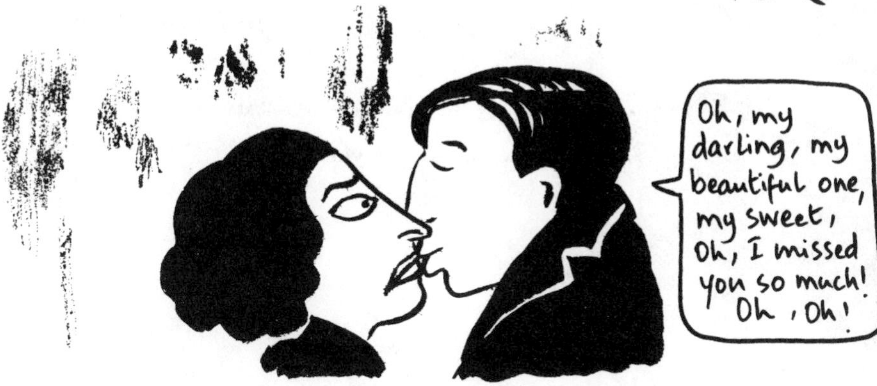
Oh, my darling, my beautiful one, my sweet, Oh, I missed you so much! Oh, Oh!

... He smelled like woman. He explained that he hadn't had the time to furnish our "Love nest". I asked him what his work was. He answered that he devoted all his time to his political activities ... He was undoubtedly busy with the diplomatic relations between his testicles and women's breasts!

All that he'd learned of western culture was to slick back his hair more and to kiss on the right and the left ...

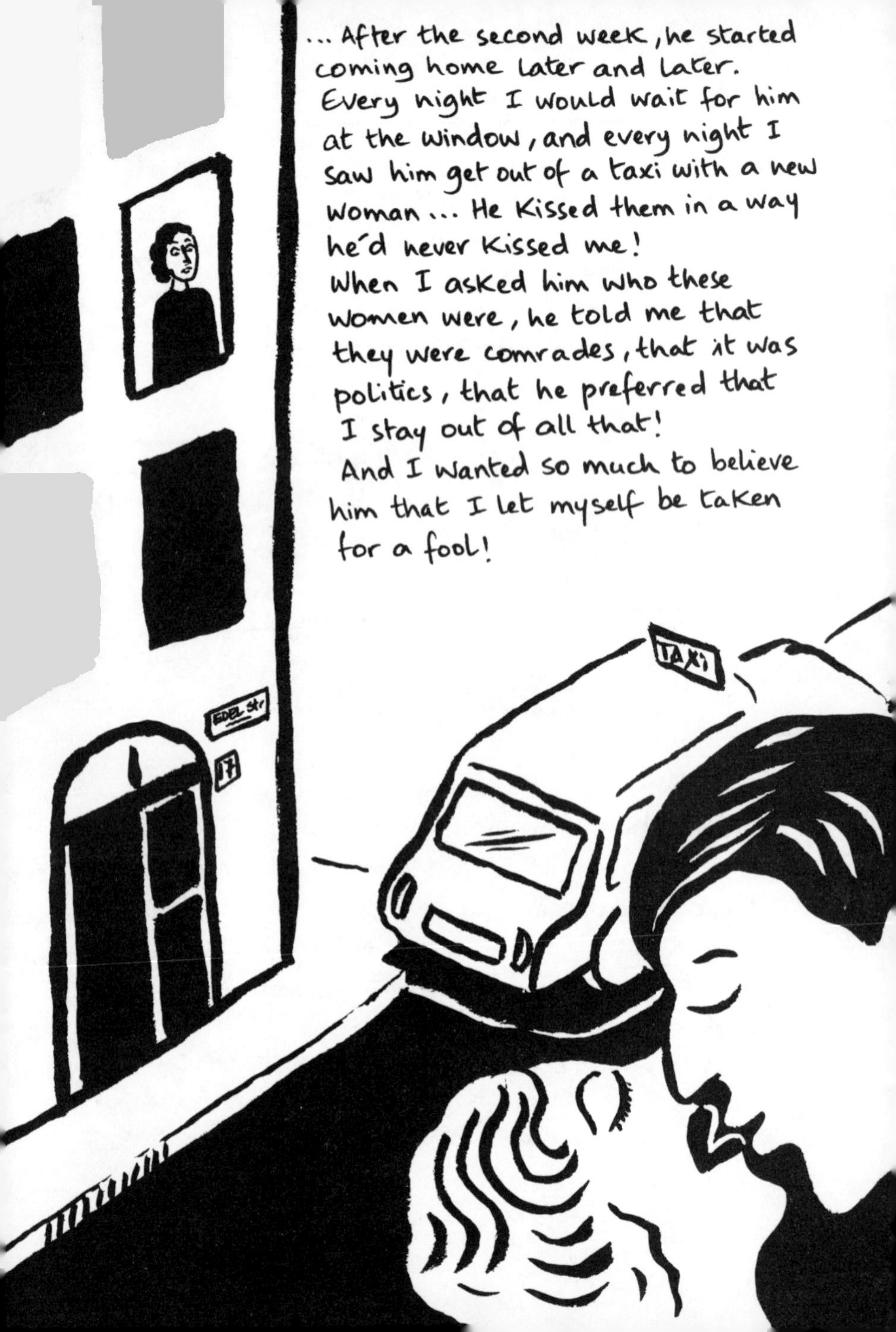
... After the second week, he started coming home later and later. Every night I would wait for him at the window, and every night I saw him get out of a taxi with a new woman... He kissed them in a way he'd never kissed me! When I asked him who these women were, he told me that they were comrades, that it was politics, that he preferred that I stay out of all that! And I wanted so much to believe him that I let myself be taken for a fool!
TAXI

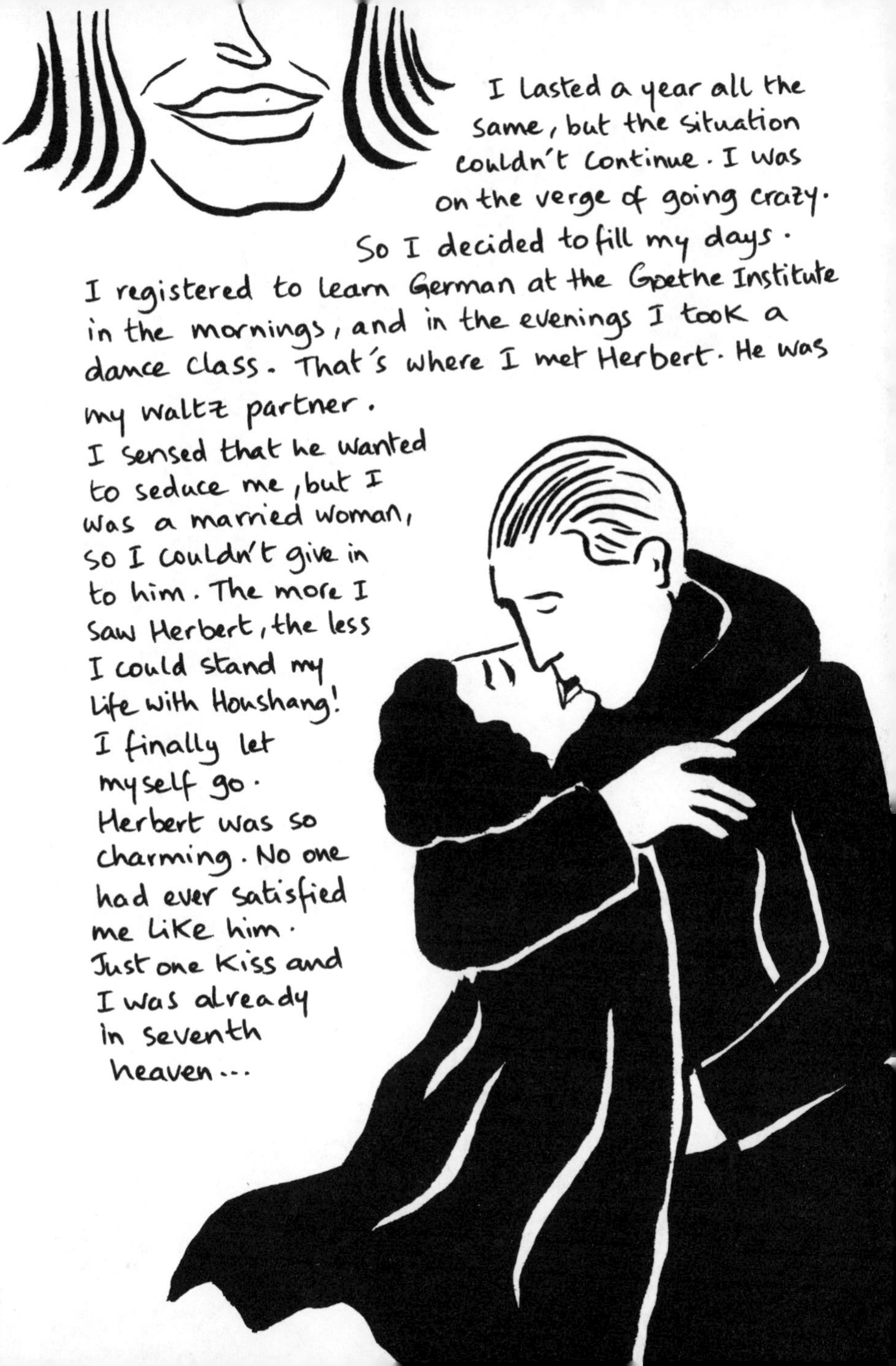
I lasted a year all the same, but the situation couldn't continue. I was on the verge of going crazy.
So I decided to fill my days.
I registered to learn German at the Goethe Institute in the mornings, and in the evenings I took a dance class. That's where I met Herbert. He was my waltz partner.
I sensed that he wanted to seduce me, but I was a married woman, so I couldn't give in to him. The more I saw Herbert, the less I could stand my life with Houshang!
I finally let myself go.
Herbert was so charming. No one had ever satisfied me like him.
Just one kiss and I was already in seventh heaven...

Thanks to him, I found the courage to leave my husband.
I'm getting out of here!!
I won't let you go!
Oh yeah?
You can't leave. You're mine!! Without you, I'll die.
SO DIE!!
SLAM!

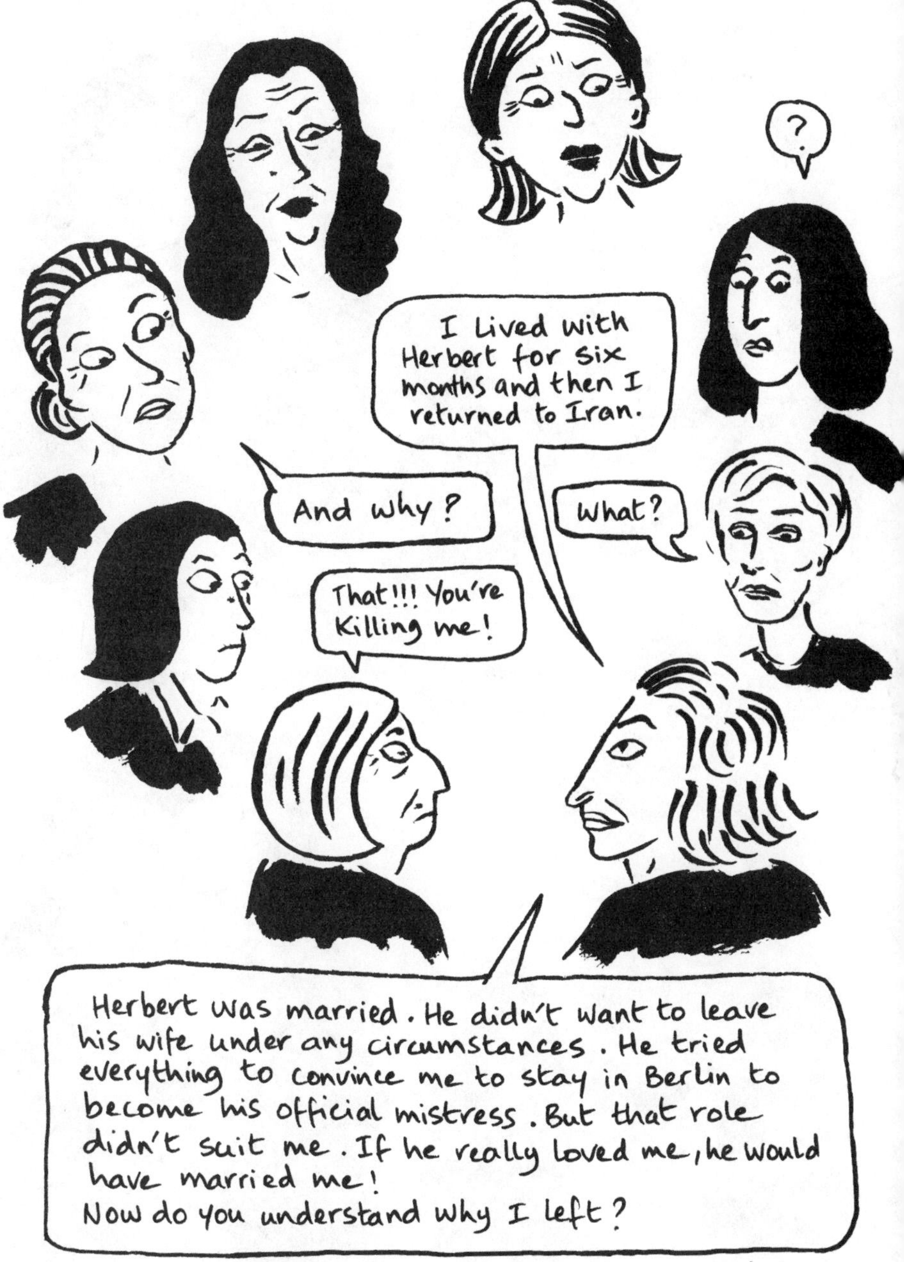
?
I Lived with Herbert for six months and then I returned to Iran.
And why?
What?
That!!! You're Killing me!
Herbert was married. He didn't want to leave his wife under any circumstances. He tried everything to convince me to stay in Berlin to become his official mistress. But that role didn't suit me. If he really loved me, he would have married me!
Now do you understand why I left?

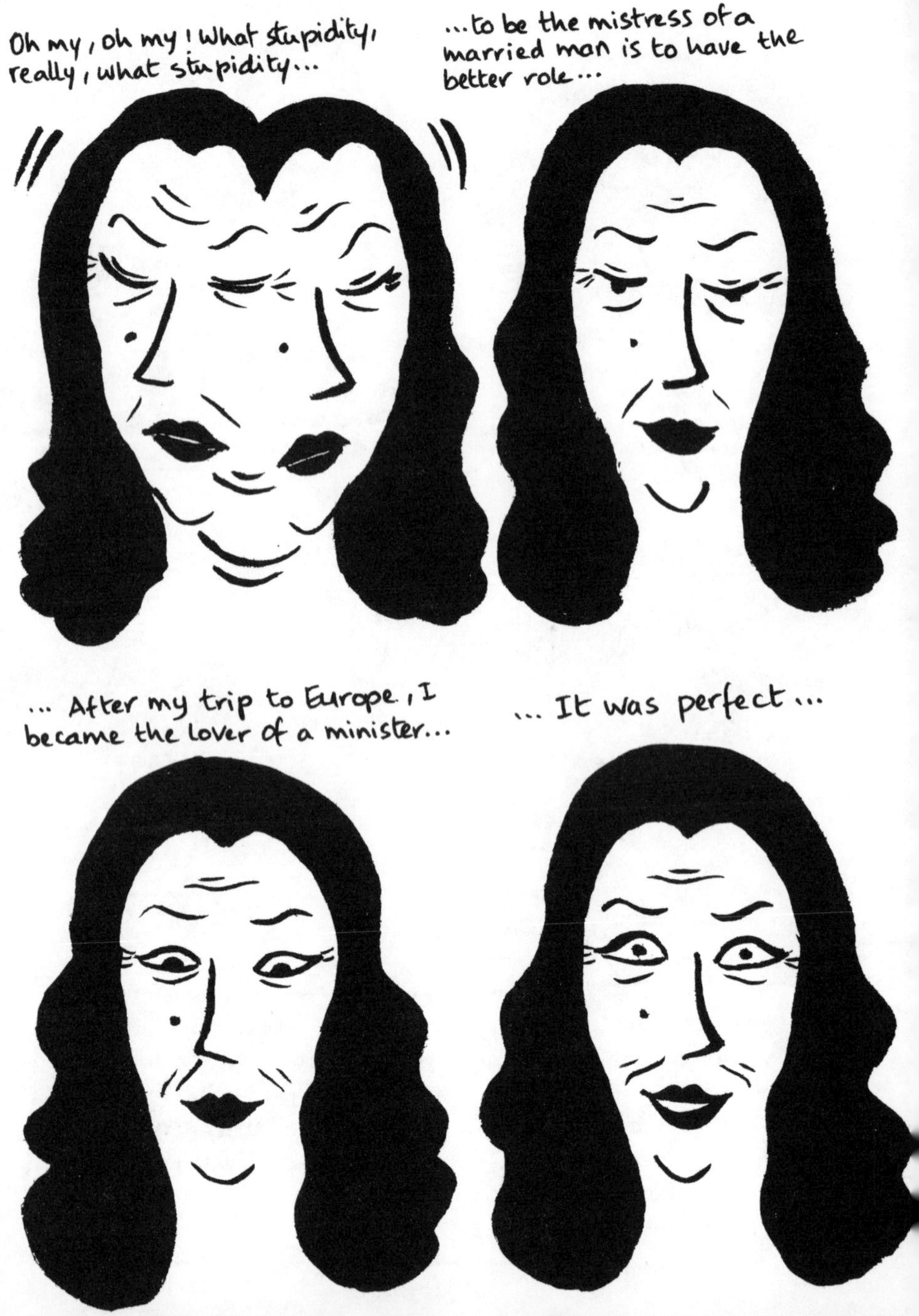
Oh my, oh my! What stupidity, really, what stupidity...
...to be the mistress of a married man is to have the better role...
... After my trip to Europe, I became the lover of a minister...
... It was perfect...

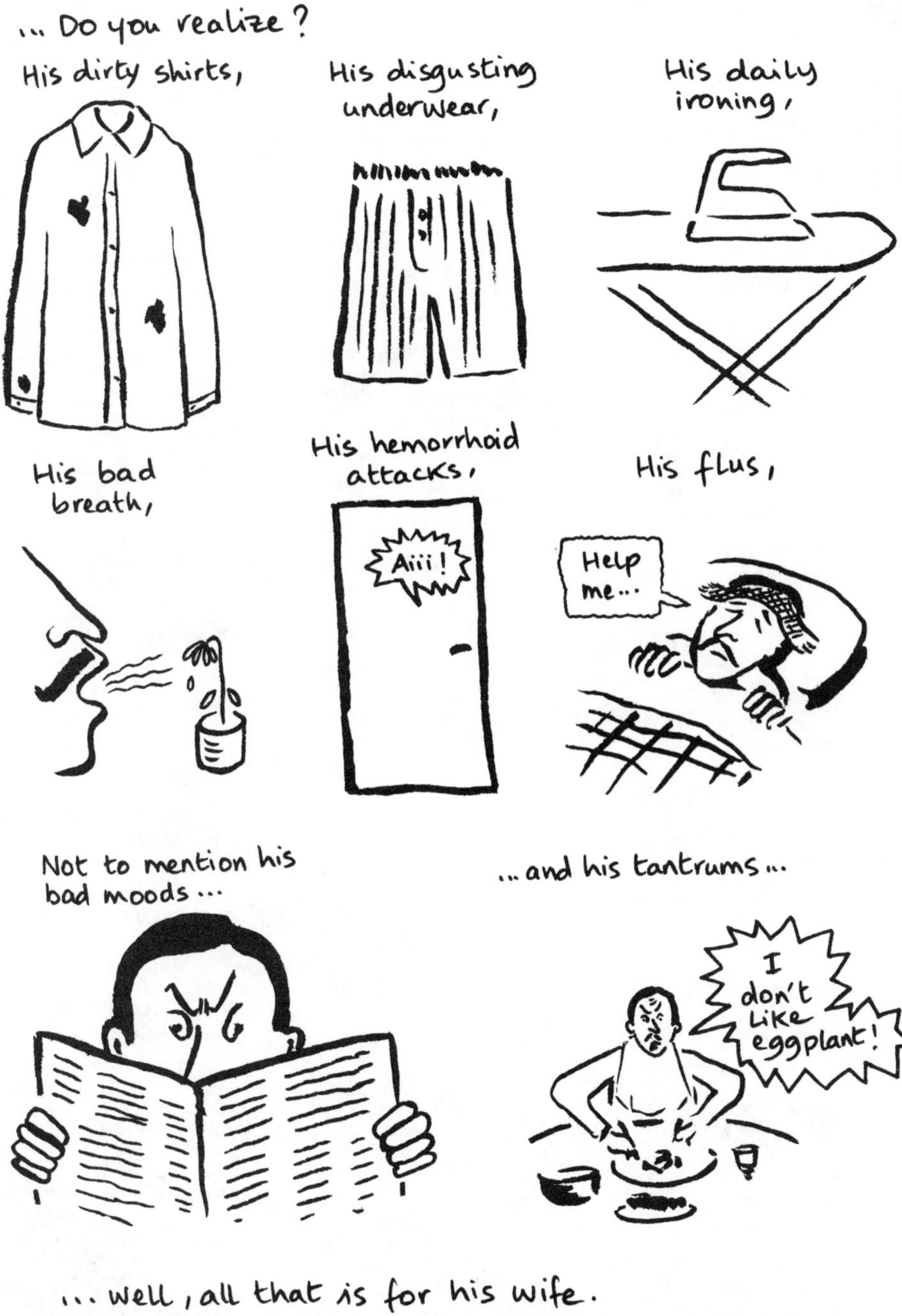
... Do you realize?
His dirty shirts,
His disgusting underwear,
His daily ironing,
His bad breath,
His hemorrhoid attacks,
Aiii!
His flus,
Help me...
Not to mention his bad moods...
... and his tantrums...
I don't like eggplant!
... well, all that is for his wife.

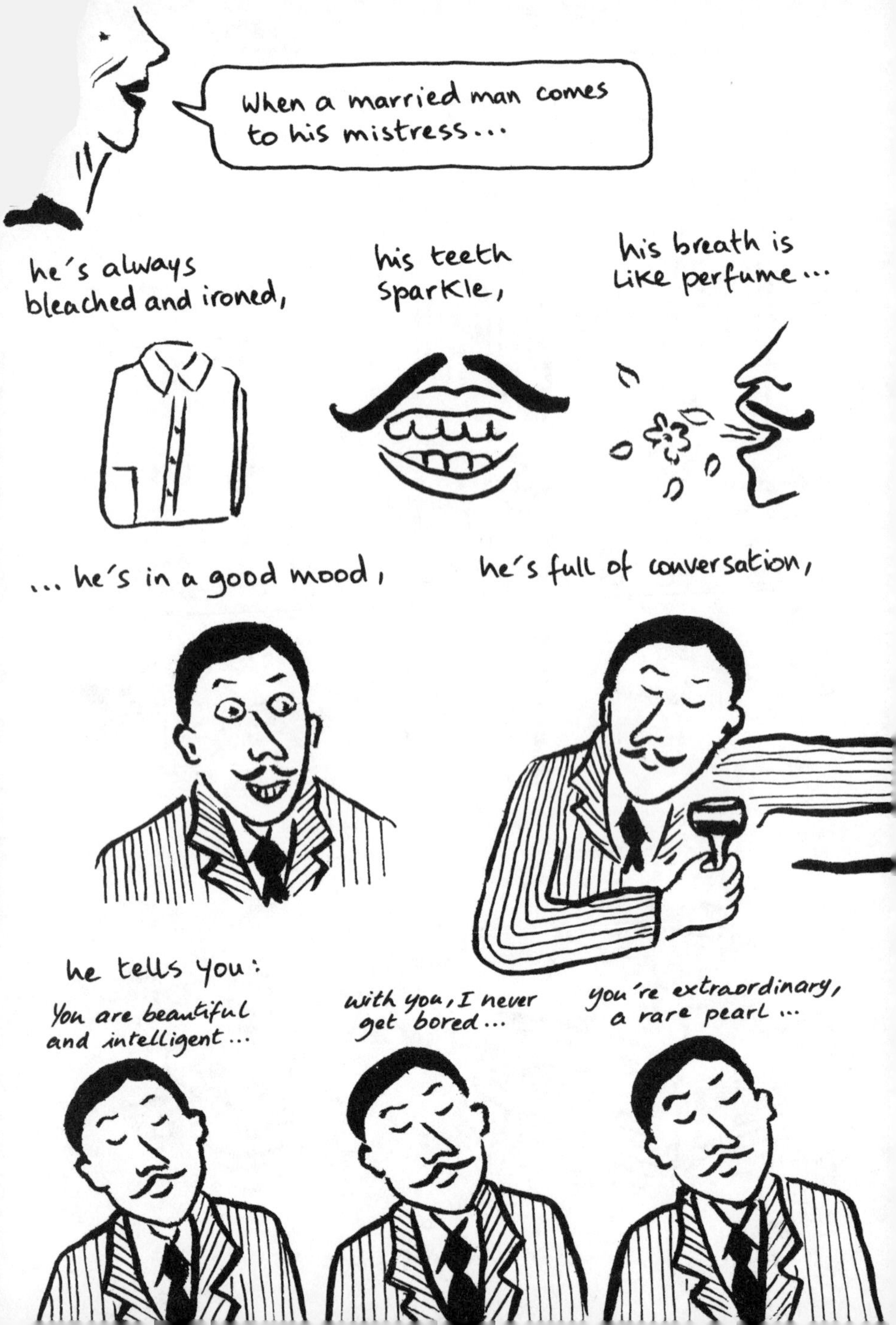

When a married man comes to his mistress...
he's always bleached and ironed,
his teeth sparkle,
his breath is like perfume...
... he's in a good mood,
he's full of conversation,
he tells you:
You are beautiful and intelligent...
with you, I never get bored...
you're extraordinary, a rare pearl...

... He is there to have a good time with you.

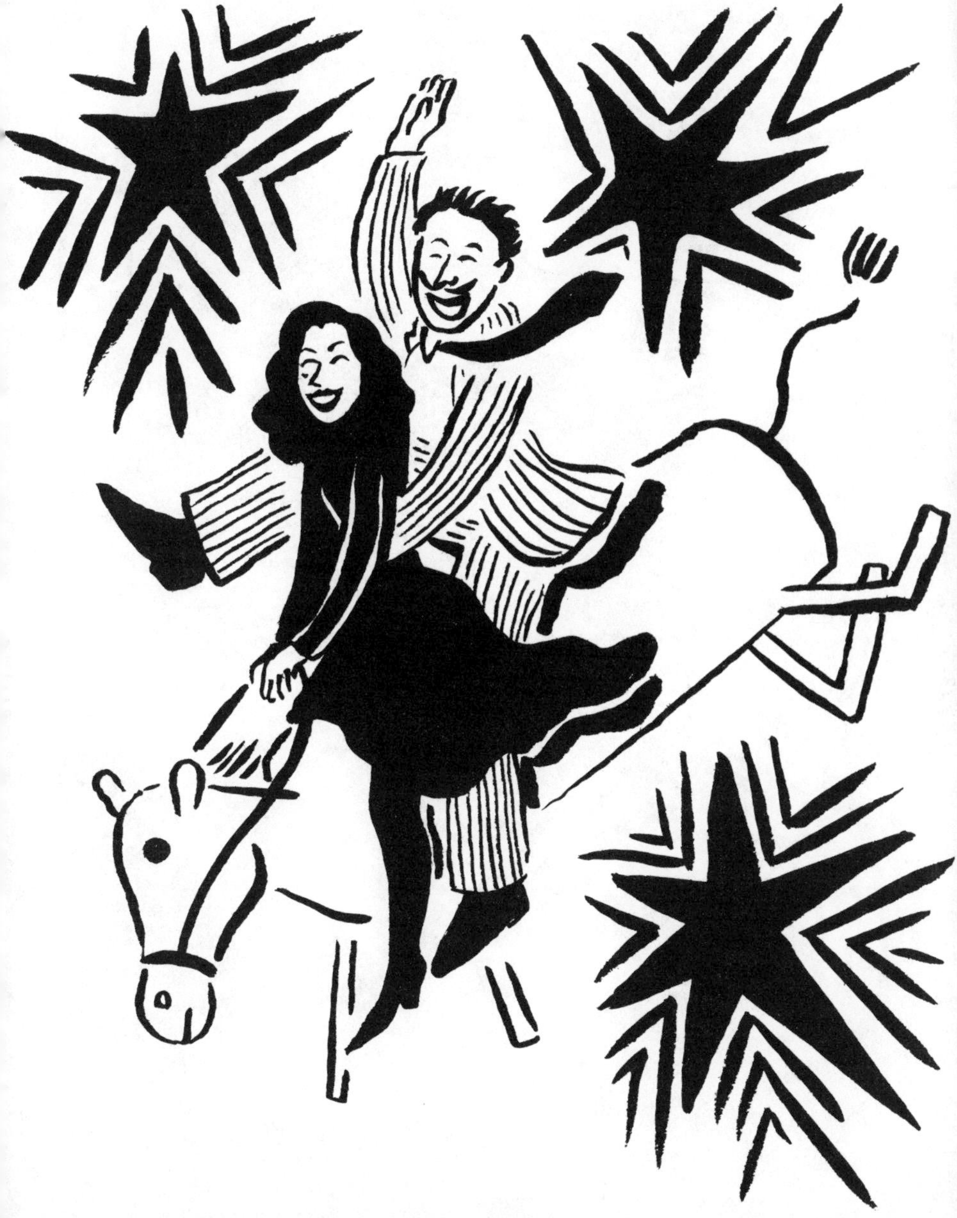

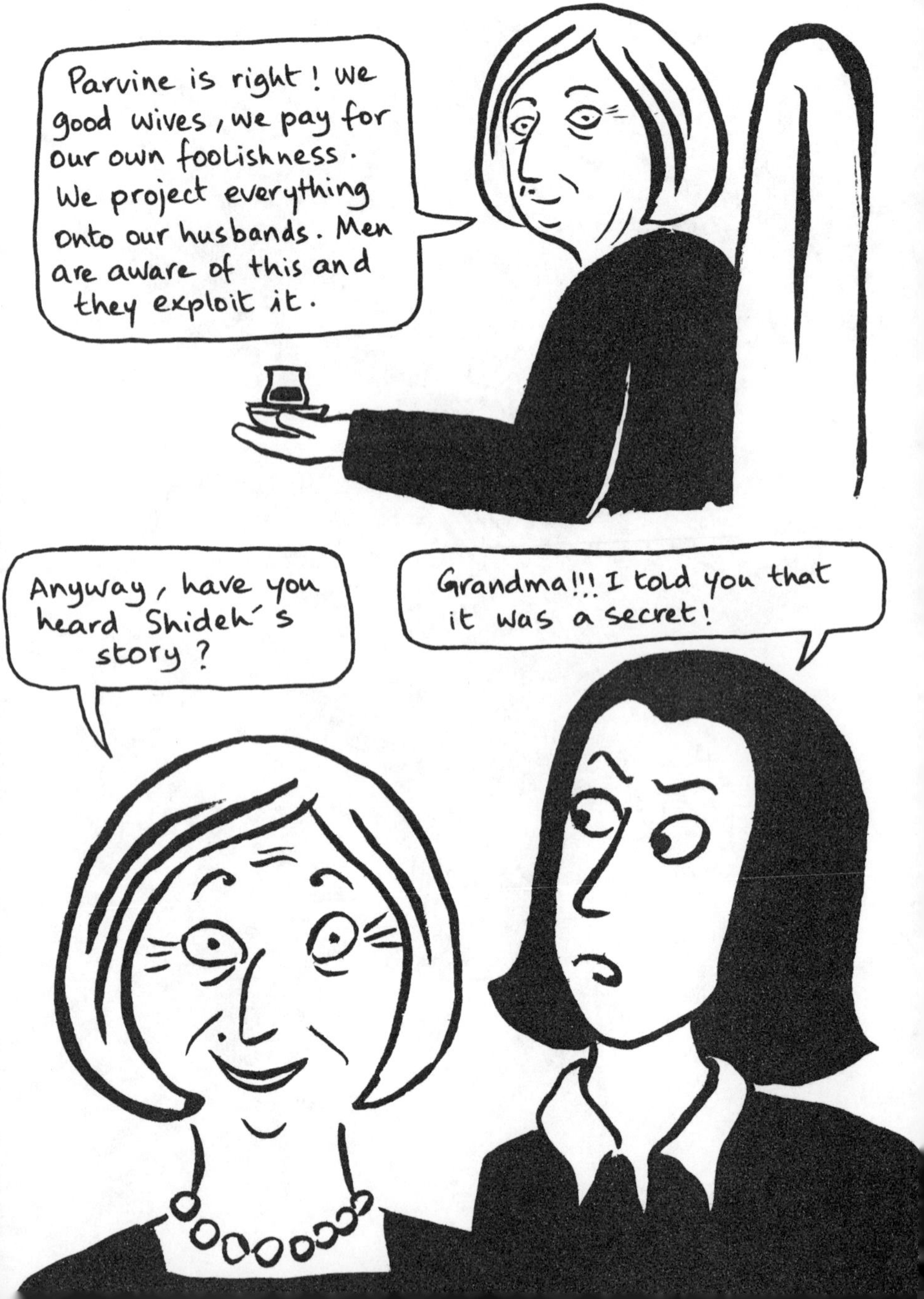
Parvine is right! We good wives, we pay for our own foolishness. We project everything onto our husbands. Men are aware of this and they exploit it.
Anyway, have you heard Shideh's story?
Grandma!!! I told you that it was a secret!

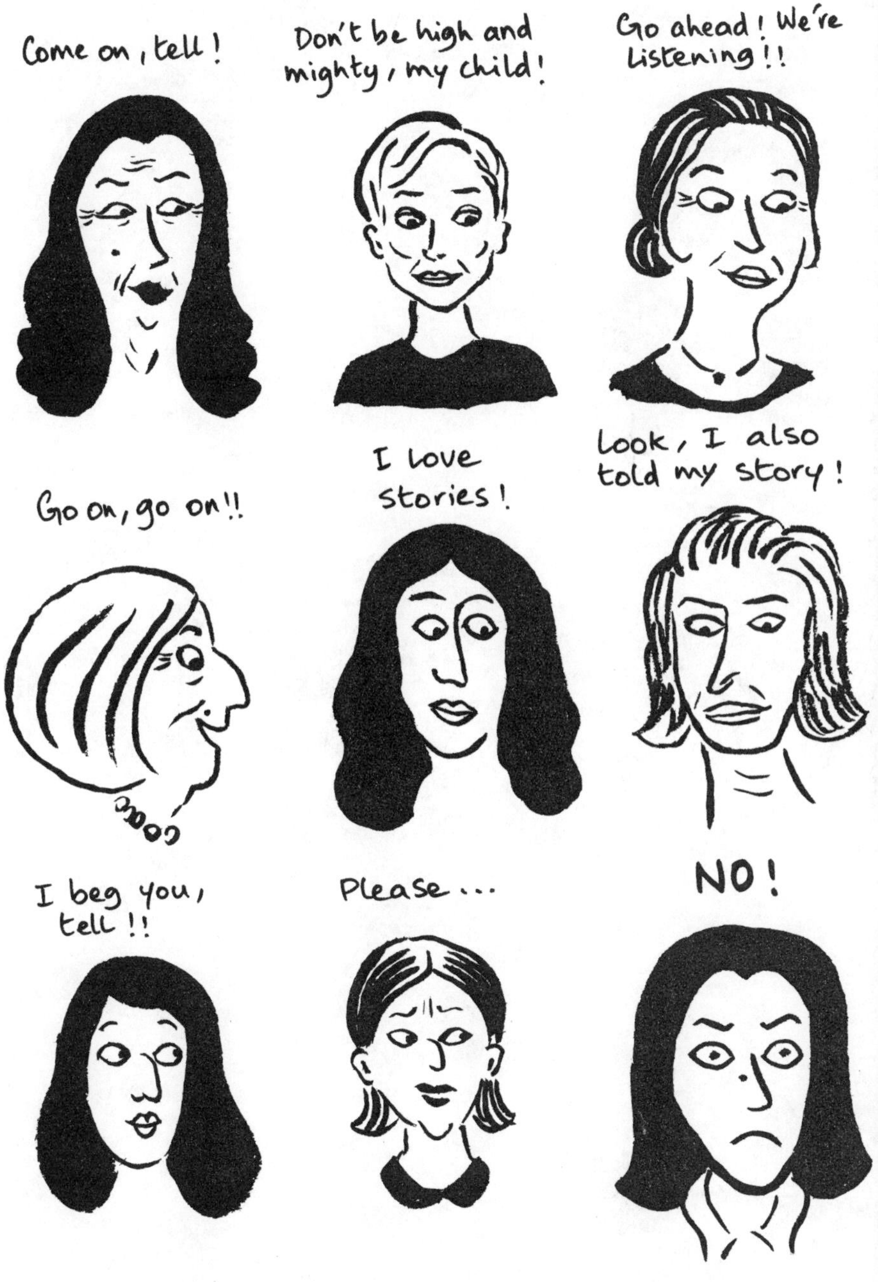

Come on, tell!
Don't be high and mighty, my child!
Go ahead! We're listening!!
Go on, go on!!
I love stories!
Look, I also told my story!
I beg you, tell!!
Please...
NO!

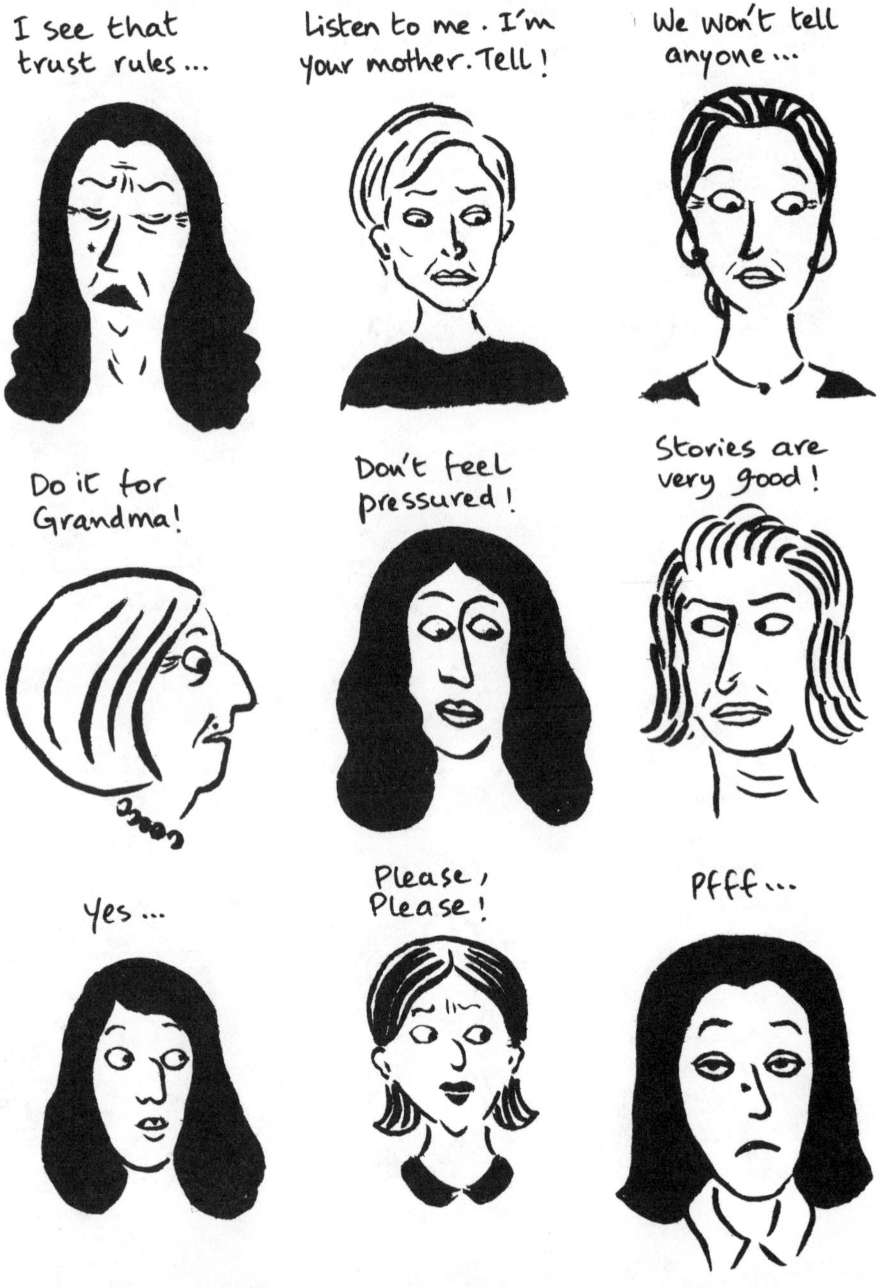
I see that trust rules...
Listen to me. I'm your mother. Tell!
We won't tell anyone...
Do it for Grandma!
Don't feel pressured!
Stories are very good!
Yes...
Please, Please!
Pfff...

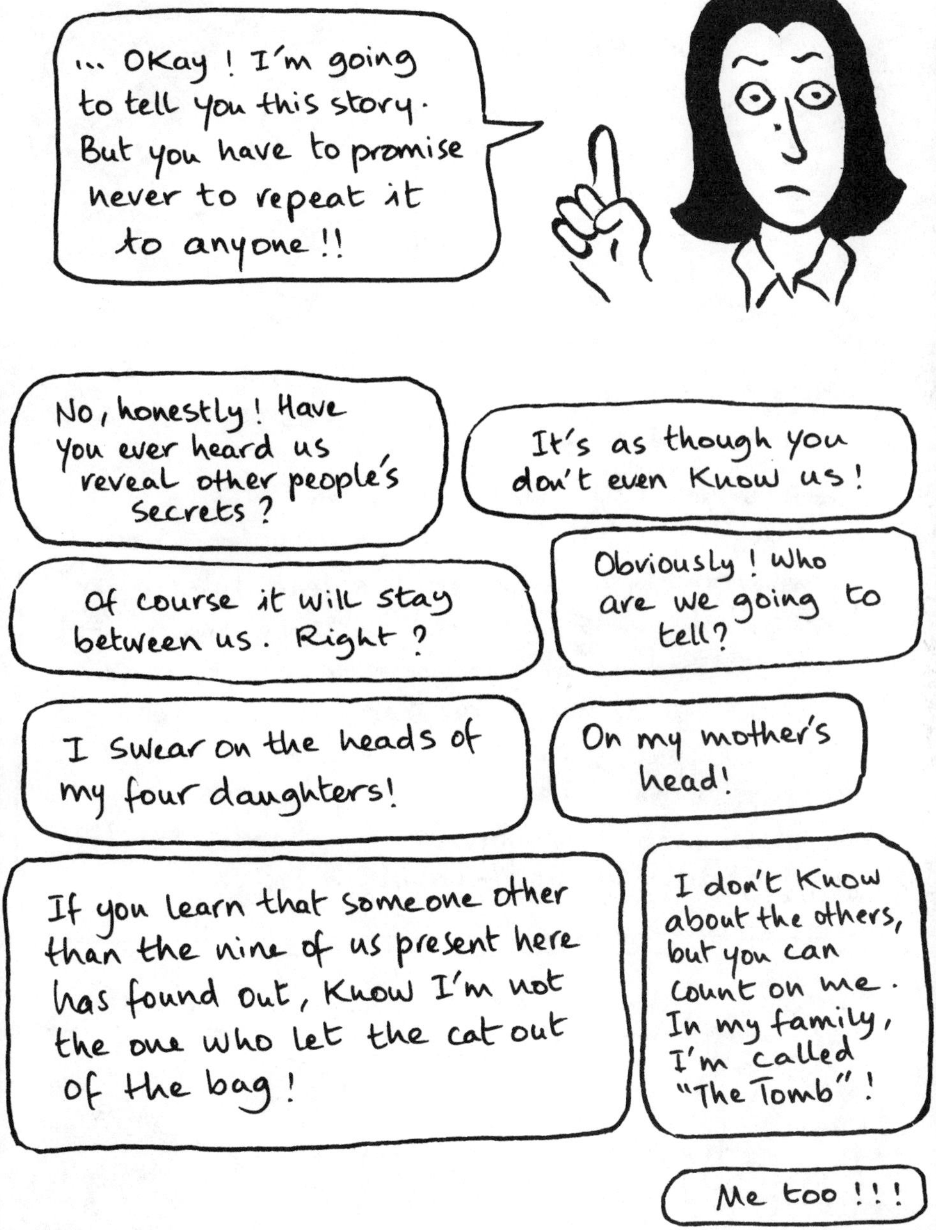
... OKay ! I'm going to tell you this story. But you have to promise never to repeat it to anyone !!
No, honestly ! Have you ever heard us reveal other people's secrets ?
It's as though you don't even Know us !
Of course it will stay between us. Right ?
Obviously ! Who are we going to tell ?
I swear on the heads of my four daughters !
On my mother's head !
If you learn that someone other than the nine of us present here has found out, Know I'm not the one who let the cat out of the bag !
I don't Know about the others, but you can count on me. In my family, I'm called "The Tomb" !
Me too !!!

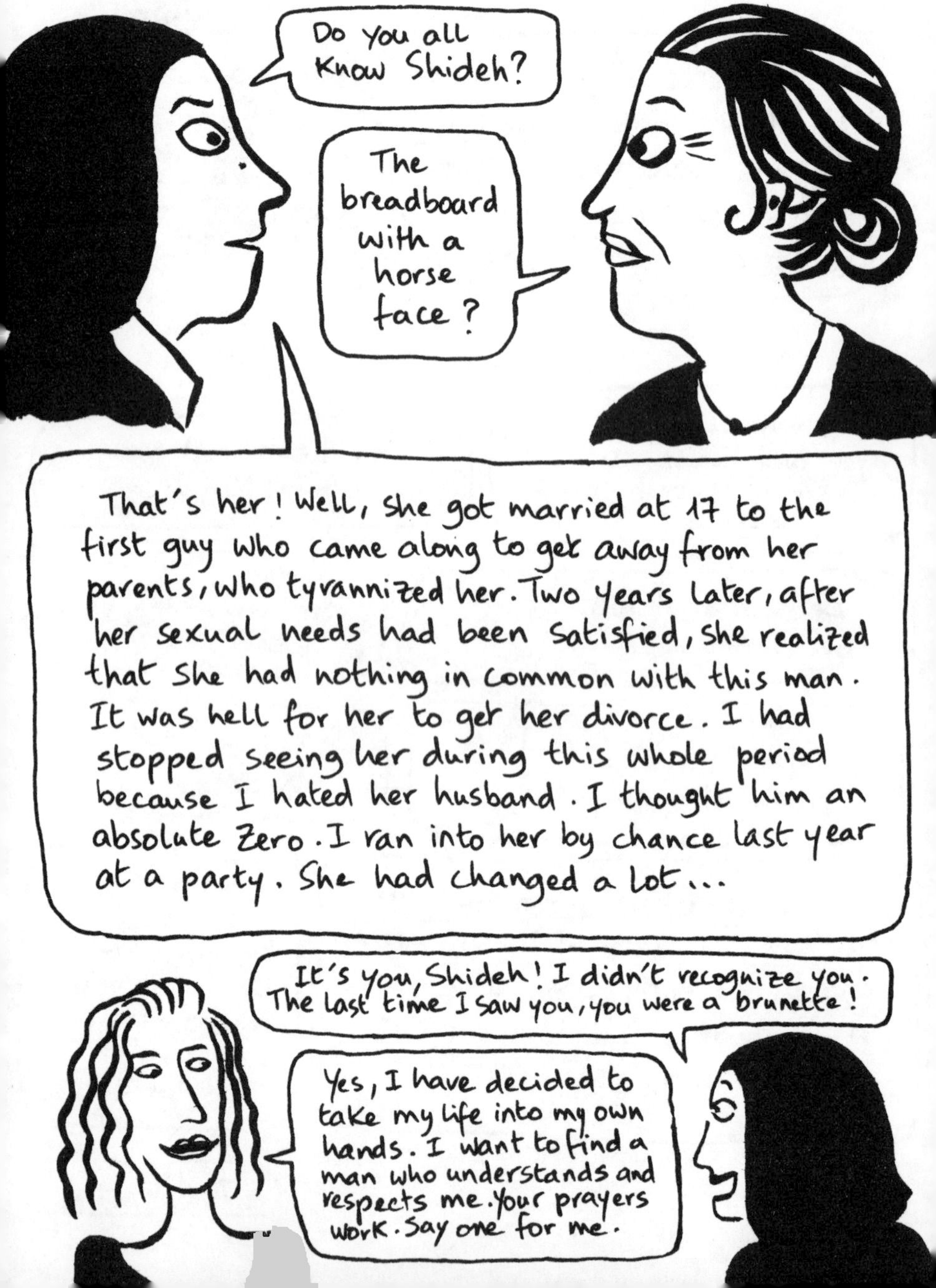
Do you all Know Shideh?
The breadboard with a horse face?
That's her! Well, she got married at 17 to the first guy who came along to get away from her parents, who tyrannized her. Two years later, after her sexual needs had been satisfied, she realized that she had nothing in common with this man. It was hell for her to get her divorce. I had stopped seeing her during this whole period because I hated her husband. I thought him an absolute zero. I ran into her by chance last year at a party. She had changed a lot...
It's you, Shideh! I didn't recognize you. The last time I saw you, you were a brunette!
Yes, I have decided to take my life into my own hands. I want to find a man who understands and respects me. Your prayers work. Say one for me.

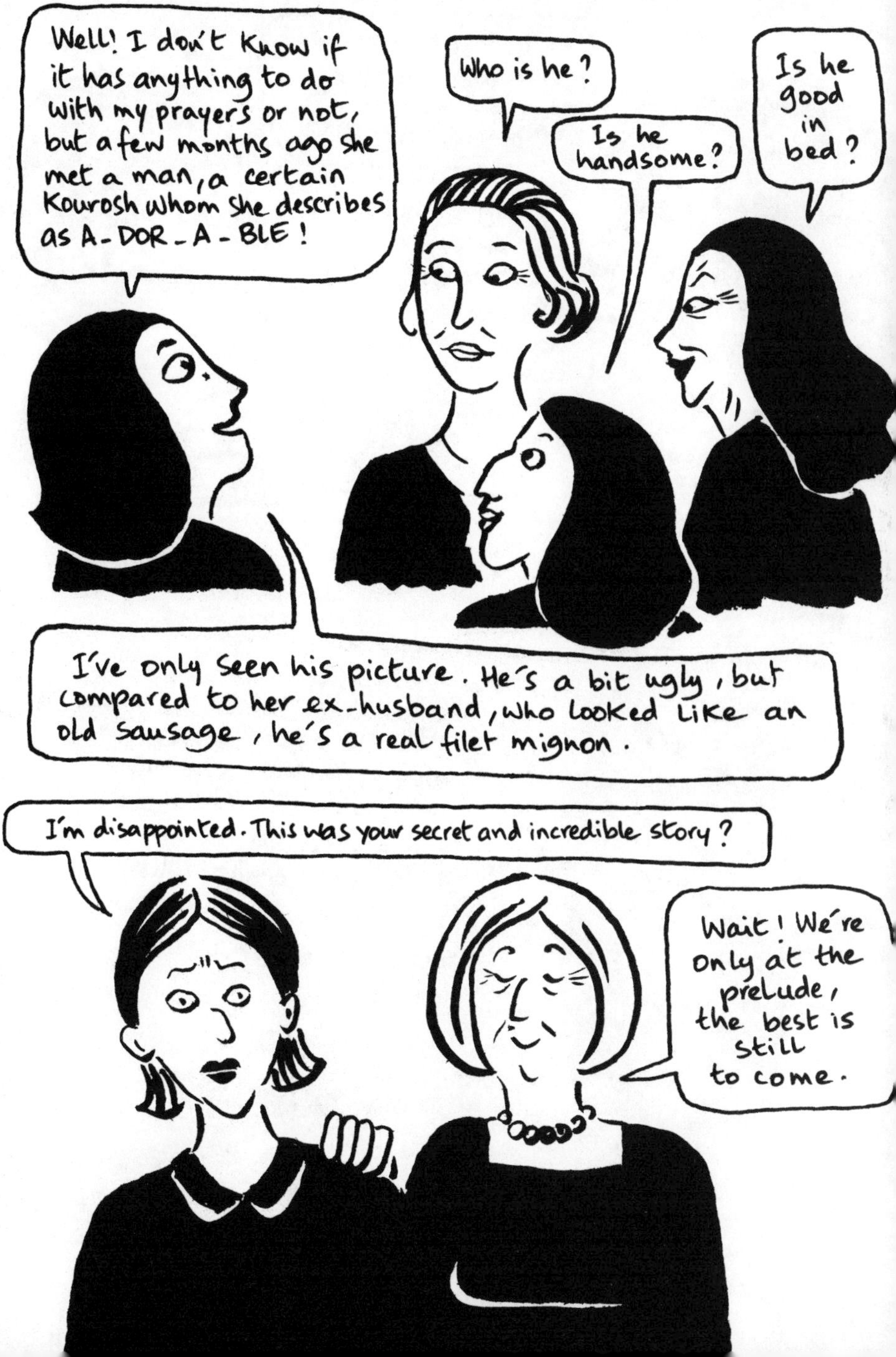
Well! I don't know if it has anything to do with my prayers or not, but a few months ago she met a man, a certain Kourosh whom she describes as A-DOR-A-BLE!
Who is he?
Is he handsome?
Is he good in bed?
I've only seen his picture. He's a bit ugly, but compared to her ex-husband, who looked like an old sausage, he's a real filet mignon.
I'm disappointed. This was your secret and incredible story?
Wait! We're only at the prelude, the best is still to come.

Even if this Kourosh is adorable and superb, there's still an enormous problem.
What Kind of problem?
His mother doesn't want him to marry Shideh!
And why not??? She's a very nice girl.
I don't think it has anything to do with Shideh. This woman has two sons. The older one is married to a divorced woman who puts him through the wringer.

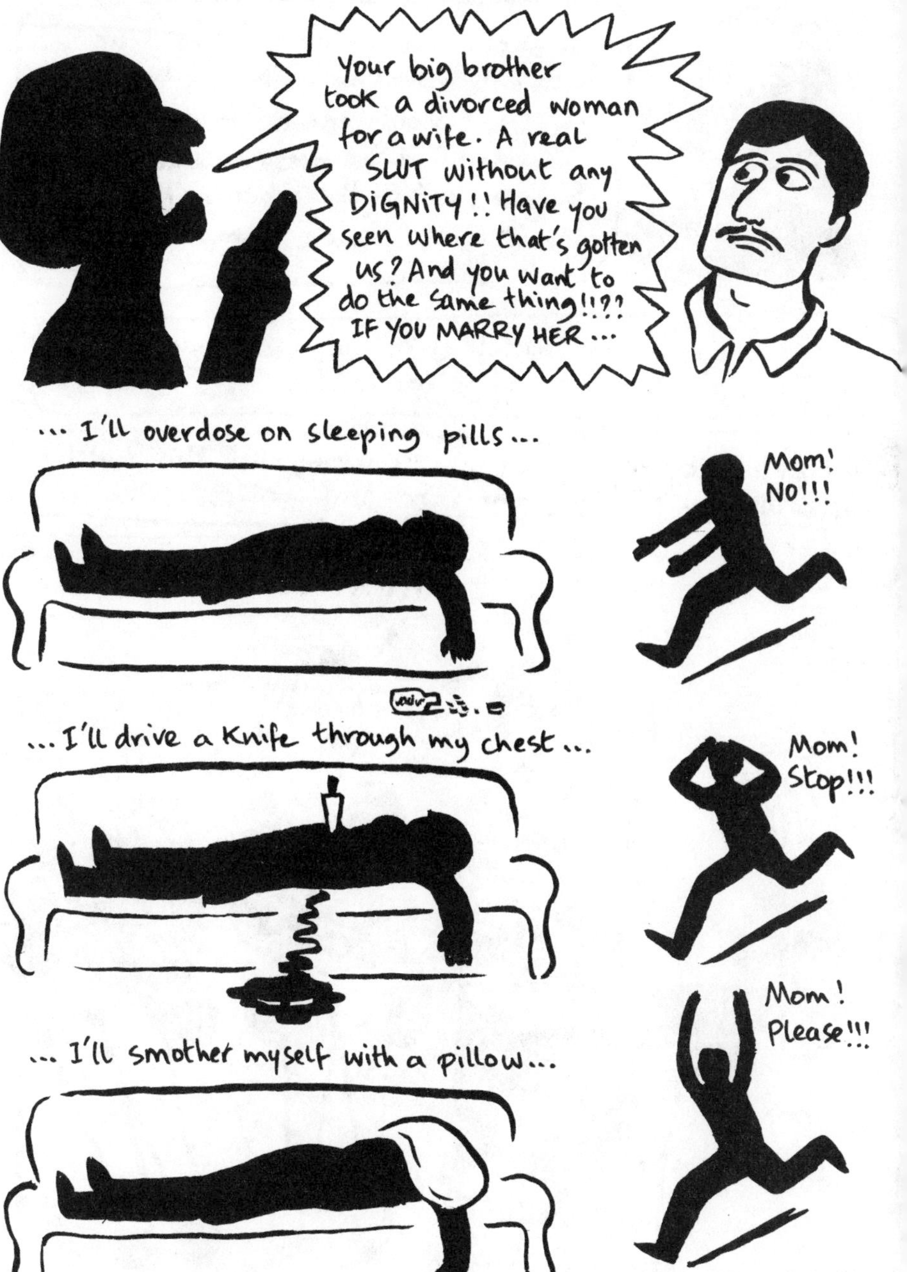
Your big brother took a divorced woman for a wife. A real SLUT without any DIGNITY!! Have you seen where that's gotten us? And you want to do the same thing!!?? IF YOU MARRY HER...
... I'll overdose on sleeping pills...
Mom! NO!!!
... I'll drive a Knife through my chest...
Mom! Stop!!!
... I'll smother myself with a pillow...
Mom! Please!!!

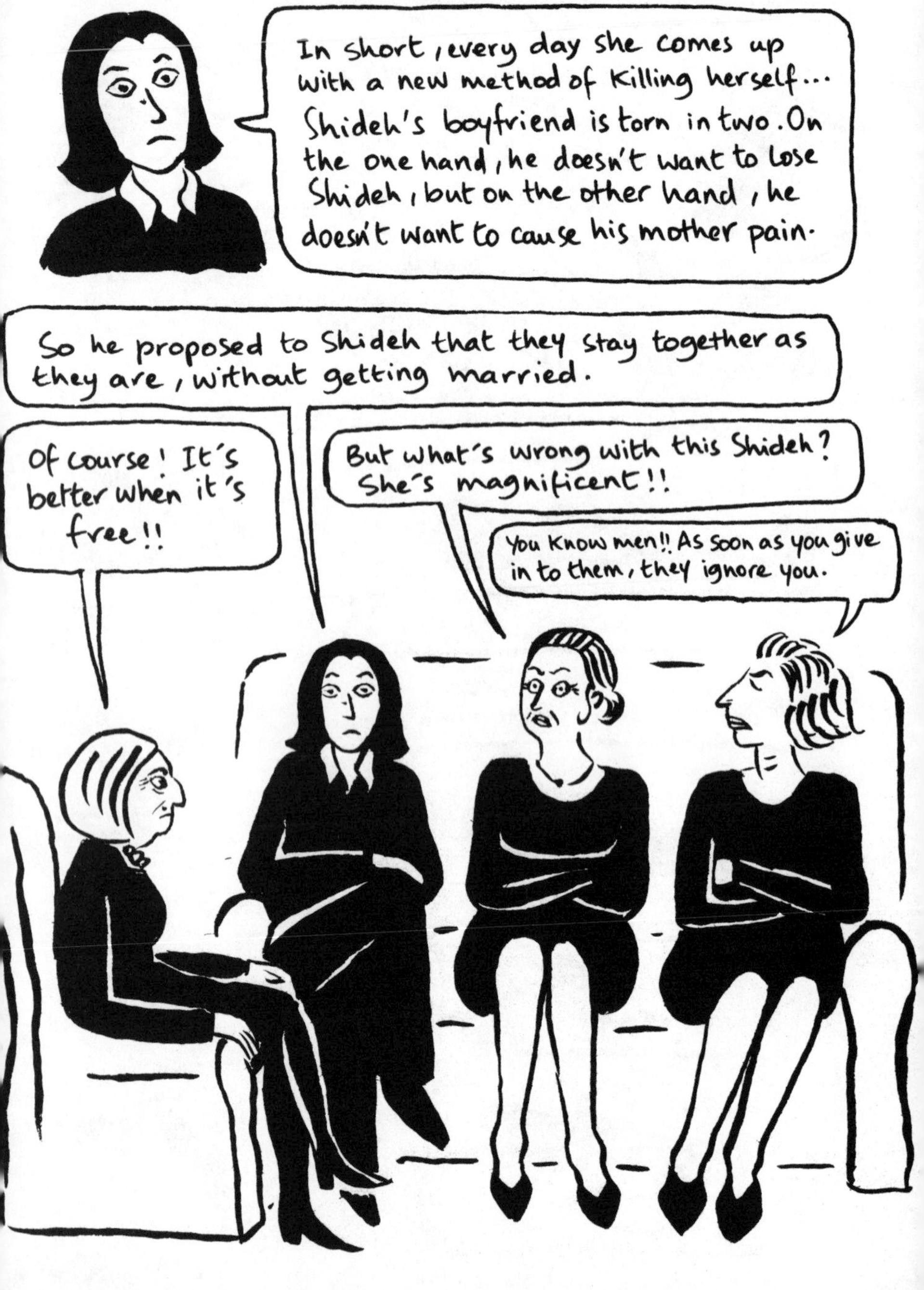
In short, every day she comes up with a new method of Killing herself... Shideh's boyfriend is torn in two. On the one hand, he doesn't want to lose Shideh, but on the other hand, he doesn't want to cause his mother pain.
So he proposed to Shideh that they stay together as they are, without getting married.
Of course! It's better when it's free!!
But what's wrong with this Shideh? She's magnificent!!
You Know men!! As soon as you give in to them, they ignore you.

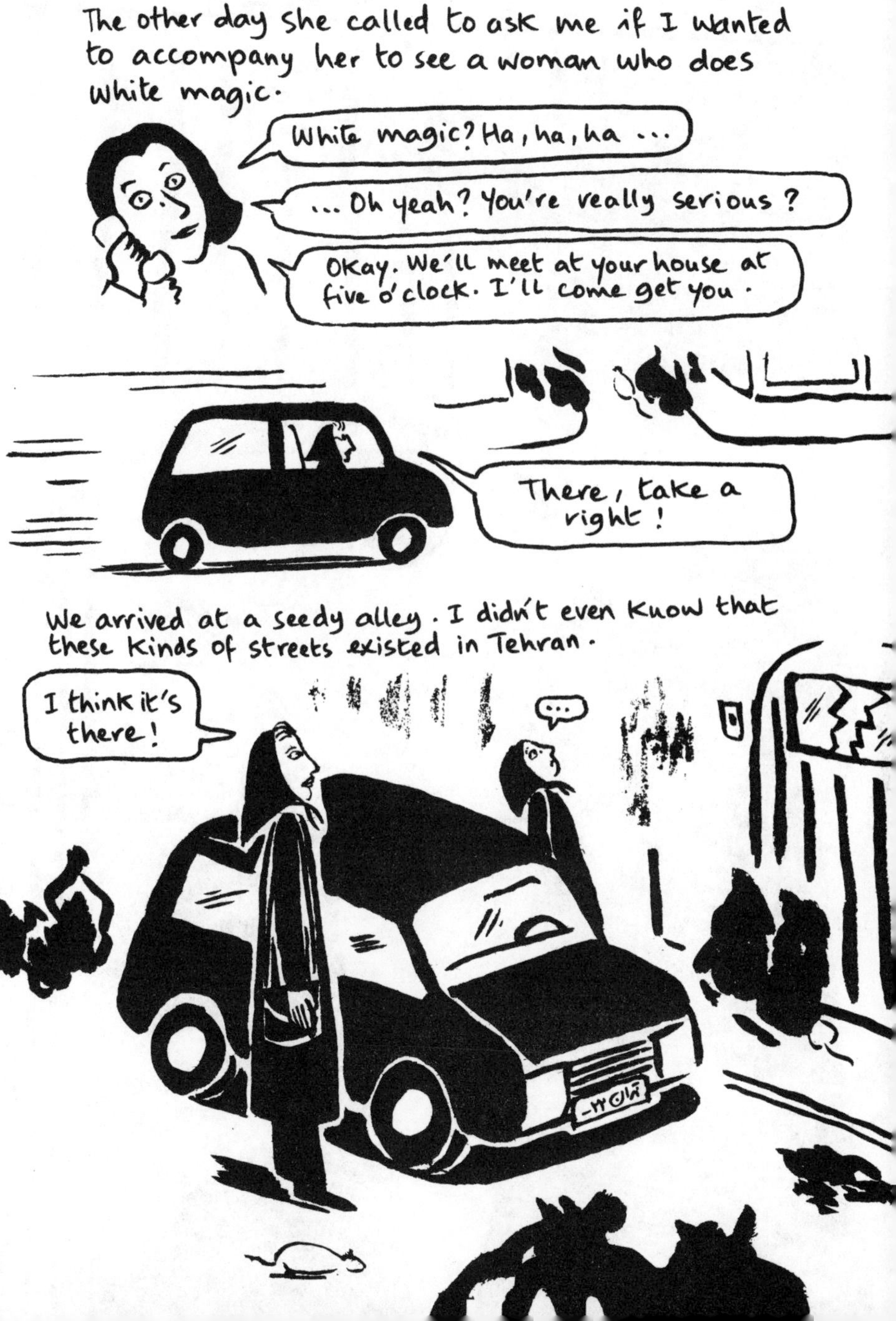
The other day she called to ask me if I wanted to accompany her to see a woman who does white magic.
White magic? Ha, ha, ha ...
... Oh yeah? You're really serious?
Okay. We'll meet at your house at five o'clock. I'll come get you.
There, take a right!
We arrived at a seedy alley. I didn't even know that these kinds of streets existed in Tehran.
I think it's there!
...

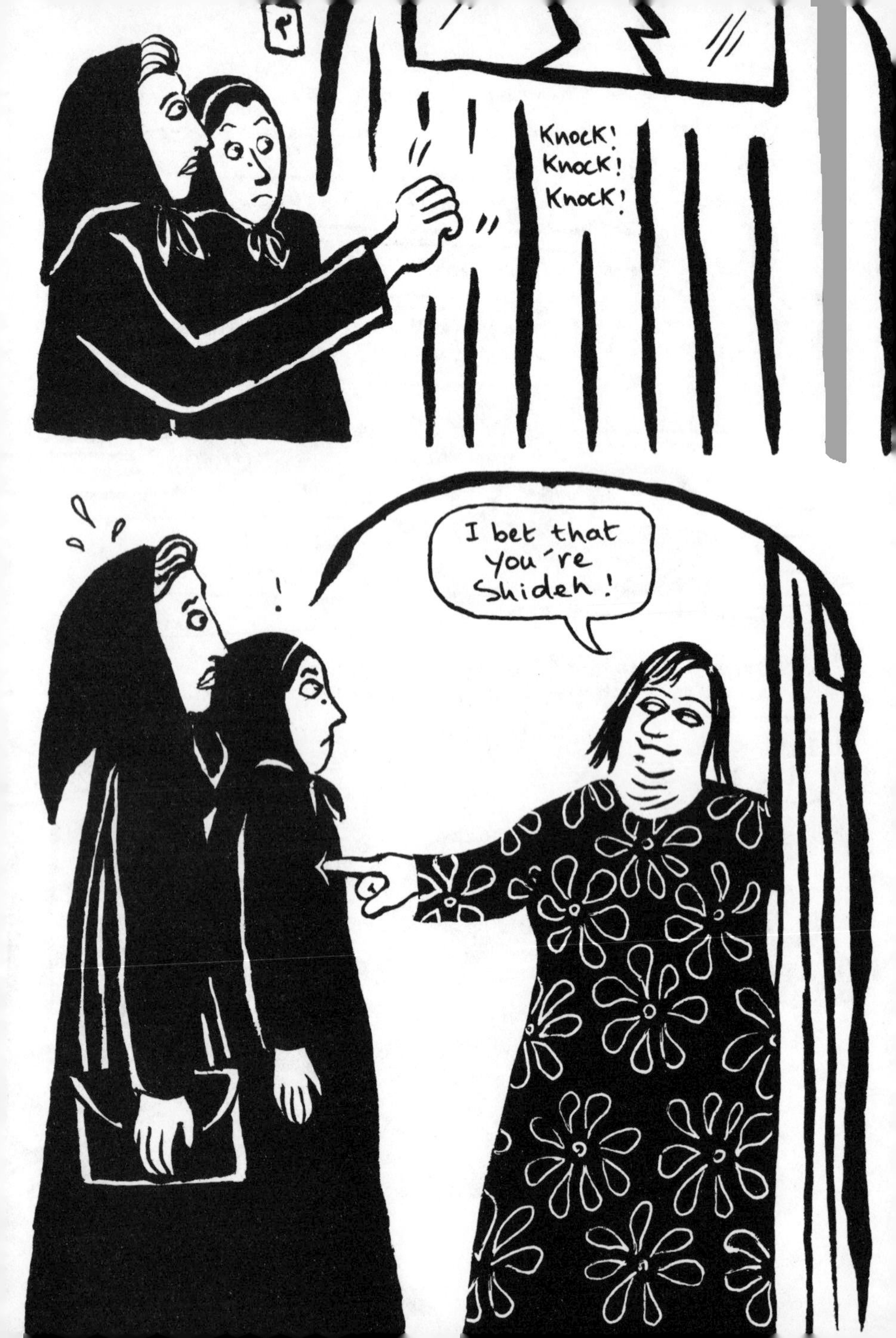
Knock! Knock! Knock!
!
I bet that you're Shideh!

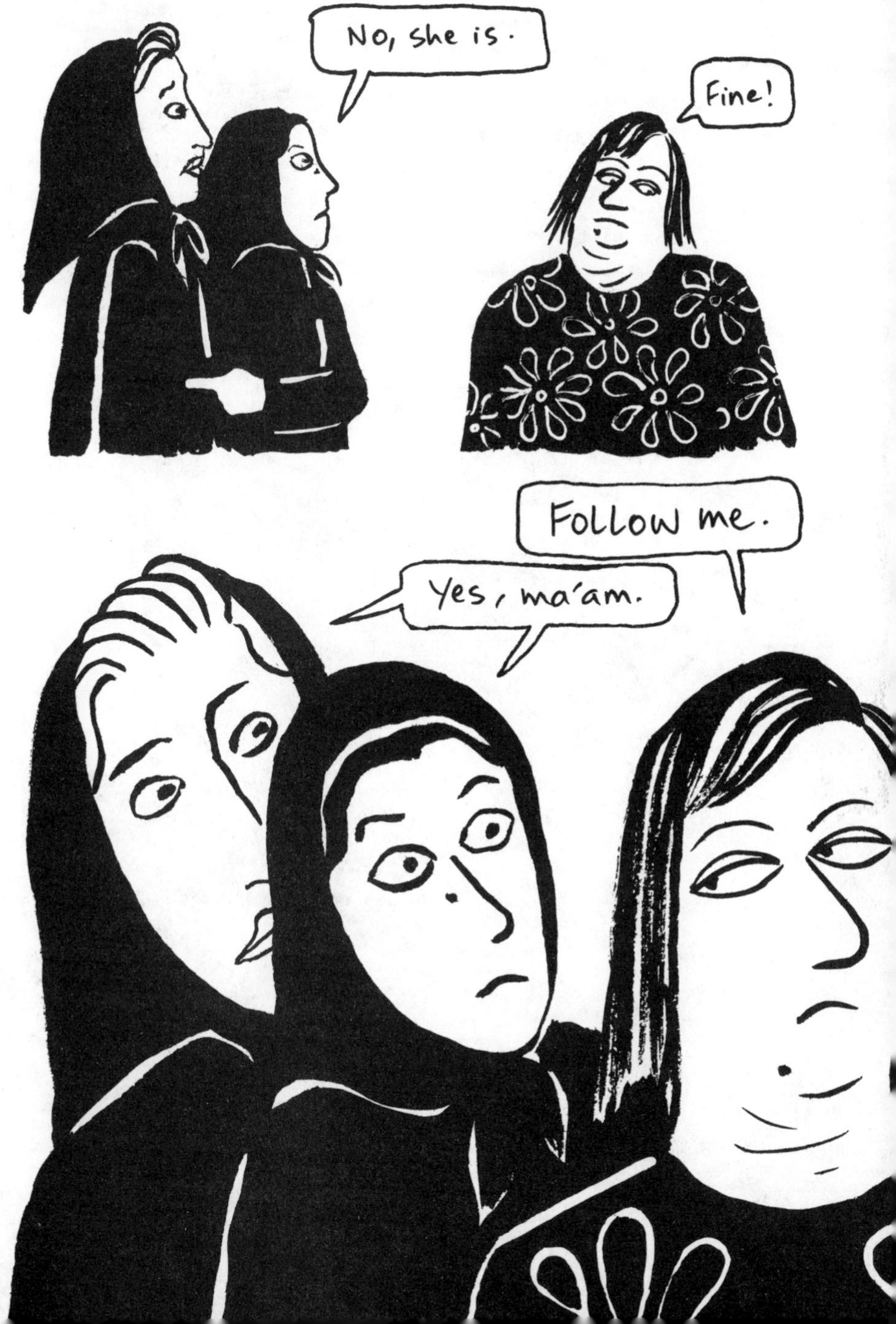
No, she is.
Fine!
Follow me.
Yes, ma'am.

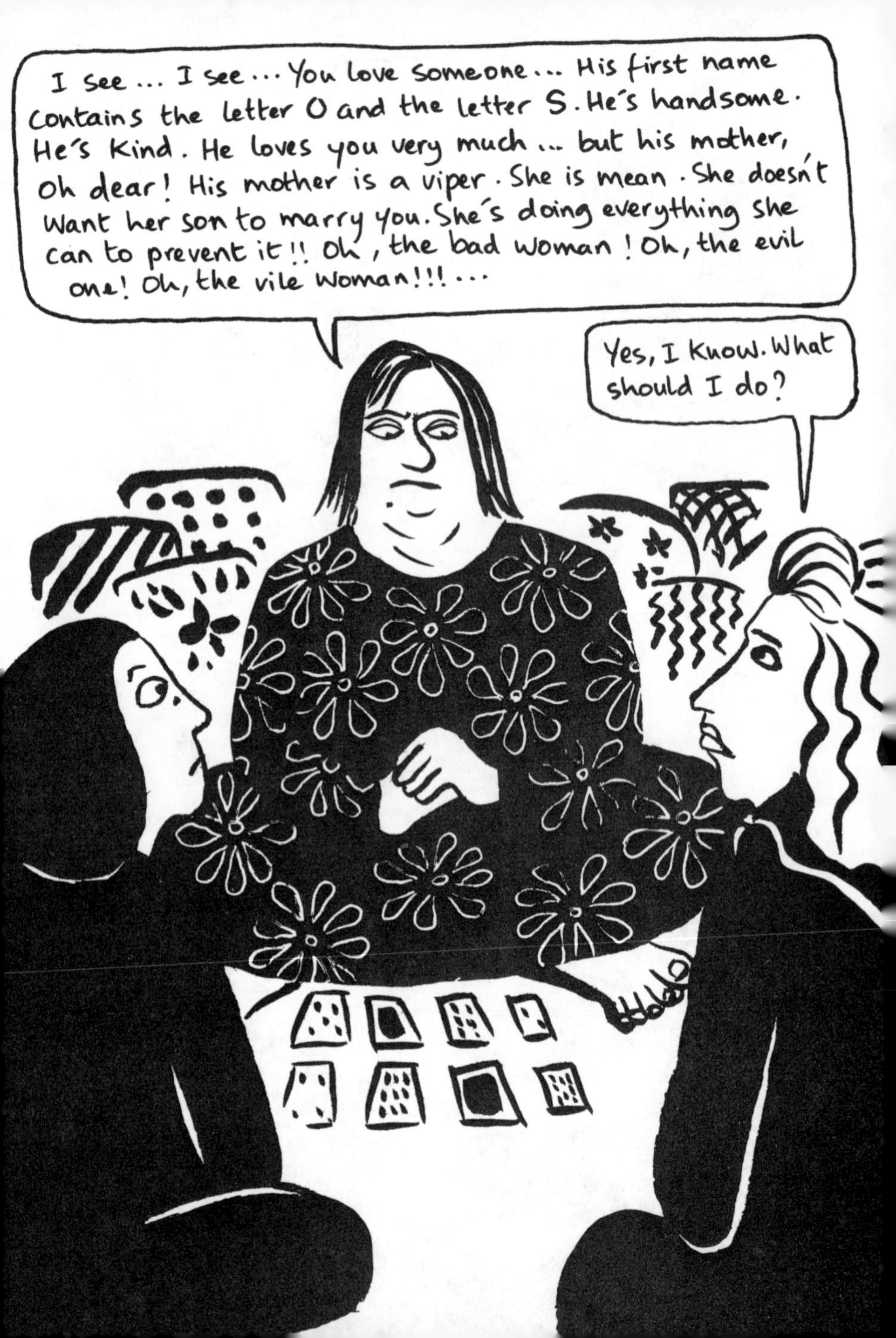
I see ... I see ... You love someone ... His first name contains the letter O and the letter S. He's handsome. He's Kind. He loves you very much ... but his mother, oh dear! His mother is a viper. She is mean. She doesn't want her son to marry you. She's doing everything she can to prevent it!! Oh, the bad woman! Oh, the evil one! Oh, the vile woman!!! ...
Yes, I Know. What should I do?

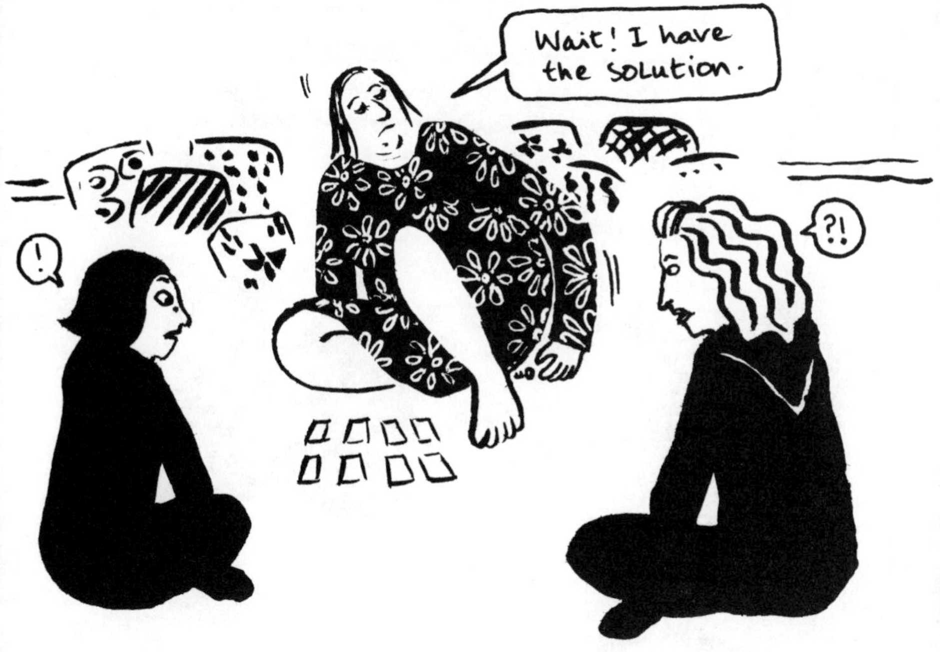
Wait! I have the solution.
!
?!

Here! Take this key. You prepare some tea. You sleep with him. Once he's ejaculated – careful! – he must come in you – you put the key in your vagina. You count to 7. Then you remove the key and put it into a cup. You pour the tea on top. You count to 7. The last step is to remove the key. Tea prepared like this should be drunk by your heart's chosen one in the 77 seconds that follow ejaculation. There, that'll be 3,000 tumans.*

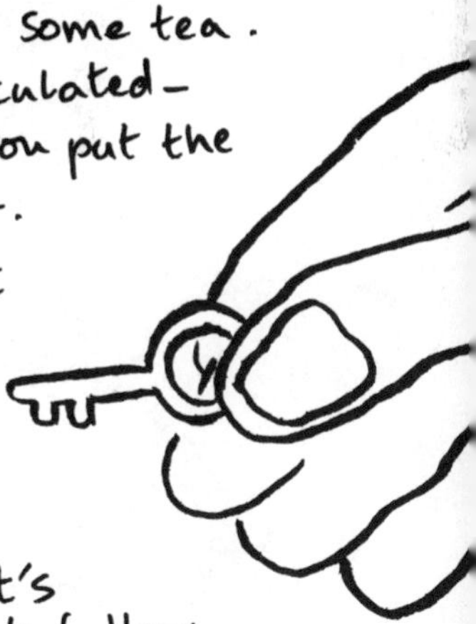

---

* equivalent to $40 in 1991 (thanks to inflation)

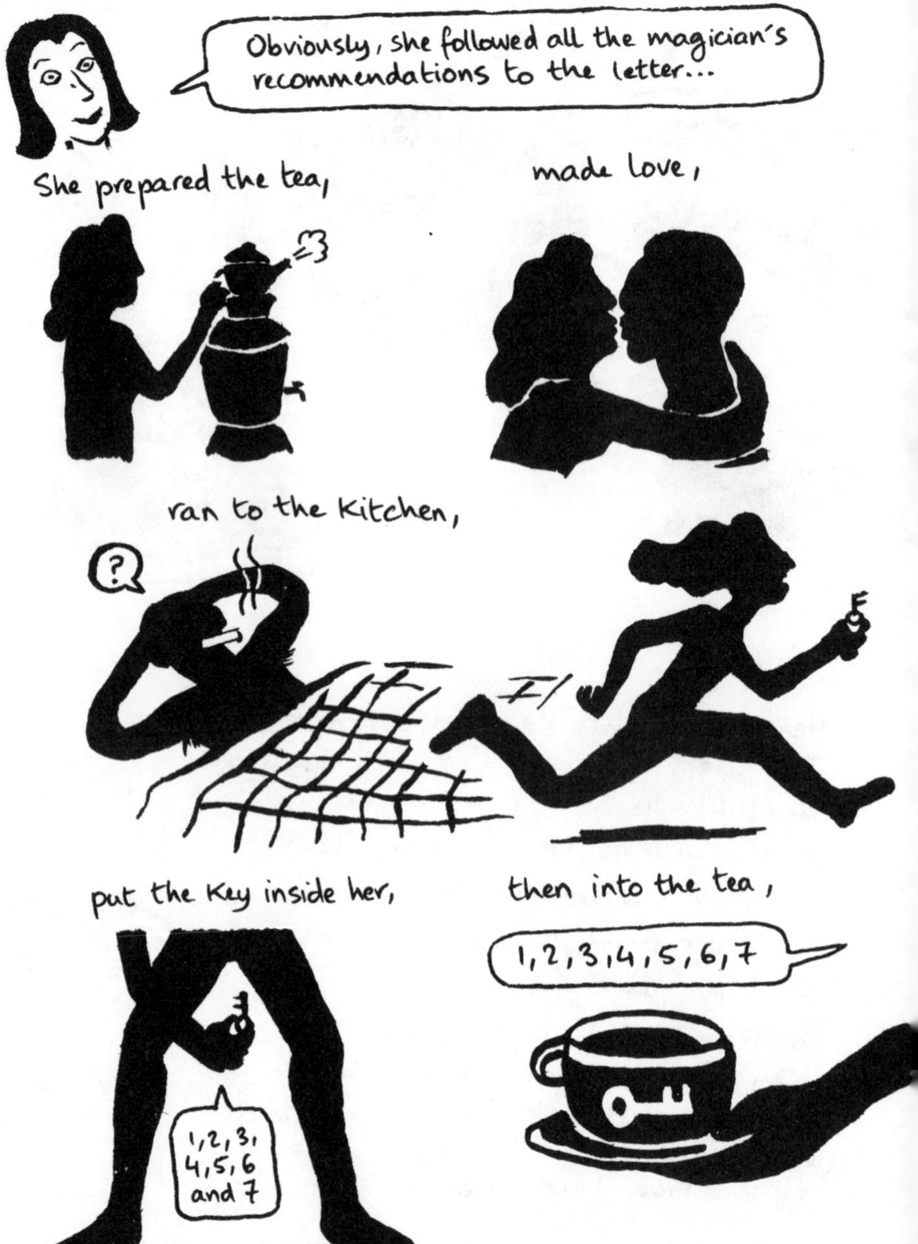

Obviously, she followed all the magician's recommendations to the letter...
She prepared the tea,
made love,
ran to the Kitchen,
?
put the Key inside her,
1,2,3, 4,5,6 and 7
then into the tea,
1,2,3,4,5,6,7

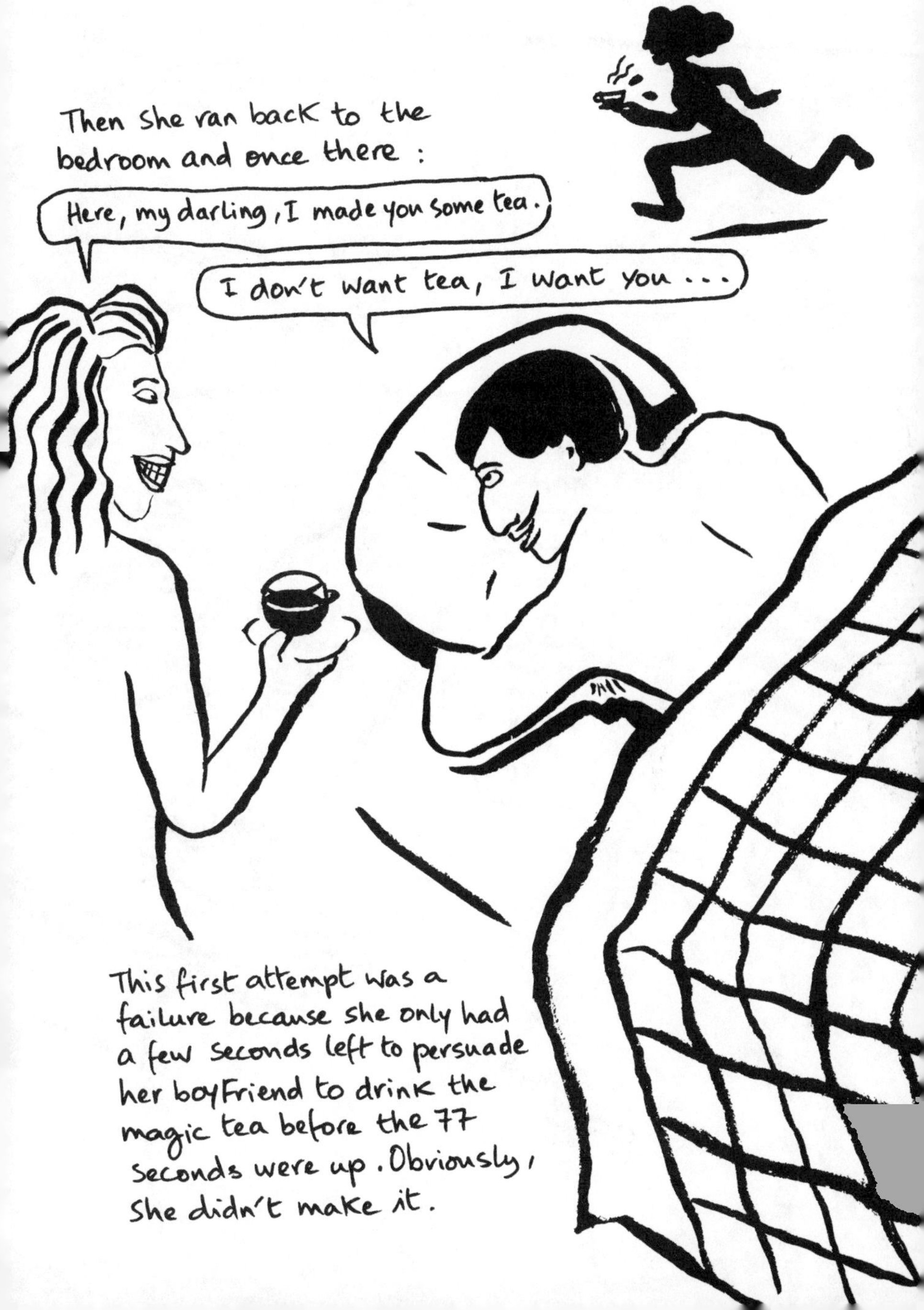
Then she ran back to the bedroom and once there :
Here, my darling, I made you some tea.
I don't want tea, I want you . . .
This first attempt was a failure because she only had a few seconds left to persuade her boyfriend to drink the magic tea before the 77 seconds were up. Obviously, she didn't make it.

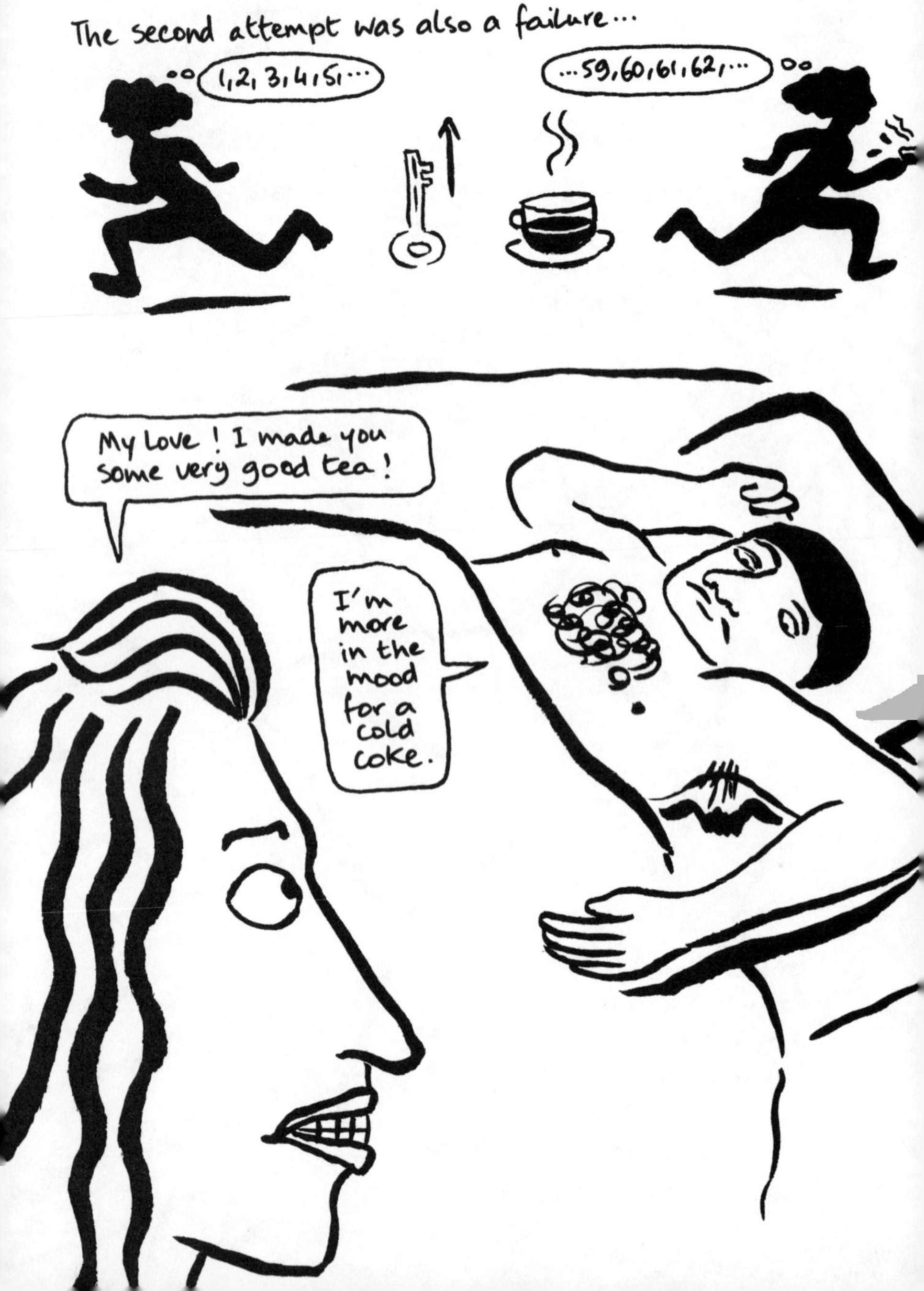
The second attempt was also a failure...
1, 2, 3, 4, 5, ...
...59, 60, 61, 62, ...
My Love! I made you some very good tea!
I'm more in the mood for a cold coke.

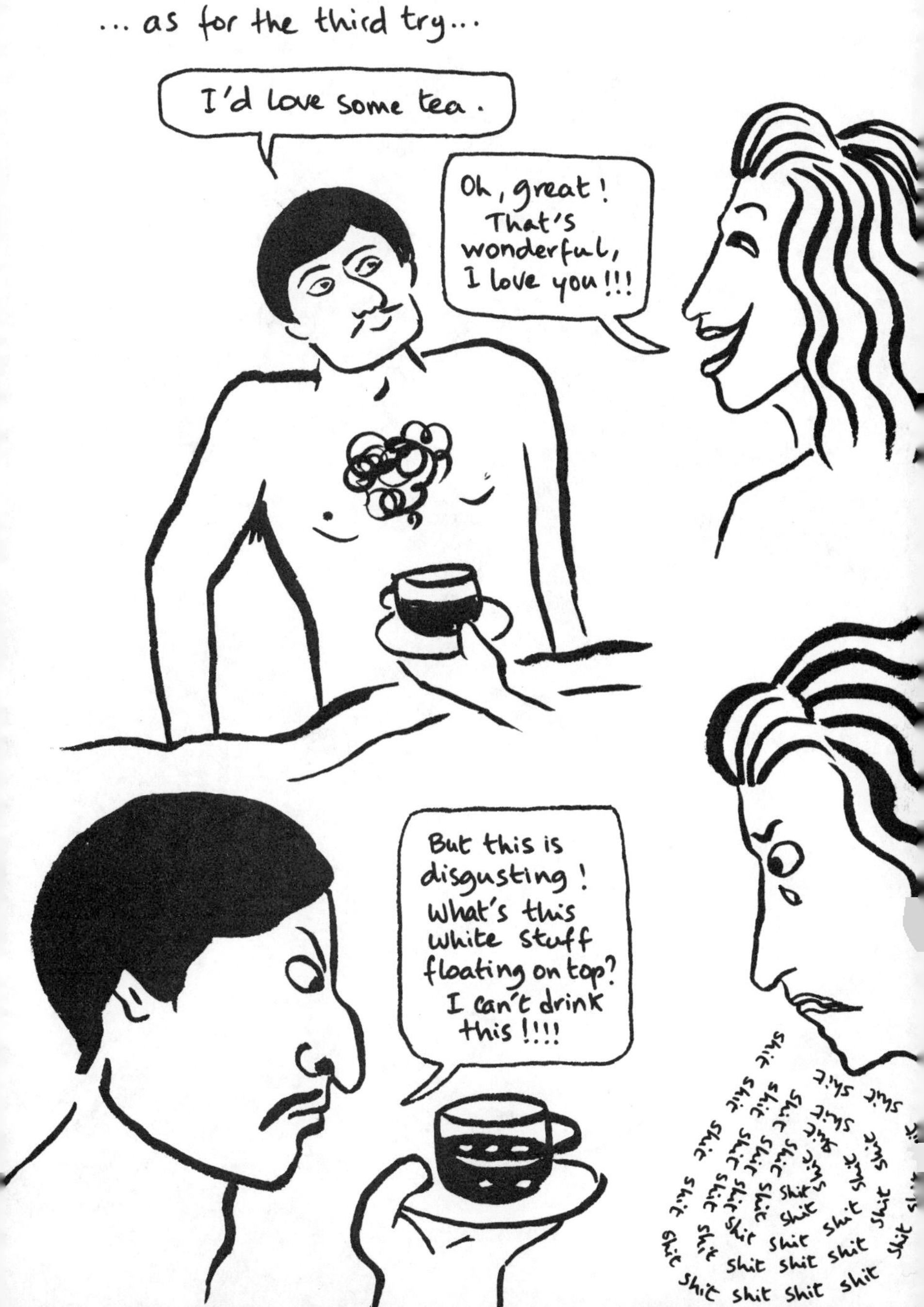
... as for the third try...
I'd love some tea.
Oh, great! That's wonderful, I love you!!!
But this is disgusting! What's this white stuff floating on top? I can't drink this!!!!
shit shit shit shit shit shit shit shit shit shit shit shit shit shit shit shit shit shit shit shit shit shit shit shit shit shit shit shit shit shit

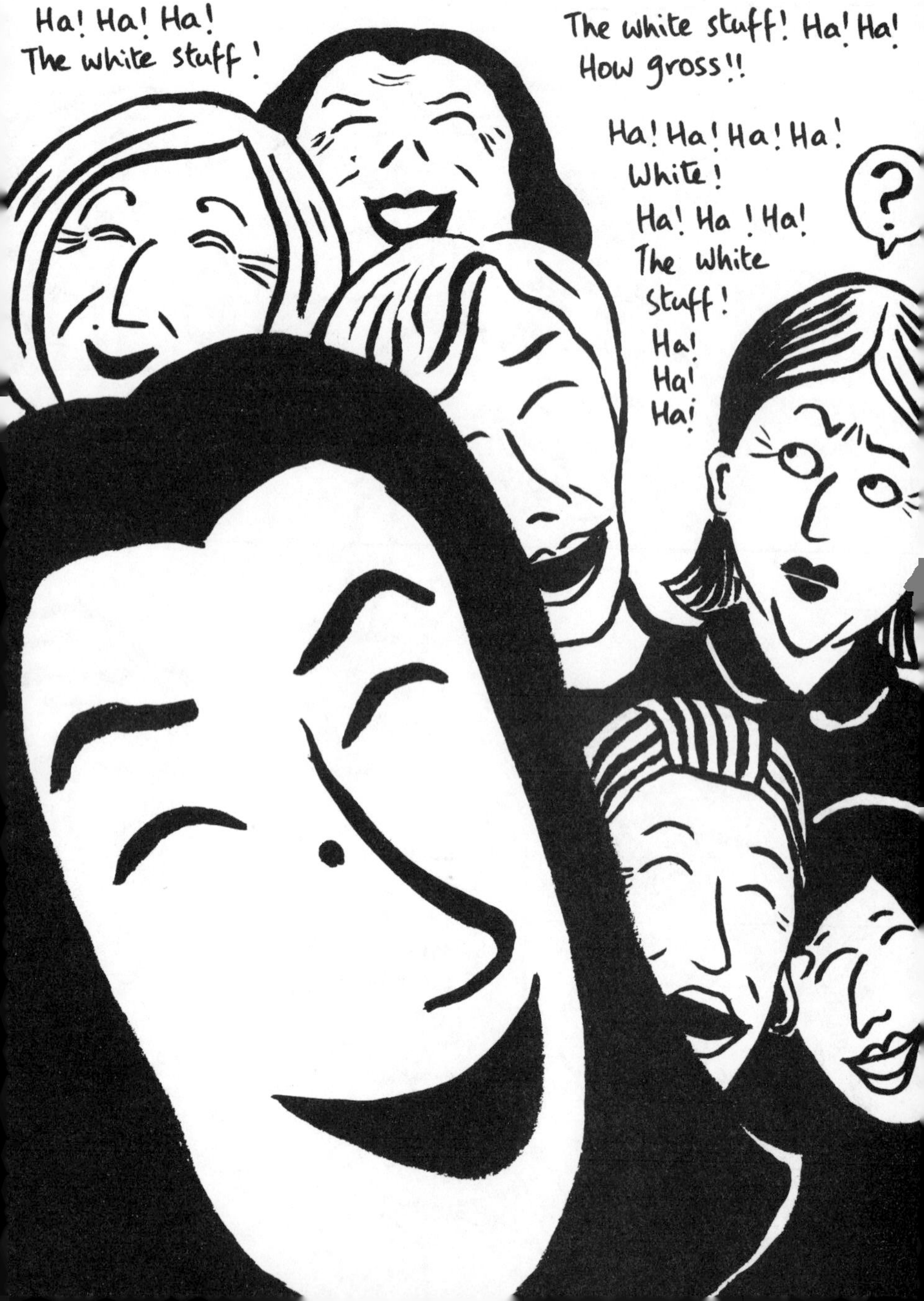
Ha! Ha! Ha!
The white stuff!
The white stuff! Ha! Ha!
How gross!!
Ha! Ha! Ha! Ha!
White!
Ha! Ha! Ha!
The white
stuff!
Ha!
Ha!
Ha!
?

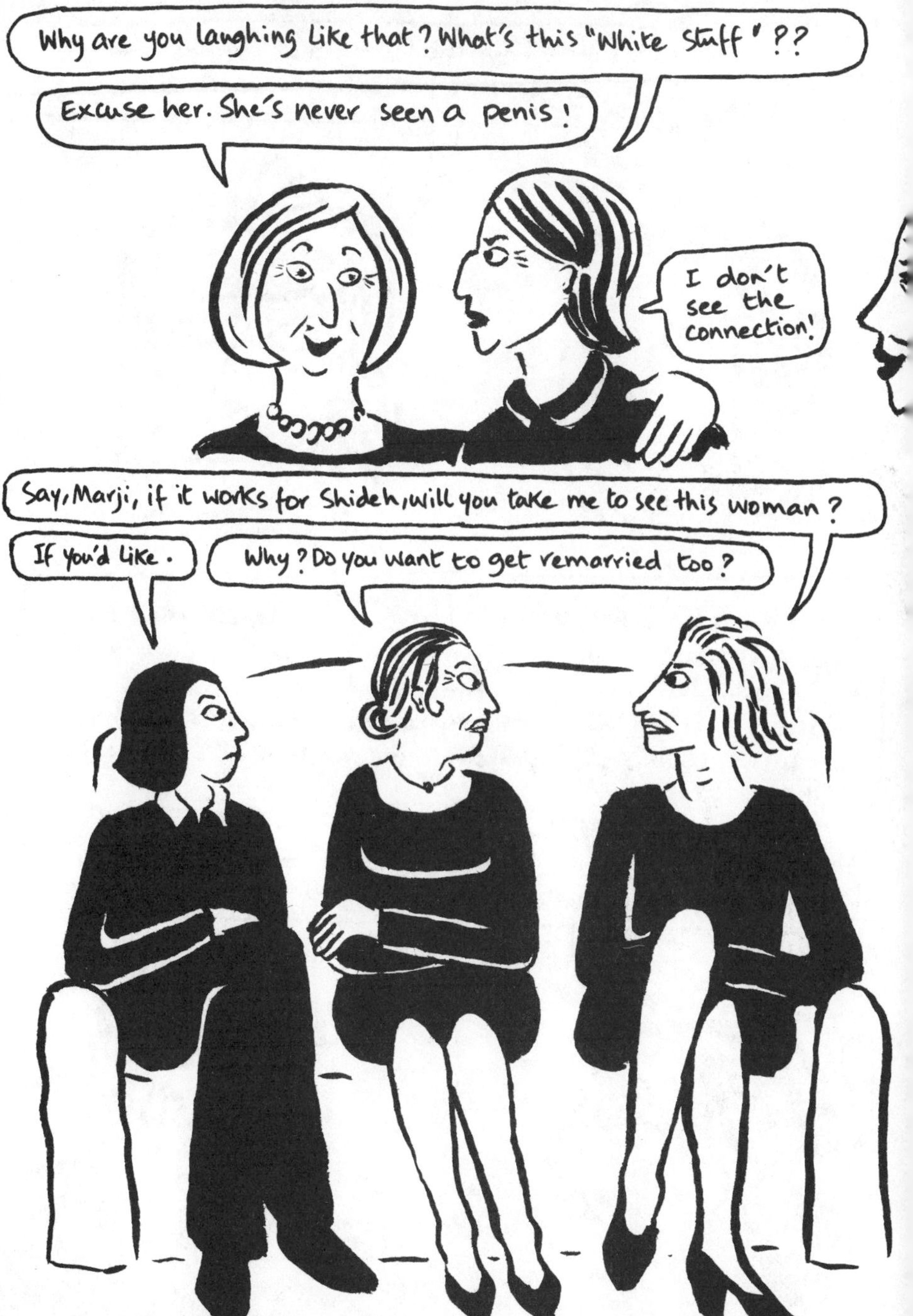
Why are you laughing like that? What's this "white stuff"??
Excuse her. She's never seen a penis!
I don't see the connection!
Say, Marji, if it works for Shideh, will you take me to see this woman?
If you'd like.
Why? Do you want to get remarried too?

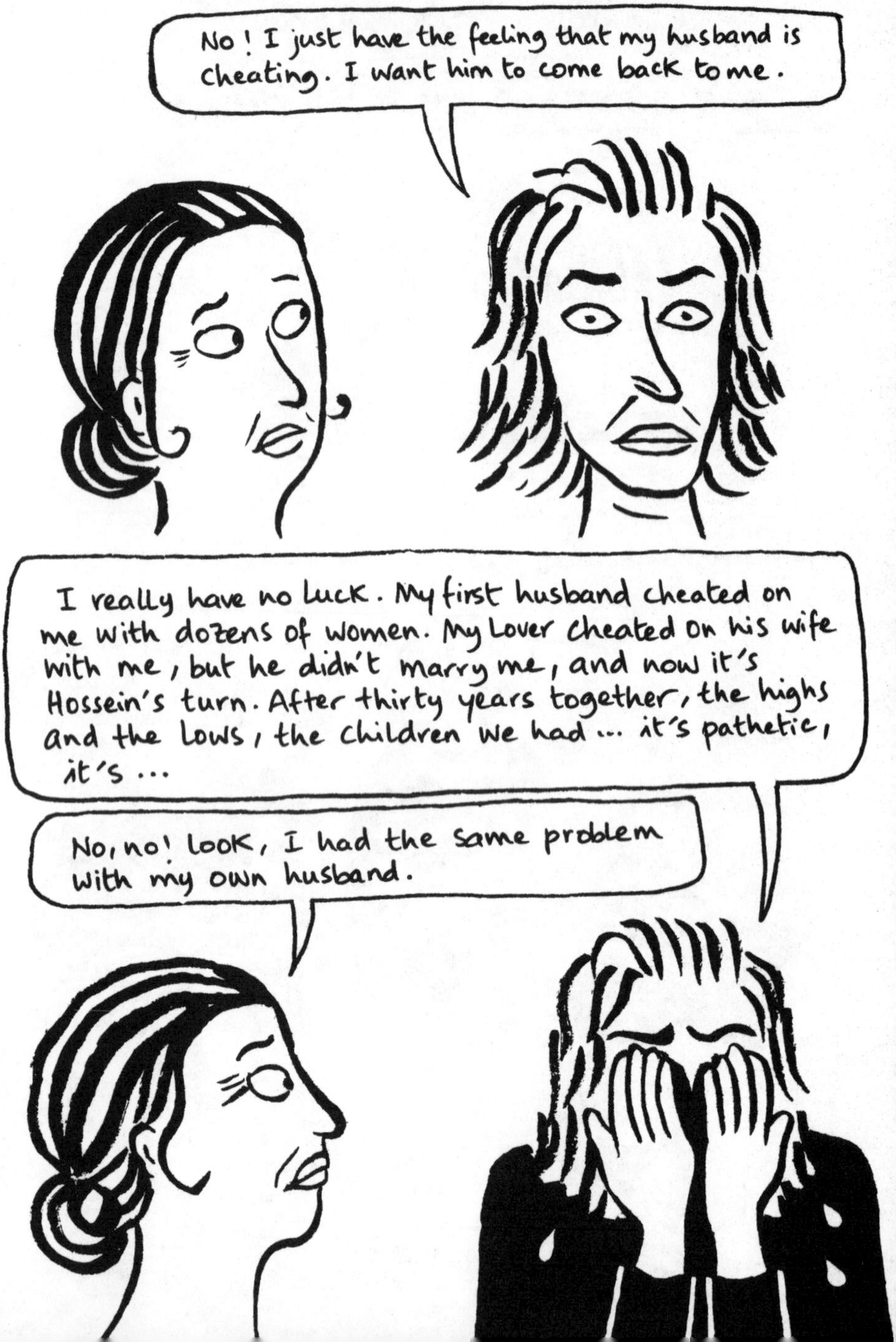
No! I just have the feeling that my husband is cheating. I want him to come back to me.
I really have no luck. My first husband cheated on me with dozens of women. My lover cheated on his wife with me, but he didn't marry me, and now it's Hossein's turn. After thirty years together, the highs and the lows, the children we had... it's pathetic, it's...
No, no! Look, I had the same problem with my own husband.

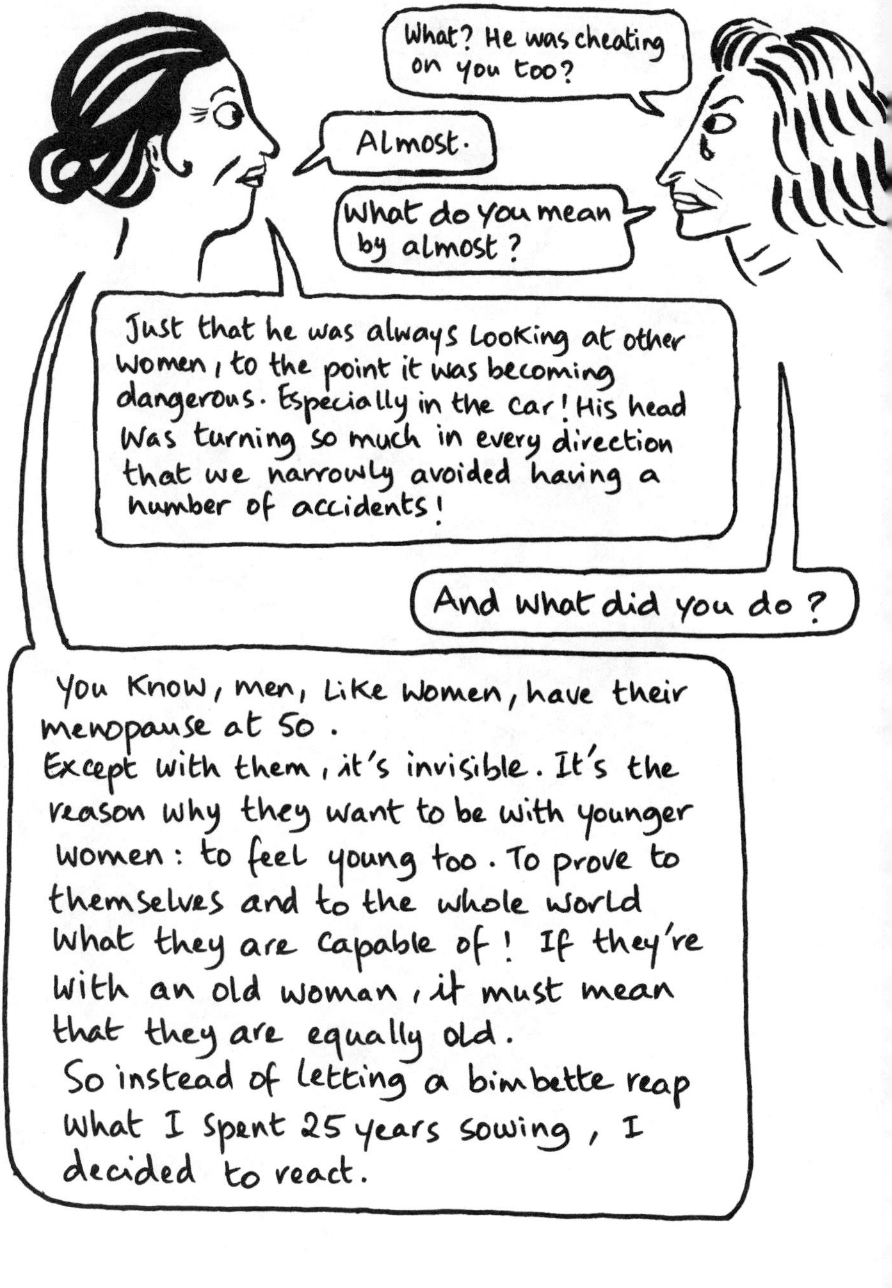
What? He was cheating on you too?
Almost.
What do you mean by almost?
Just that he was always looking at other women, to the point it was becoming dangerous. Especially in the car! His head was turning so much in every direction that we narrowly avoided having a number of accidents!
And what did you do?
You know, men, like women, have their menopause at 50.
Except with them, it's invisible. It's the reason why they want to be with younger women: to feel young too. To prove to themselves and to the whole world what they are capable of! If they're with an old woman, it must mean that they are equally old.
So instead of letting a bimbette reap what I spent 25 years sowing, I decided to react.

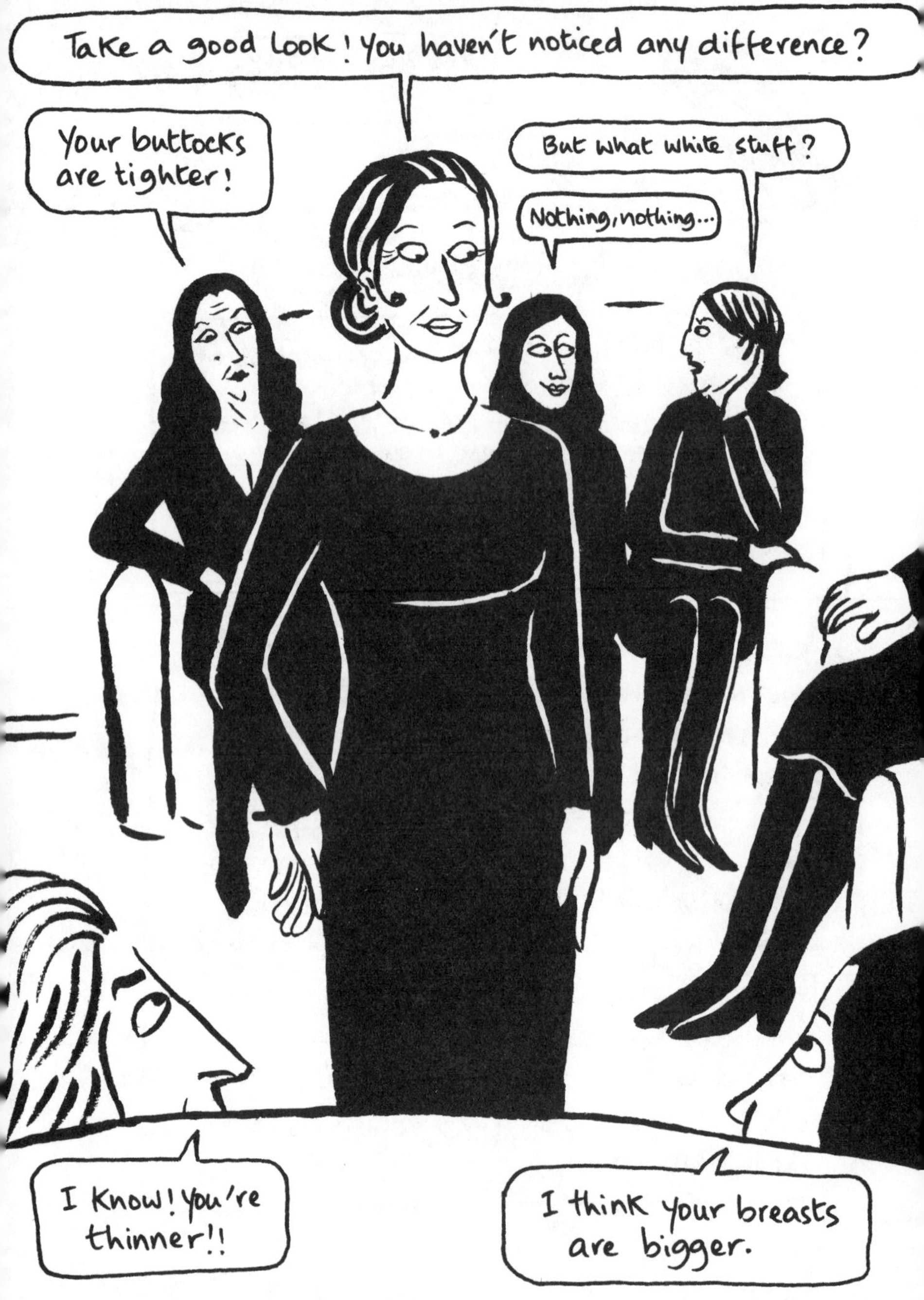
Take a good look! You haven't noticed any difference?
Your buttocks are tighter!
But what white stuff?
Nothing, nothing...
I know! You're thinner!!
I think your breasts are bigger.

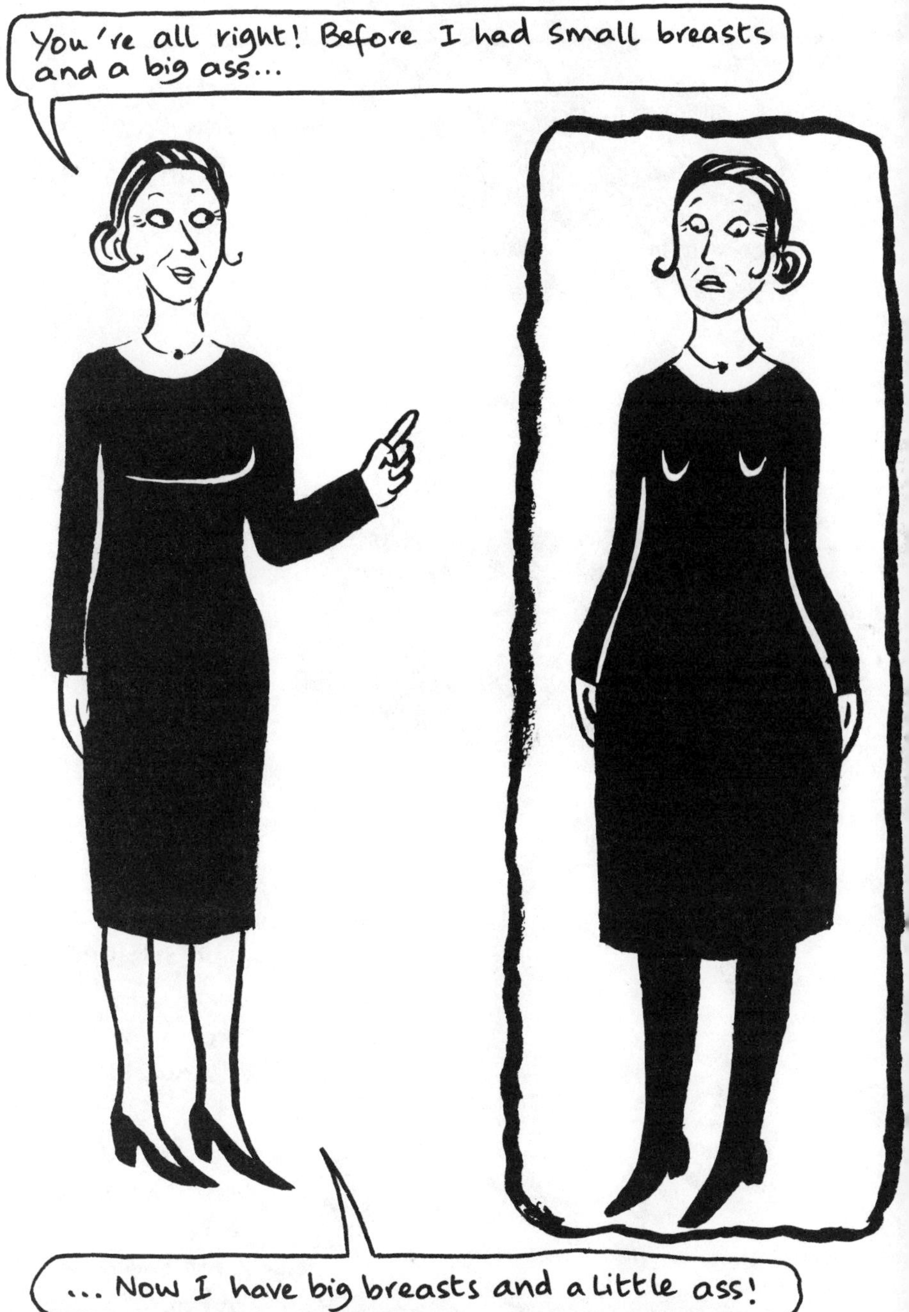
You're all right! Before I had small breasts and a big ass...
... Now I have big breasts and a little ass!

Yes, Ladies!
I had my fat
removed from here.
...And I had it
injected here.
At present, my breasts are
my husband's sole object
of attention.
He can't stop telling me
that I'm beautiful and
desirable, that I look
like Brigitte Bardot, that
I'm the best thing that ever
happened to him in his
life, that this, that
that...

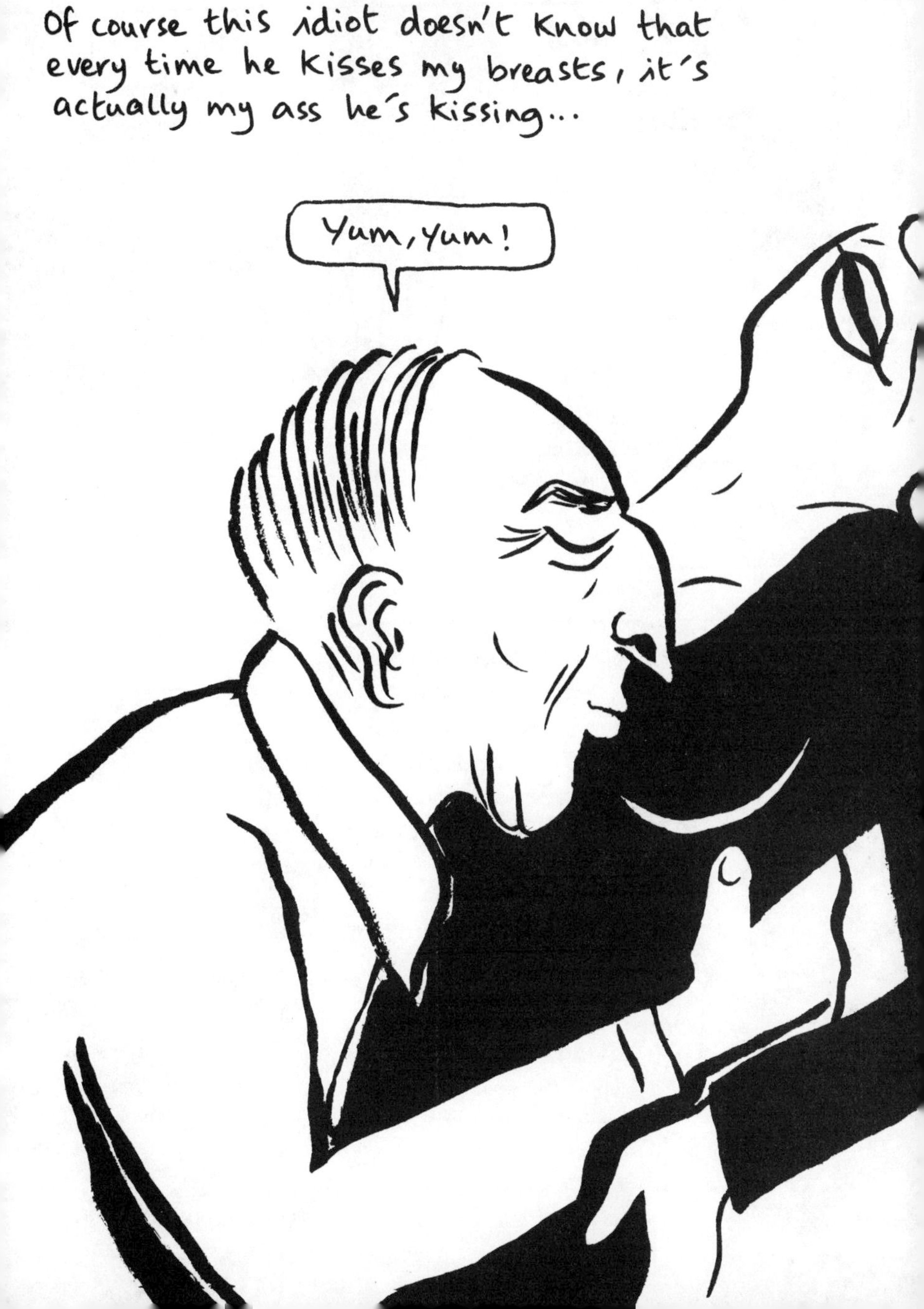
Of course this idiot doesn't know that every time he kisses my breasts, it's actually my ass he's kissing...
Yum, yum!

Bravo!
Well Said!!
I'm still amazed by the results of your operation. If I had known, I wouldn't have deprived myself so. That is to say, in my time one only had the nose redone.
What? You had your nose redone? I always thought that...

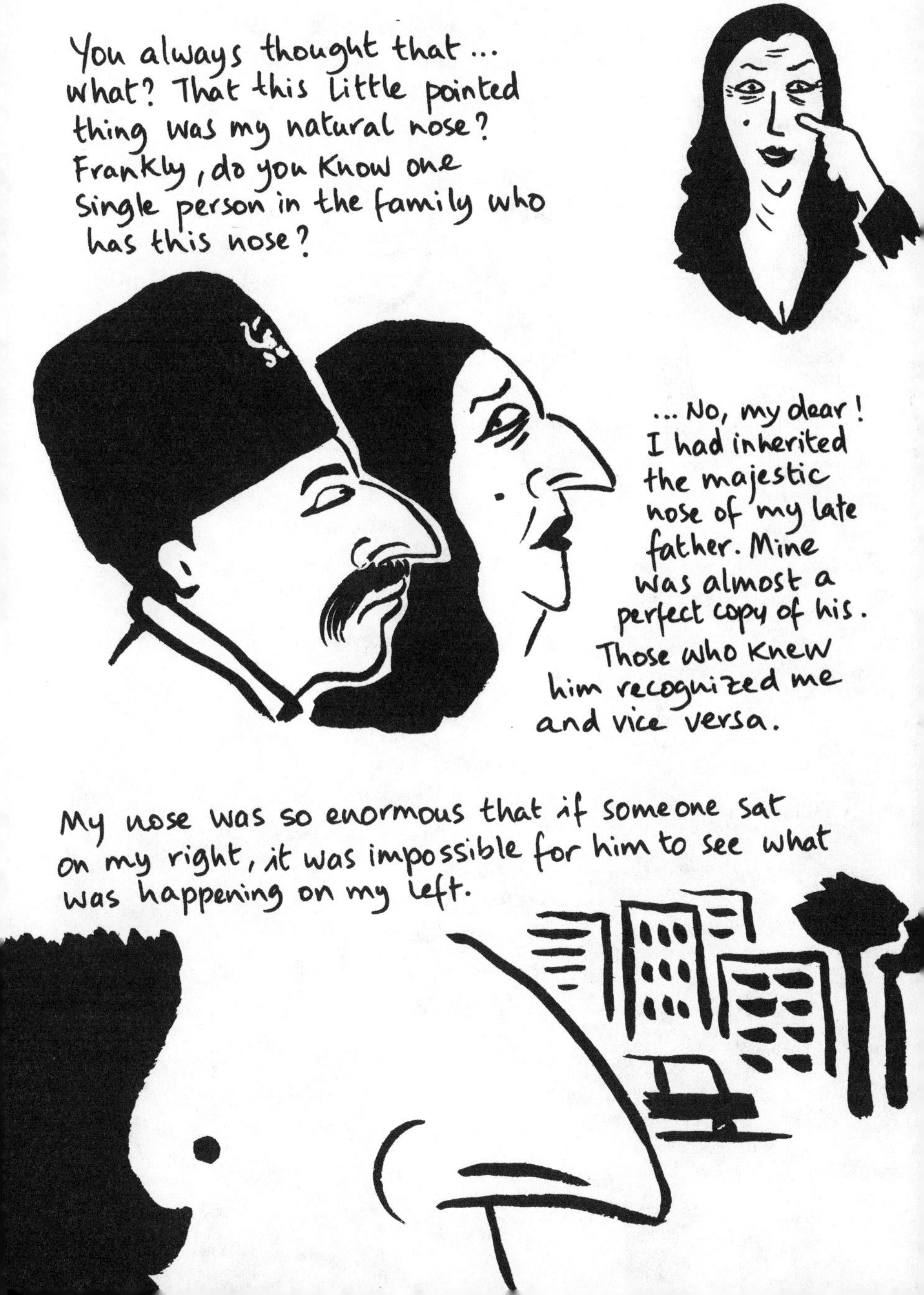
You always thought that... what? That this little pointed thing was my natural nose? Frankly, do you know one single person in the family who has this nose?
... No, my dear! I had inherited the majestic nose of my late father. Mine was almost a perfect copy of his. Those who knew him recognized me and vice versa.
My nose was so enormous that if someone sat on my right, it was impossible for him to see what was happening on my left.

Listen, my dear, the nose is Key. When you meet someone new, what do you look at first? His face, of course.
Now you take a face's oval and you draw two perpendicular lines to find its center. What's in the center of a face? A nose!!
I concluded that since the nose is the most central element of the face, it logically became the most essential element.
To have a beautiful nose is thus of major importance.

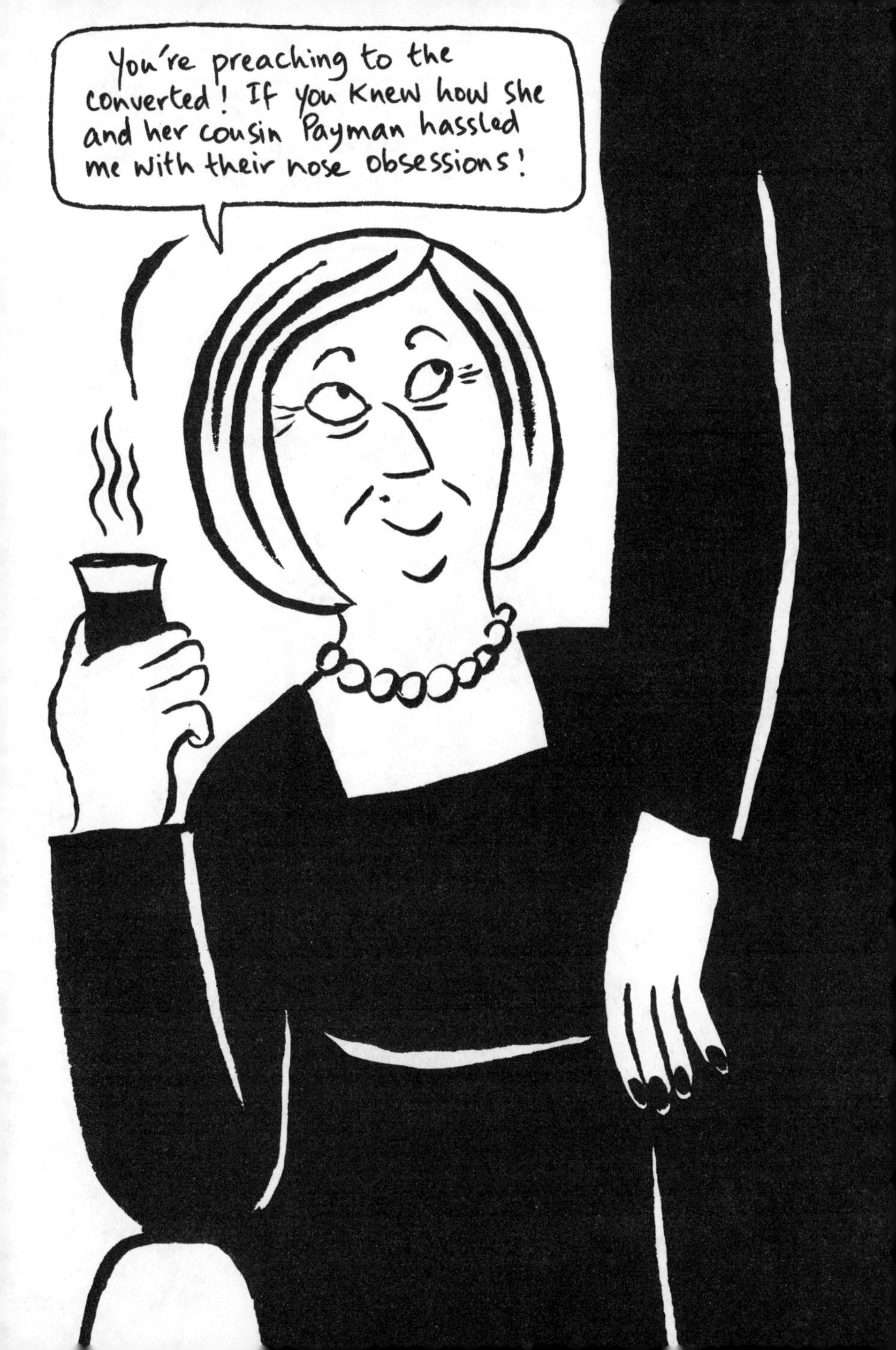
You're preaching to the converted! If you knew how she and her cousin Payman hassled me with their nose obsessions!

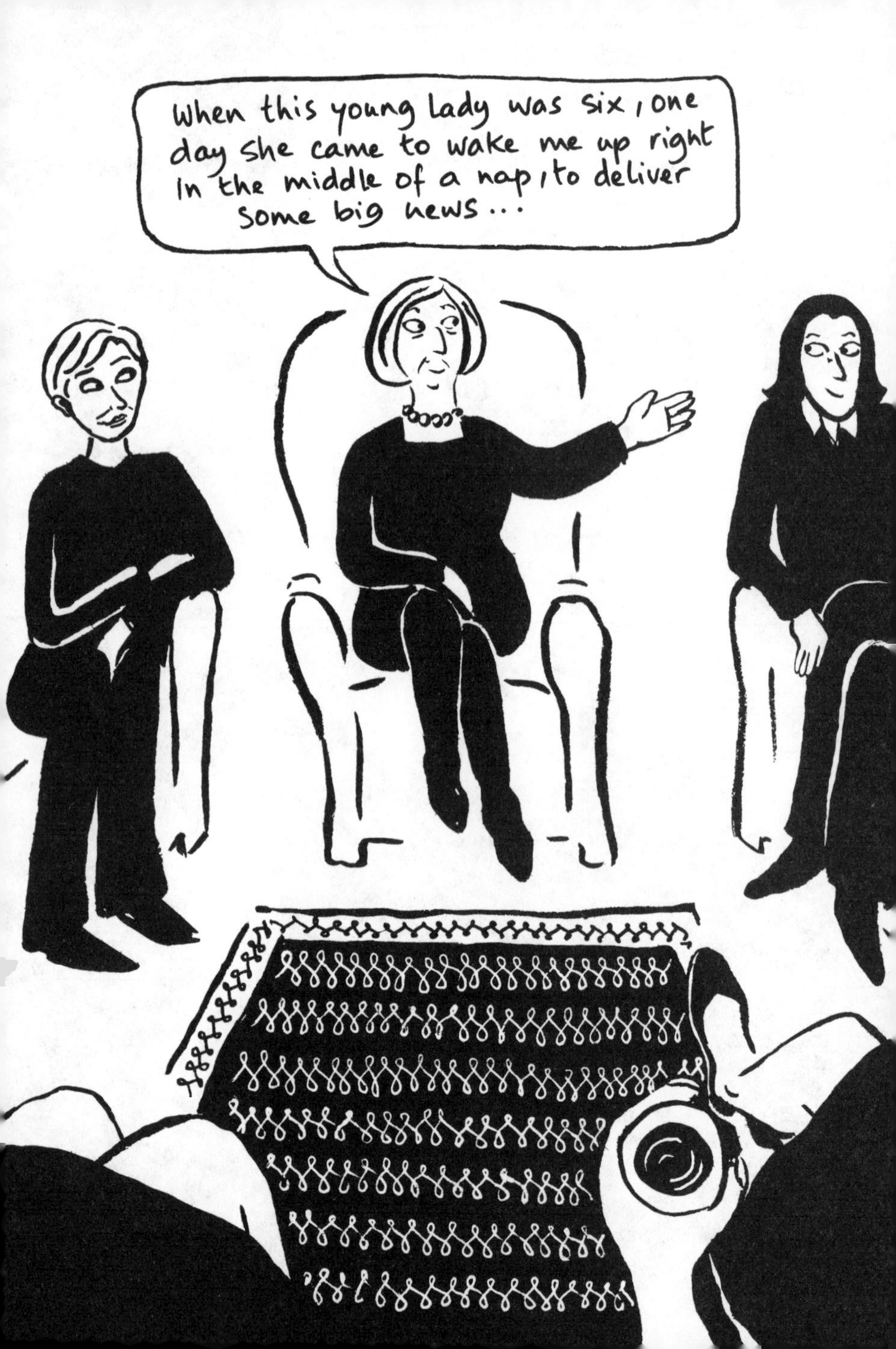
When this young lady was six, one day she came to wake me up right in the middle of a nap, to deliver some big news...

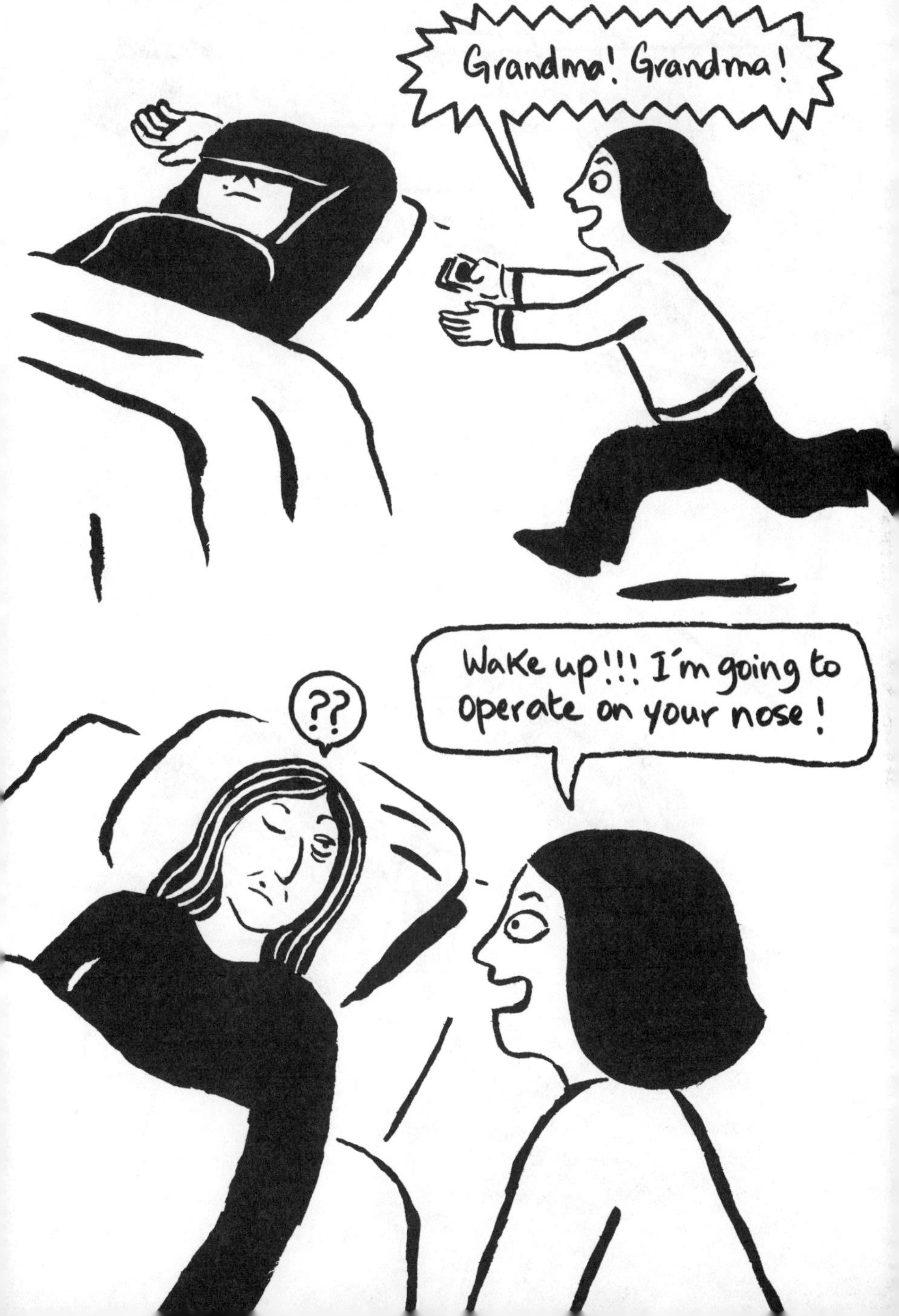
Grandma! Grandma!
??
Wake up!!! I'm going to operate on your nose!

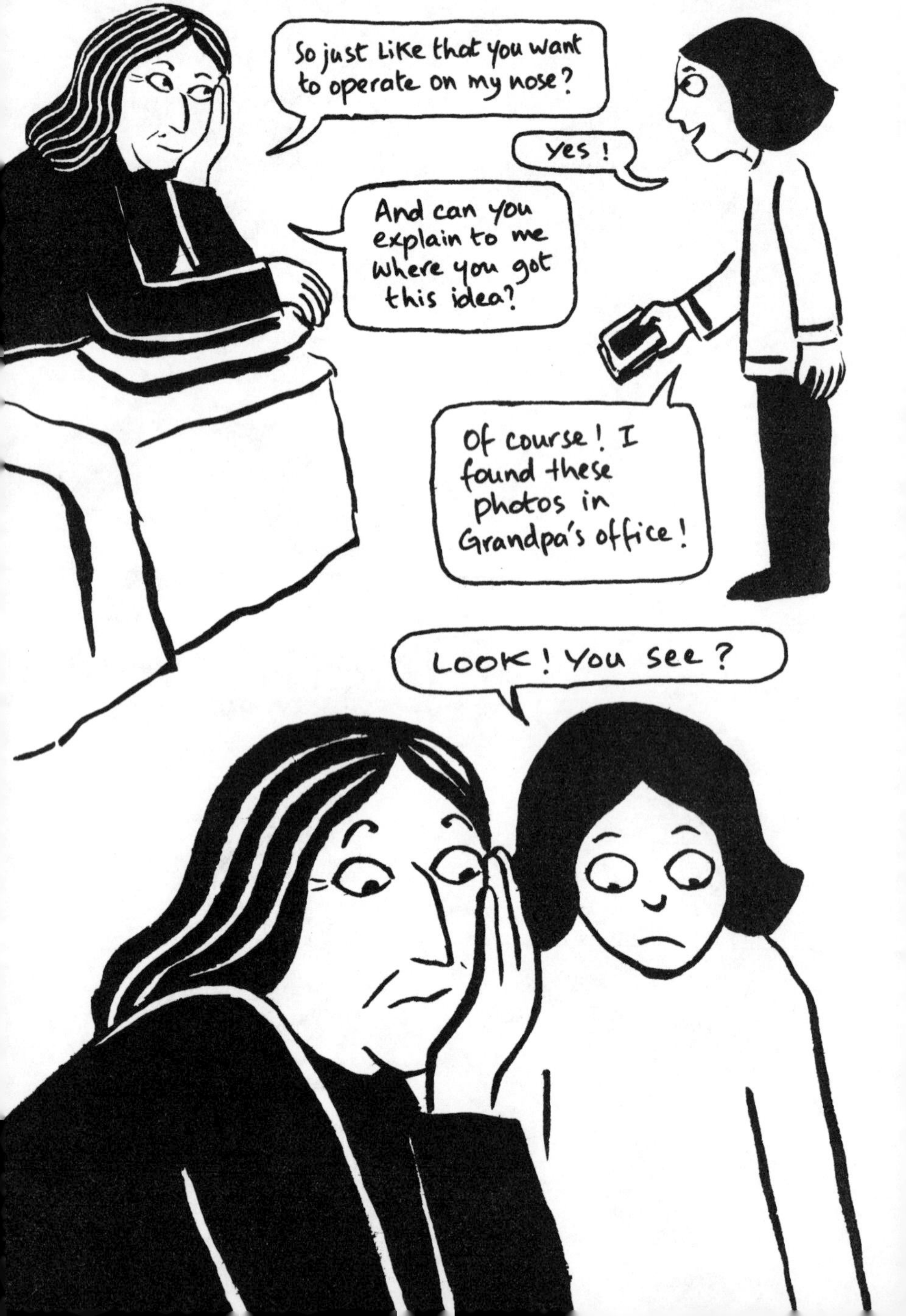
So just like that you want to operate on my nose?
Yes!
And can you explain to me where you got this idea?
Of course! I found these photos in Grandpa's office!
LOOK! You see?

Look here! That's Eli before her operation
That's Eli after
Fariba before
Fariba after
Nouchine before
Nouchine after

So I told myself since your nose is super-ugly, I could redo it for you.

!

And you're the one who will perform the operation?

Oh no! It will be a plastic surgeon...

...

...And also don't worry about the money. I've spoken to Payman about it. We're going to find a solution.

Ah! Because Payman also thinks that my nose is "super-ugly"?

Of course! Everyone thinks so.

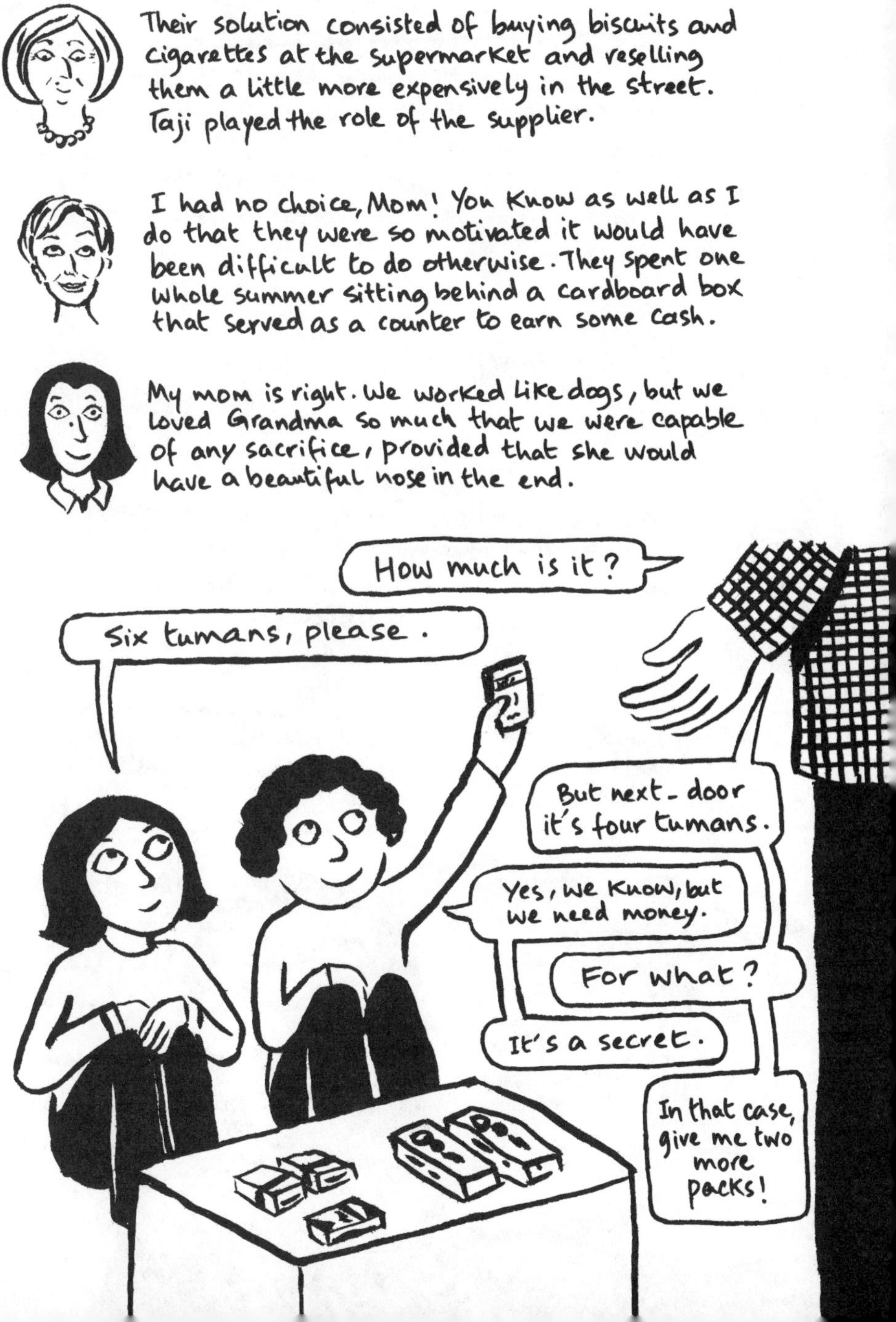
Their solution consisted of buying biscuits and cigarettes at the supermarket and reselling them a little more expensively in the street. Taji played the role of the supplier.
I had no choice, Mom! You know as well as I do that they were so motivated it would have been difficult to do otherwise. They spent one whole summer sitting behind a cardboard box that served as a counter to earn some cash.
My mom is right. We worked like dogs, but we loved Grandma so much that we were capable of any sacrifice, provided that she would have a beautiful nose in the end.
How much is it?
Six tumans, please.
But next-door it's four tumans.
Yes, we know, but we need money.
For what?
It's a secret.
In that case, give me two more packs!

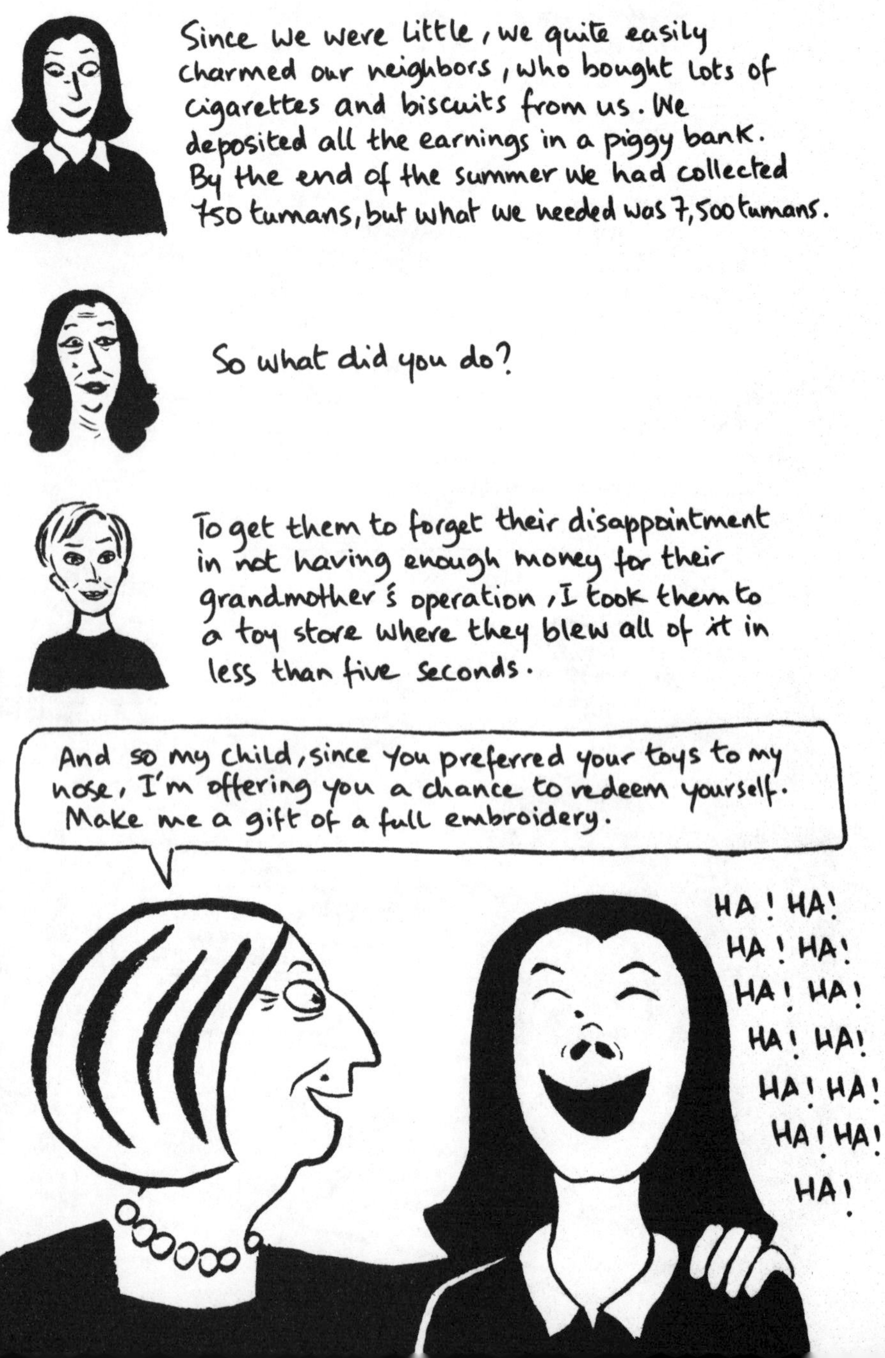
Since we were little, we quite easily charmed our neighbors, who bought lots of cigarettes and biscuits from us. We deposited all the earnings in a piggy bank. By the end of the summer we had collected 750 tumans, but what we needed was 7,500 tumans.
So what did you do?
To get them to forget their disappointment in not having enough money for their grandmother's operation, I took them to a toy store where they blew all of it in less than five seconds.
And so my child, since you preferred your toys to my nose, I'm offering you a chance to redeem yourself. Make me a gift of a full embroidery.
HA! HA! HA! HA! HA! HA! HA! HA! HA! HA! HA! HA! HA!

Hee! Hee! Hee! I love this expression!!
Hee! Hee! Hee! Hee! full embroidery!
Oh, because you know what it is?
Just because she's never seen a penis doesn't mean she doesn't know anything about anything!
You joke, but it's practiced much more than you think!
WHAT??? There are a lot of women who do it?

Obviously! Women's morals are relaxing! Today's girls are no longer virgins before marriage. They do everything like men and get sewn up again to get married! This way, everyone is happy!
And the men! What do the men do? They get themselves sewn up too?
It's not the same...
Ha! Ha! Ha! You know? There's not only the full embroidery where they completely block you! Ha! Ha! Ha! There's also partial embroidery! Ha! Ha! Ha!...
... The other day I was at a funeral. After the cemetery, everyone gathered at the home of the deceased's family. There were two women having a discussion next to me. I'll admit to the fact that I listened to their conversation...
I heard that you were living in Europe.
That's right. I live in Luxemburg.
PFF...

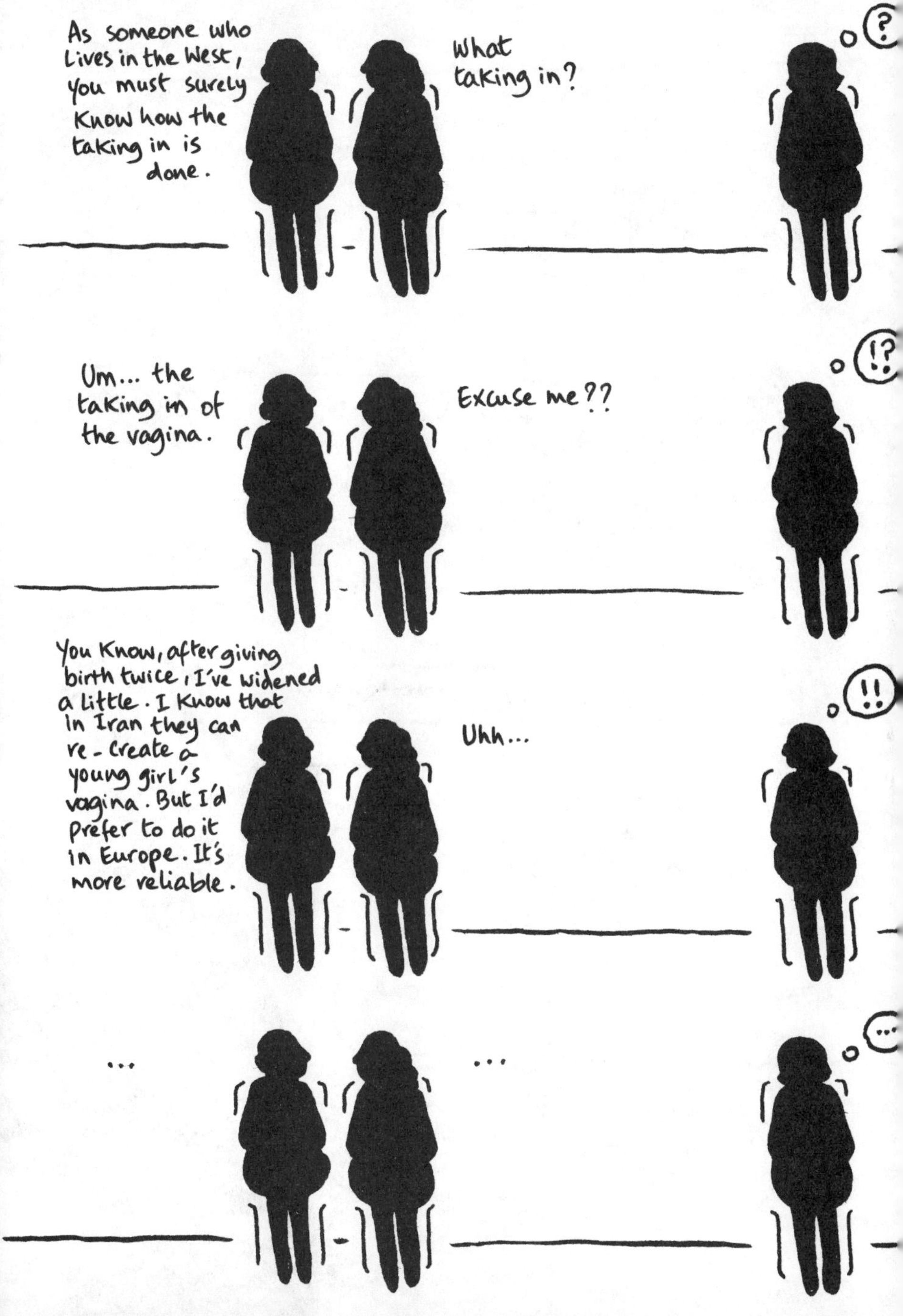
As someone who lives in the West, you must surely know how the taking in is done.
What taking in?
?
Um... the taking in of the vagina.
Excuse me??
!?
You know, after giving birth twice, I've widened a little. I know that in Iran they can re-create a young girl's vagina. But I'd prefer to do it in Europe. It's more reliable.
Uhh...
!!
...
...
...

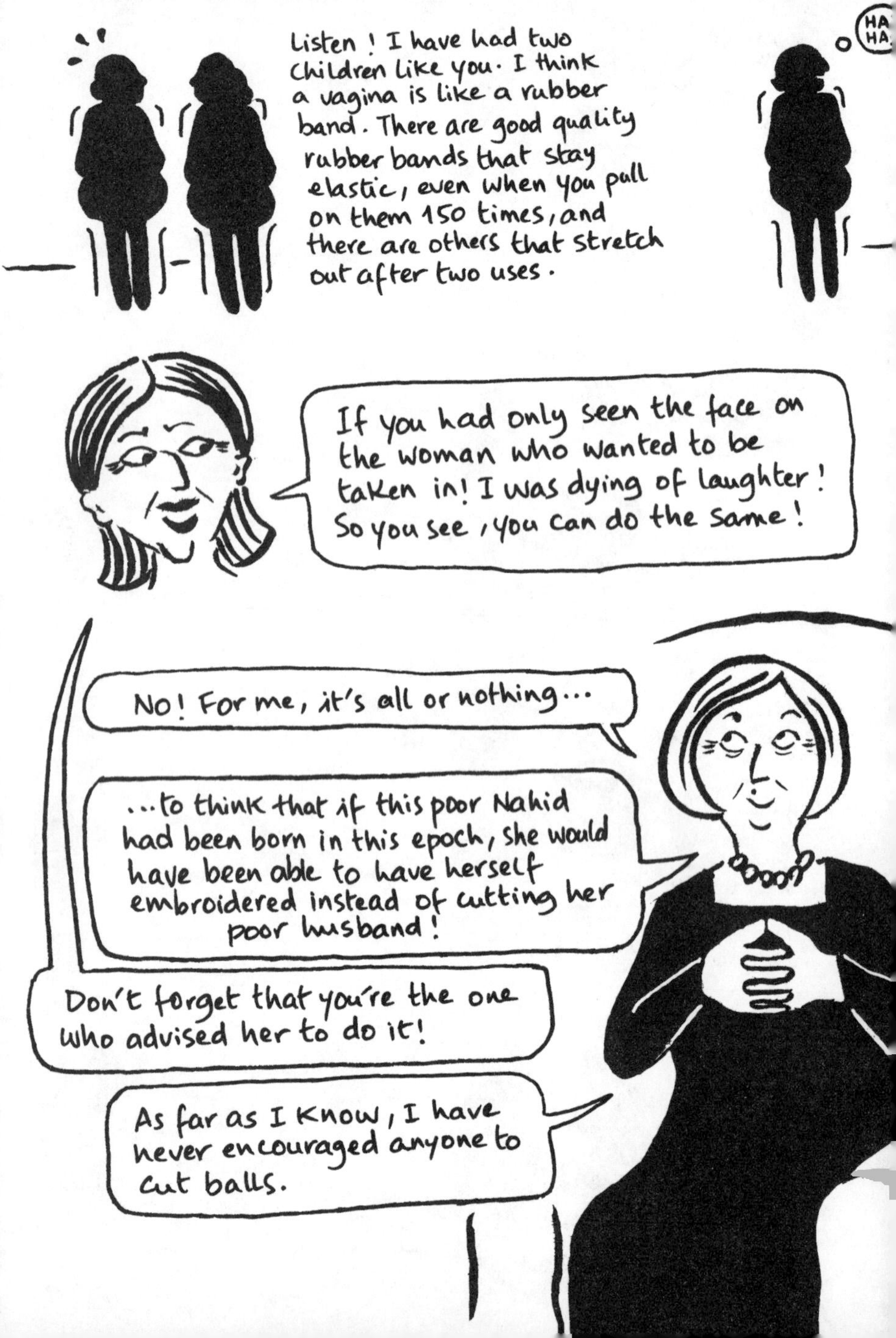
Listen! I have had two children like you. I think a vagina is like a rubber band. There are good quality rubber bands that stay elastic, even when you pull on them 150 times, and there are others that stretch out after two uses.
HA HA
If you had only seen the face on the woman who wanted to be taken in! I was dying of laughter! So you see, you can do the same!
No! For me, it's all or nothing...
...to think that if this poor Nahid had been born in this epoch, she would have been able to have herself embroidered instead of cutting her poor husband!
Don't forget that you're the one who advised her to do it!
As far as I know, I have never encouraged anyone to cut balls.

And why is it the women who have to be virgins? Why suffer torment to satisfy an asshole? Because the man who demands "virginity" from a woman is nothing but an asshole! Why don't we behave as westerners do!? For them, since the problem of sex is resolved, they can move on to other things! This is the reason they progress!!!
In this same west, the members of high society, like the aristocrats, have the same point of view as we do on the subject. To them, virginity is highly prized.
It's because aristocrats are all degenerates! You just have to look at my family!

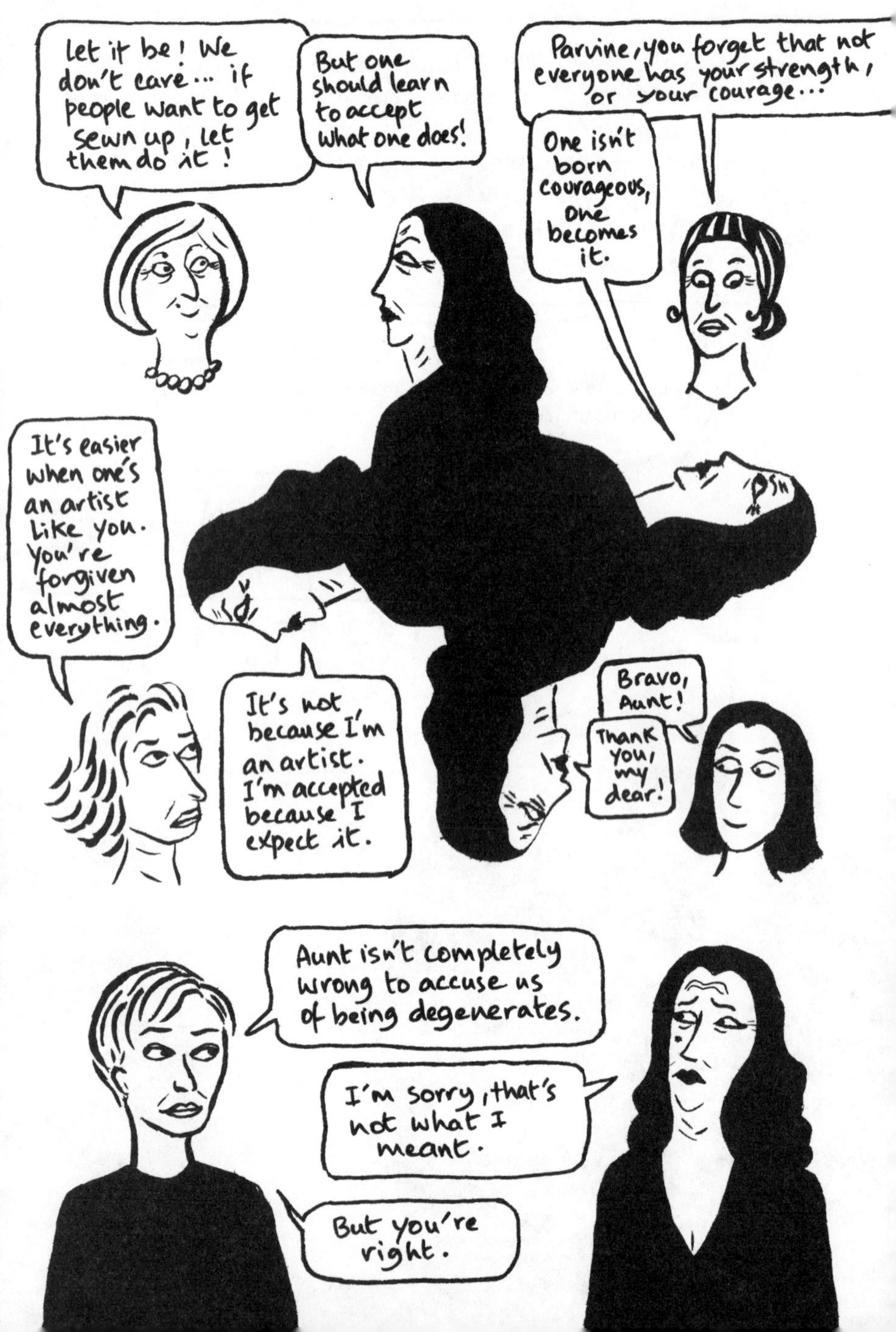
Let it be! We don't care... if people want to get sewn up, let them do it!
But one should learn to accept what one does!
Parvine, you forget that not everyone has your strength, or your courage...
One isn't born courageous, one becomes it.
It's easier when one's an artist like you. You're forgiven almost everything.
It's not because I'm an artist. I'm accepted because I expect it.
Bravo, Aunt!
Thank you, my dear!
Aunt isn't completely wrong to accuse us of being degenerates.
I'm sorry, that's not what I meant.
But you're right.

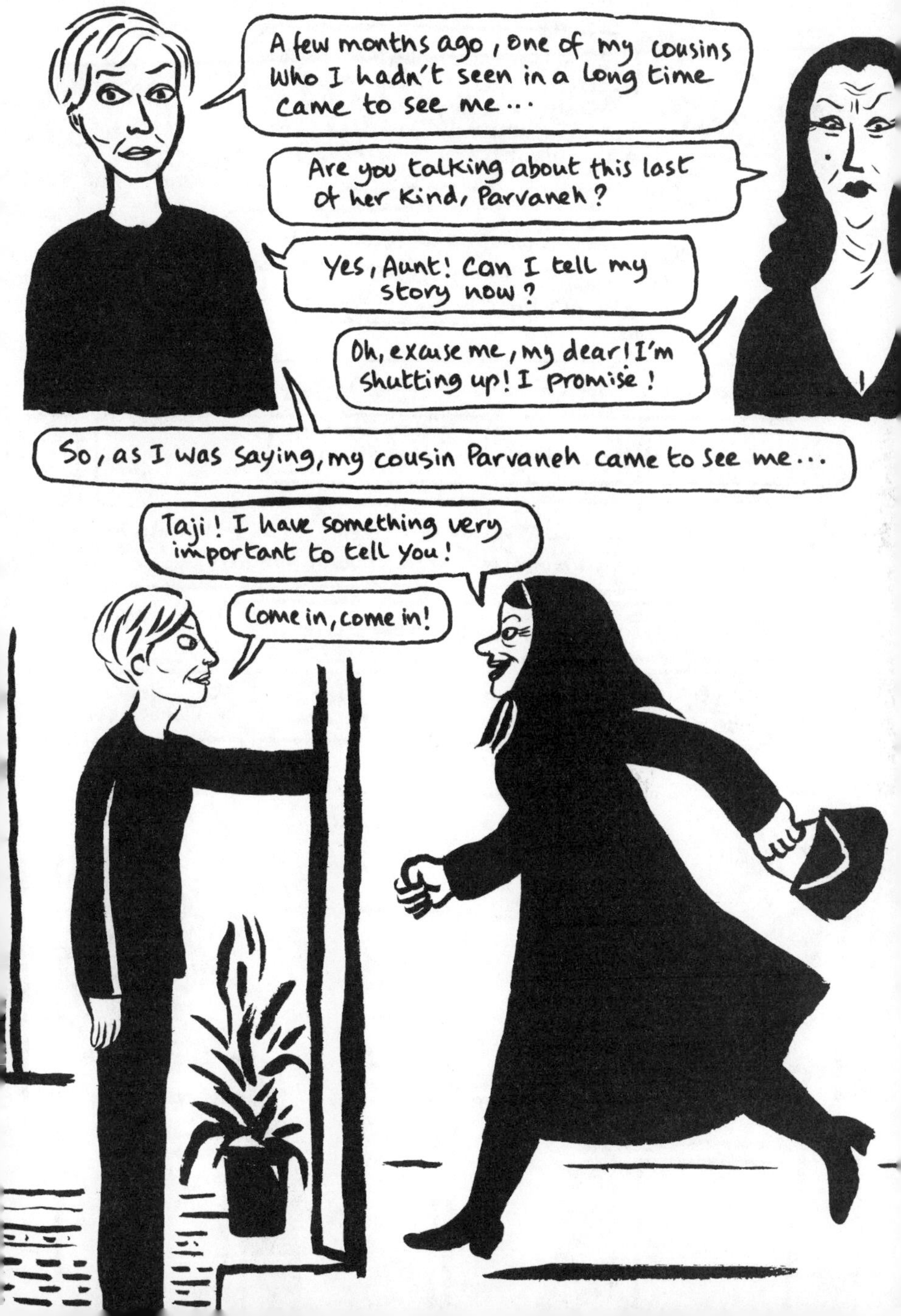
A few months ago, one of my cousins who I hadn't seen in a long time came to see me...
Are you talking about this last of her kind, Parvaneh?
Yes, Aunt! Can I tell my story now?
Oh, excuse me, my dear! I'm shutting up! I promise!
So, as I was saying, my cousin Parvaneh came to see me...
Taji! I have something very important to tell you!
Come in, come in!

Ohmydearmyfamilyohmy daughterisgoingtogetmarriedsheis goingtomarryaguywhohas livedinEnglandhiswholelife and whowantstomarryherohmy...
I don't understand a word of what you're saying! Come sit down, take off your veil, come...
Bahar is getting married! Do you realize? My daughter is getting married!!!
But she just got her highschool diploma!
The gentleman who is going to marry her is a MULTIMILLIONAIRE! He owns seven houses in London, two in Monaco.
A multimillionaire in London? But how old is he?
Forty-one! He's lived in England for the last 25 years. He was at the Royal College. At his age, a man knows what he wants!
Ah, Taji! It's super, it's fantastic! I'm so happy!

Can you explain to me why a man of 41 who has lived in Europe practically his whole life and who is educated wants to marry a girl of 18?
Well, you know how western girls are... They're no longer pure, starting at ages ten, eleven. He's an Iranian. He has certain values, and it's all to his credit!
Listen, Parvaneh! Since you came to see me, I suppose that I have the right to give my opinion: Look, I think that you are on your way to making a big mistake! Bahar is very young. Let her study, be independent, become someone! You yourself married the man of your choice. Give her the opportunity and the time to grow up and decide for herself.
And the result? Every time I fight with "the man of my choice," he reproaches me for having run after him, meaning that a good girl would have waited for him to ask for her hand.
No, Taji! She will be married. She'll still have the advantage of her youth, unlike me who gets called "old bag" all the time!

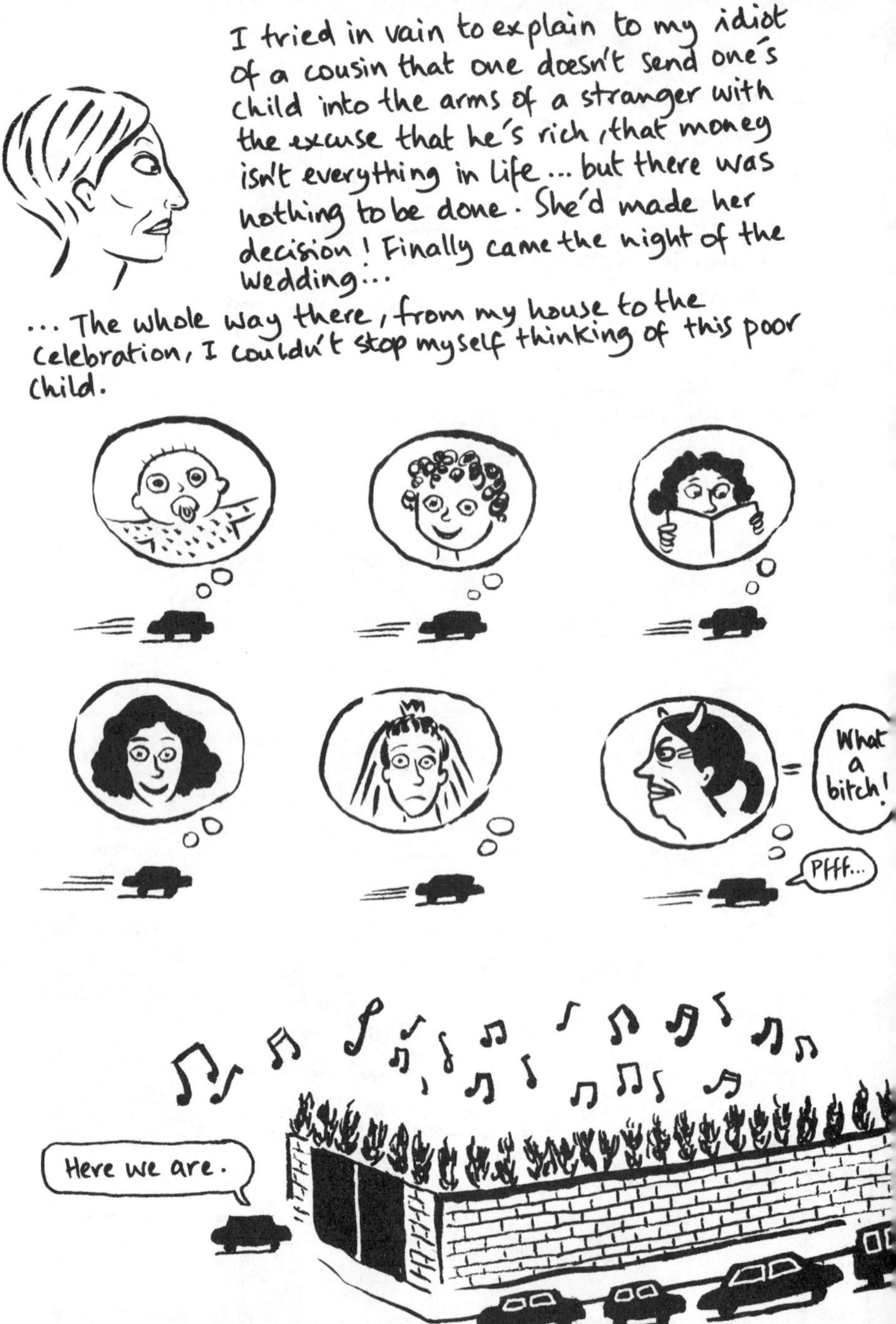
I tried in vain to explain to my idiot of a cousin that one doesn't send one's child into the arms of a stranger with the excuse that he's rich, that money isn't everything in life ... but there was nothing to be done. She'd made her decision! Finally came the night of the wedding...
... The whole way there, from my house to the celebration, I couldn't stop myself thinking of this poor child.
What a bitch!
Pfff...
Here we are.

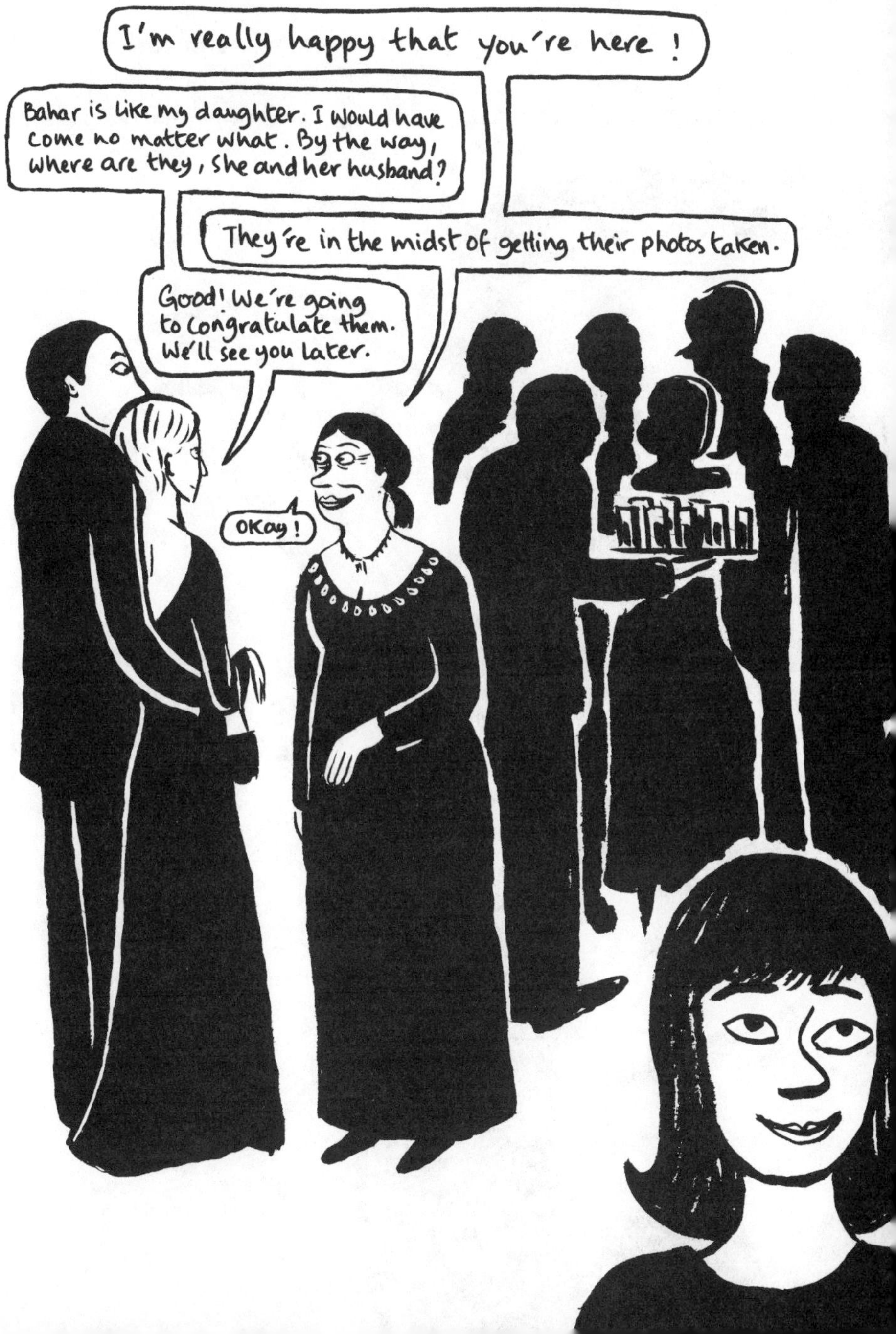
I'm really happy that you're here!
Bahar is like my daughter. I would have come no matter what. By the way, where are they, she and her husband?
They're in the midst of getting their photos taken.
Good! We're going to congratulate them. We'll see you later.
OKay!

So Ebi and I went to congratulate the newlyweds
and there, what did we see ???...
Not Bahar sitting on a sofa with her husband at her side...

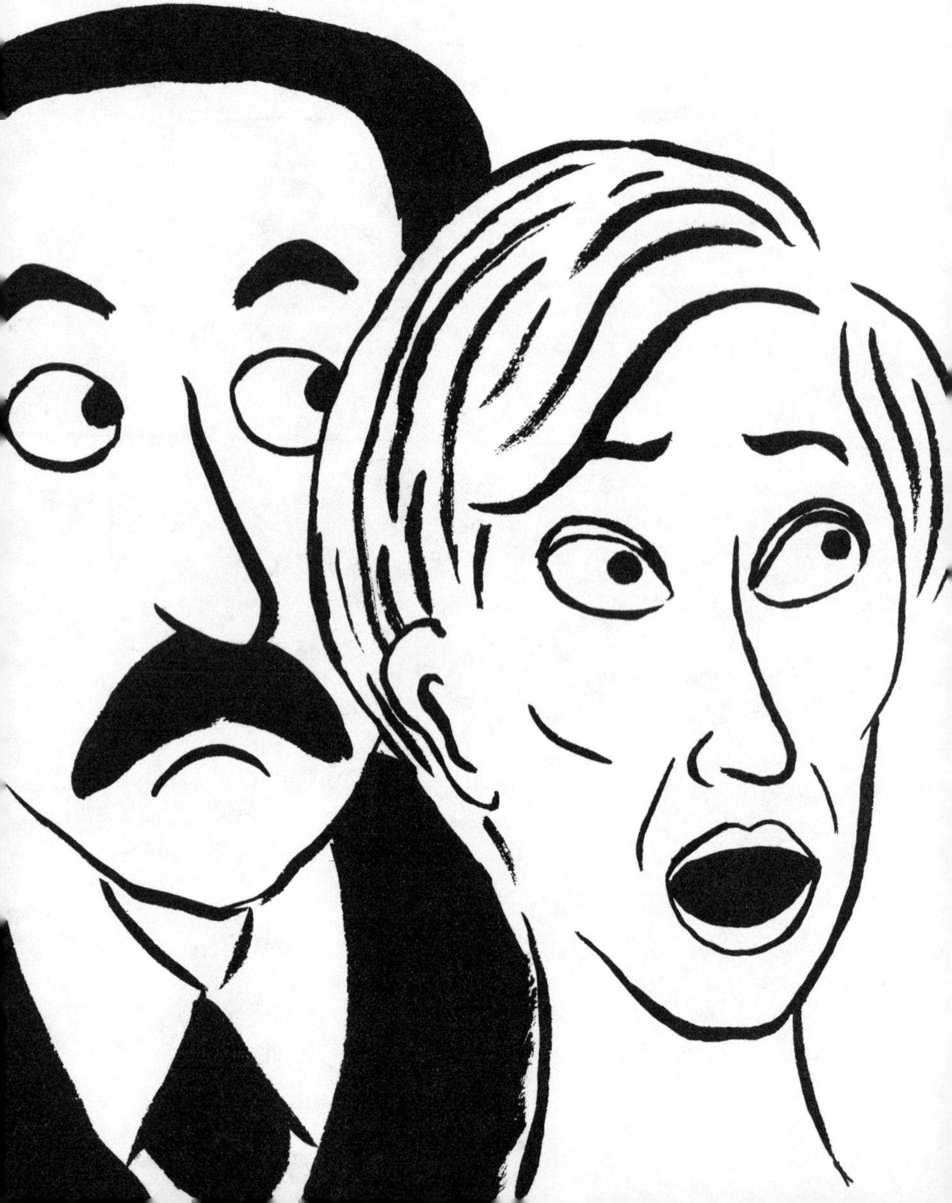

... But a picture of her husband!!!

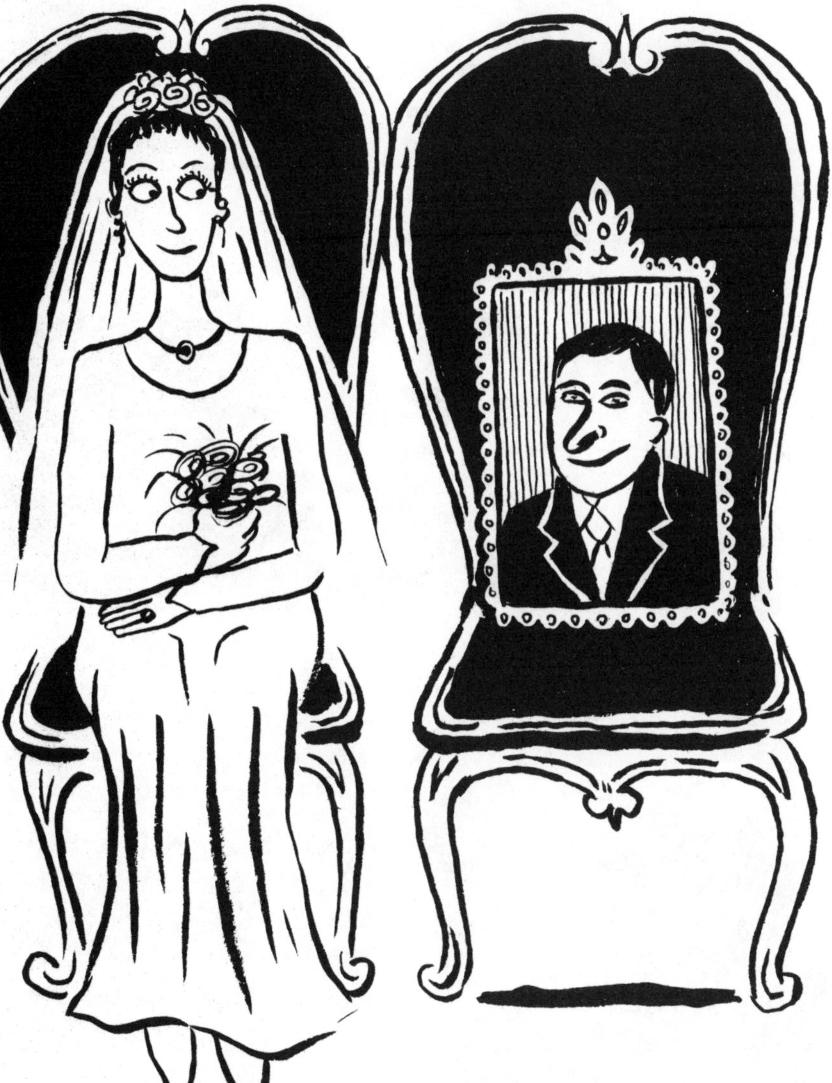

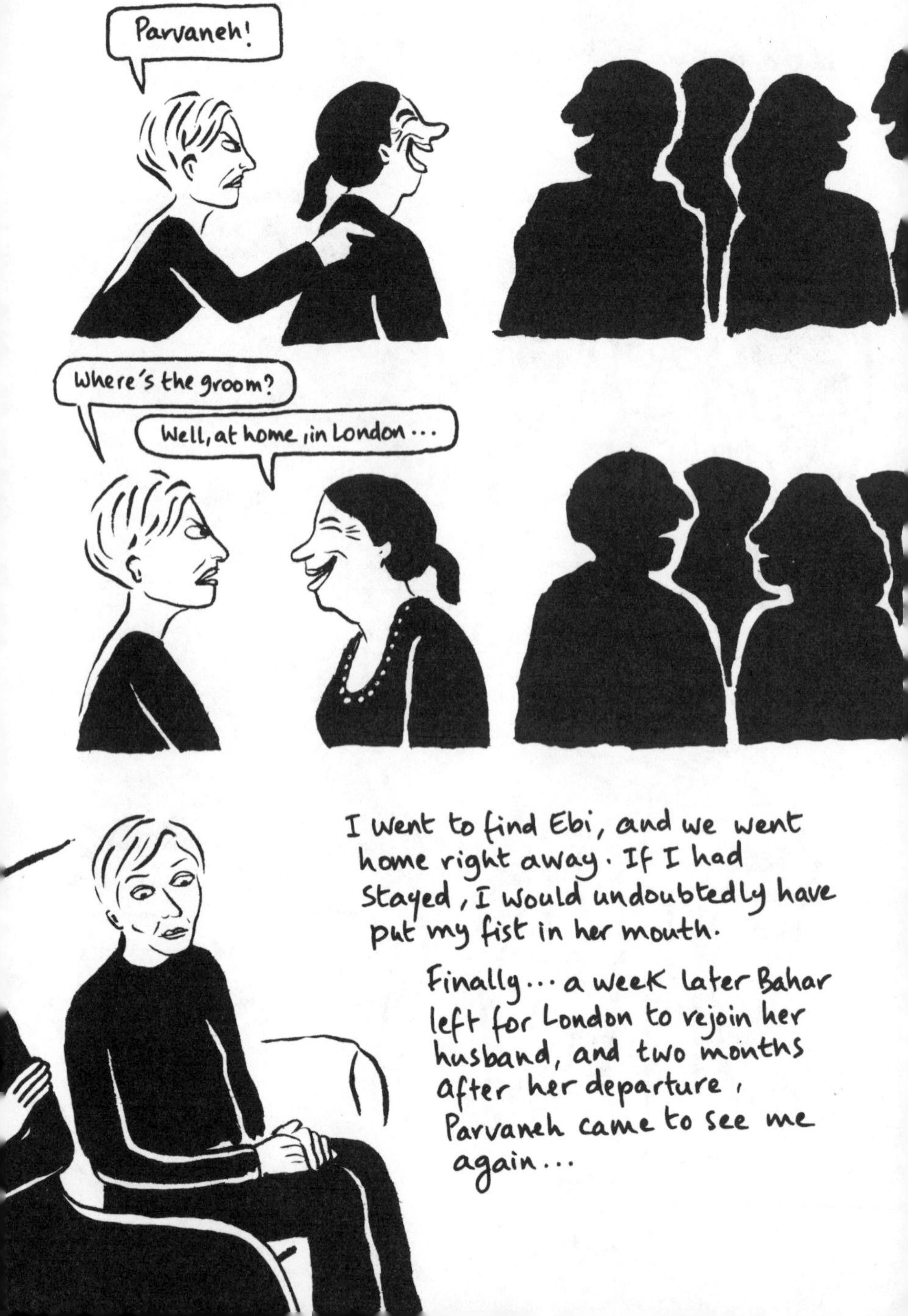
Parvaneh!
Where's the groom?
Well, at home, in London...
I went to find Ebi, and we went home right away. If I had stayed, I would undoubtedly have put my fist in her mouth.
Finally... a week later Bahar left for London to rejoin her husband, and two months after her departure, Parvaneh came to see me again...

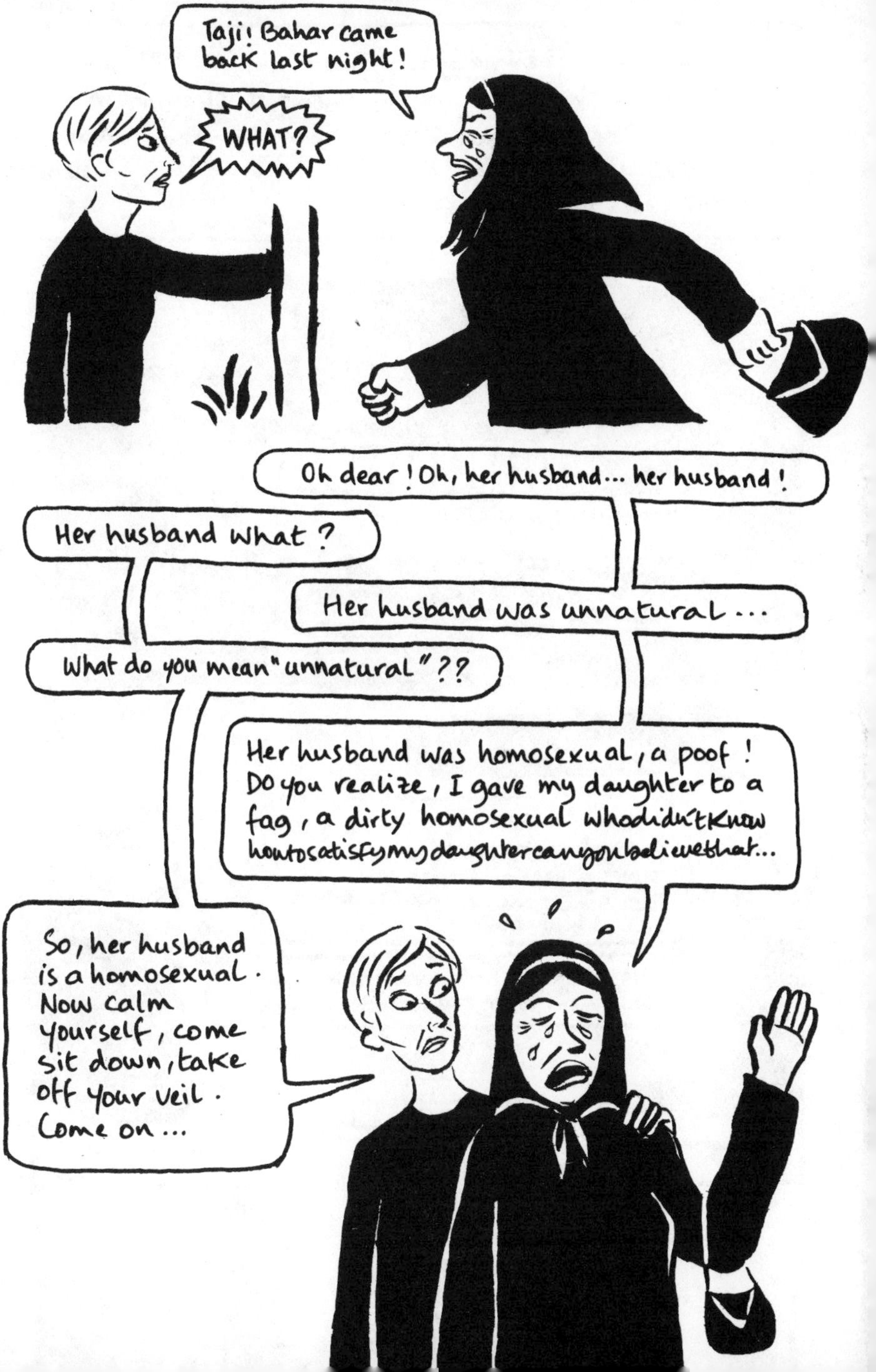
Taji! Bahar came back last night!
WHAT?
Oh dear! Oh, her husband... her husband!
Her husband what?
Her husband was unnatural...
What do you mean "unnatural"??
Her husband was homosexual, a poof! DO you realize, I gave my daughter to a fag, a dirty homosexual whodidn'tknow howtosatisfymydaughtercanyoubelievethat...
So, her husband is a homosexual. Now calm yourself, come sit down, take off your veil. Come on...

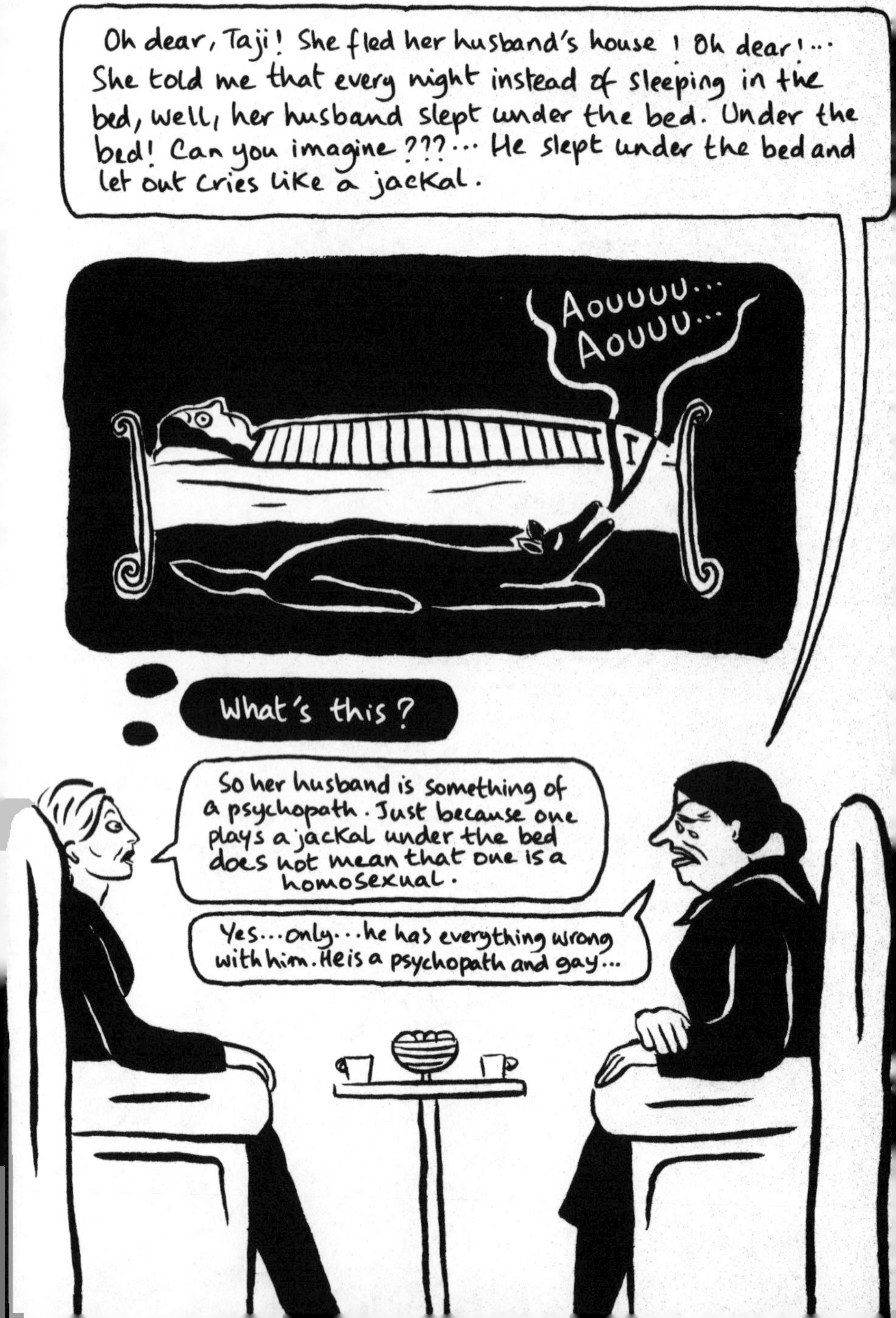

Oh dear, Taji! She fled her husband's house! Oh dear!... She told me that every night instead of sleeping in the bed, well, her husband slept under the bed. Under the bed! Can you imagine???... He slept under the bed and let out cries like a jackal.
Aouuuu... Aouuu...
What's this?
So her husband is something of a psychopath. Just because one plays a jackal under the bed does not mean that one is a homosexual.
Yes...only...he has everything wrong with him. He is a psychopath and gay...

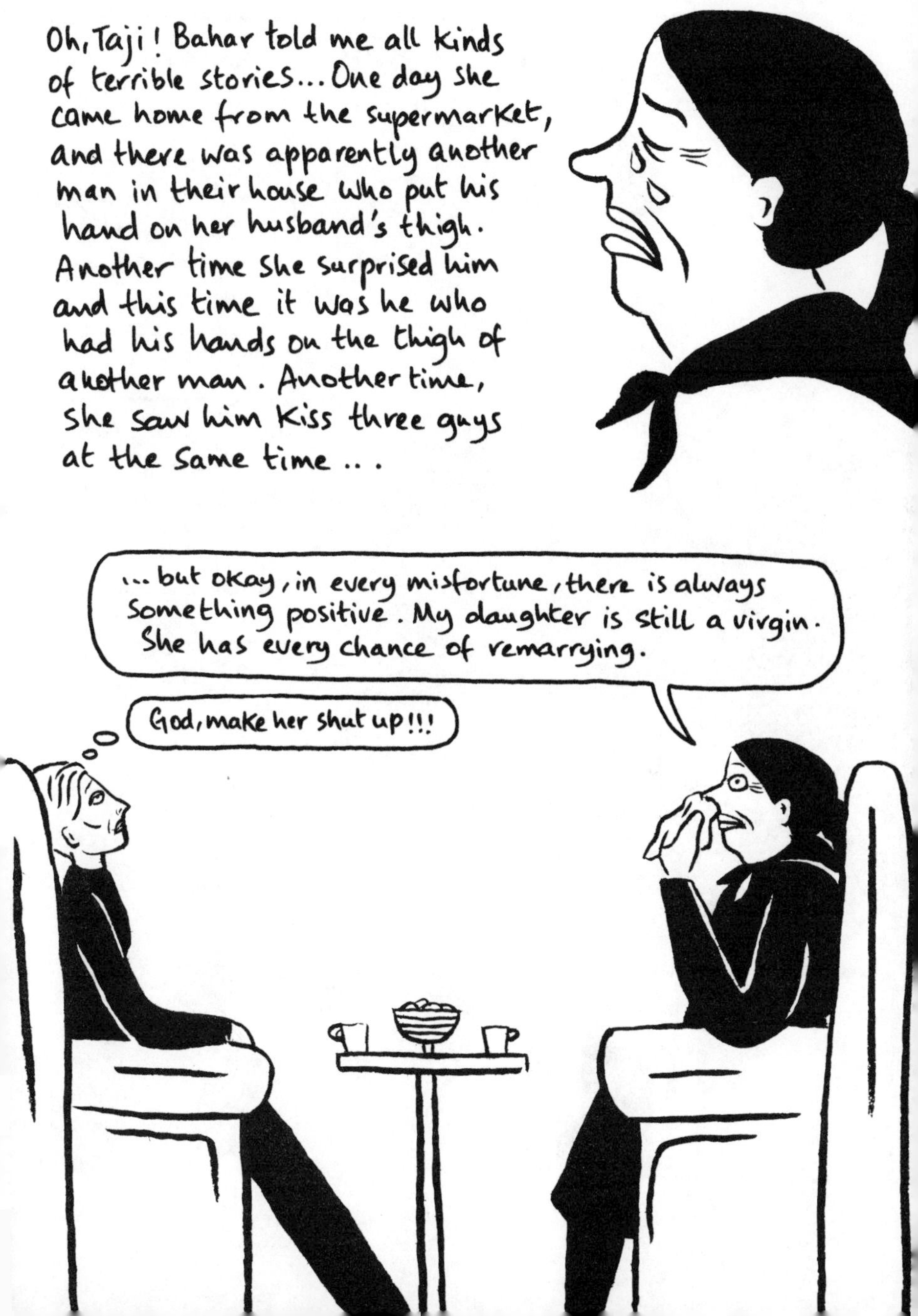
Oh, Taji! Bahar told me all kinds of terrible stories... One day she came home from the supermarket, and there was apparently another man in their house who put his hand on her husband's thigh. Another time she surprised him and this time it was he who had his hands on the thigh of another man. Another time, she saw him kiss three guys at the same time...
...but okay, in every misfortune, there is always something positive. My daughter is still a virgin. She has every chance of remarrying.
God, make her shut up!!!

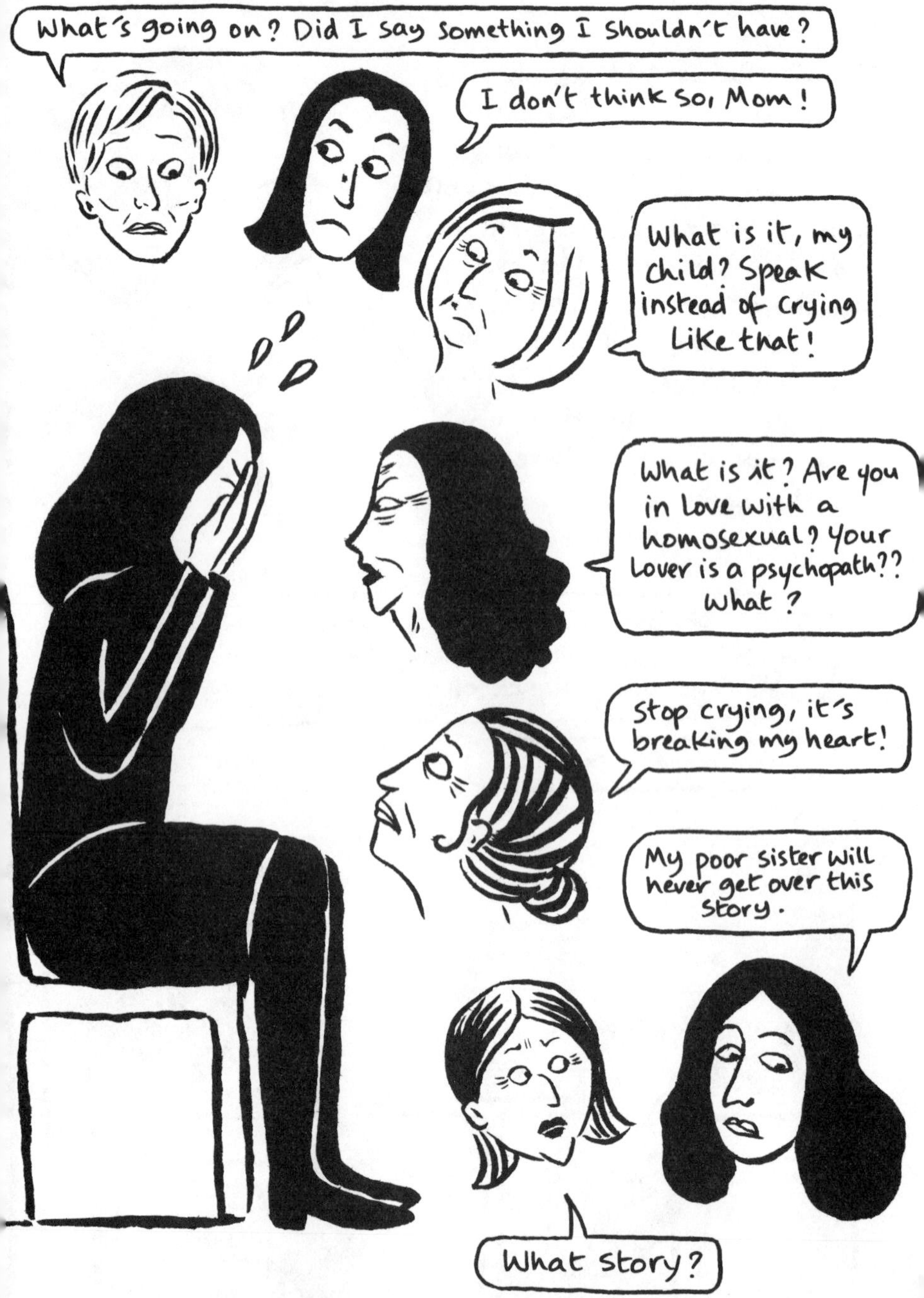
What's going on? Did I say something I shouldn't have?
I don't think so, Mom!
What is it, my child? Speak instead of crying like that!
What is it? Are you in love with a homosexual? Your lover is a psychopath?? What?
Stop crying, it's breaking my heart!
My poor sister will never get over this story.
What story?

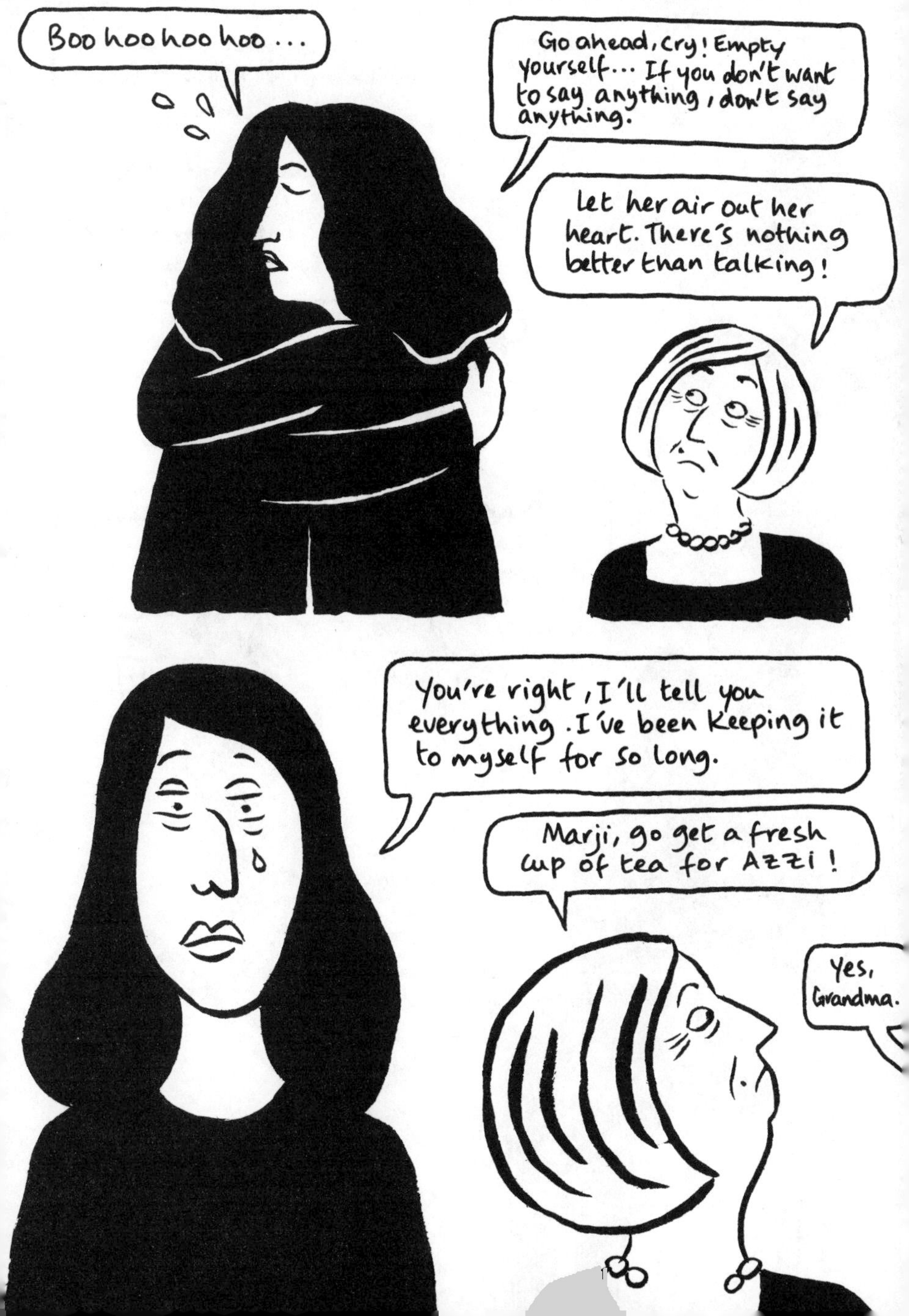
Boo hoo hoo hoo...
Go ahead, cry! Empty yourself... If you don't want to say anything, don't say anything.
Let her air out her heart. There's nothing better than talking!
You're right, I'll tell you everything. I've been keeping it to myself for so long.
Marji, go get a fresh cup of tea for Azzi!
Yes, Grandma.

Azzi was our neighbor.
She had moved into our building two years before. She lived with her sister and her parents. She was very kind and very discreet. So discreet that no one knew anything about her life.
... year of studying to be a nurse. One day, when I got back from school, my mother told me that one of our neighbors had come to see her to ask for my hand for her nephew, who lived in Switzerland and who was looking to marry a good Iranian girl from a good family.

My parents told me that the decision was entirely up to me. I thought about it for a long time. I also talked about it a lot with my sister and my girlfriends.
If I were in your place, I'd be wary.
In your place, I wouldn't hesitate for a single second. You have the chance to live in Europe, to not wear the veil anymore! To be free!!! ... What more could you want?
Here, in Iran, we have no future. Go ahead, get married, leave!!

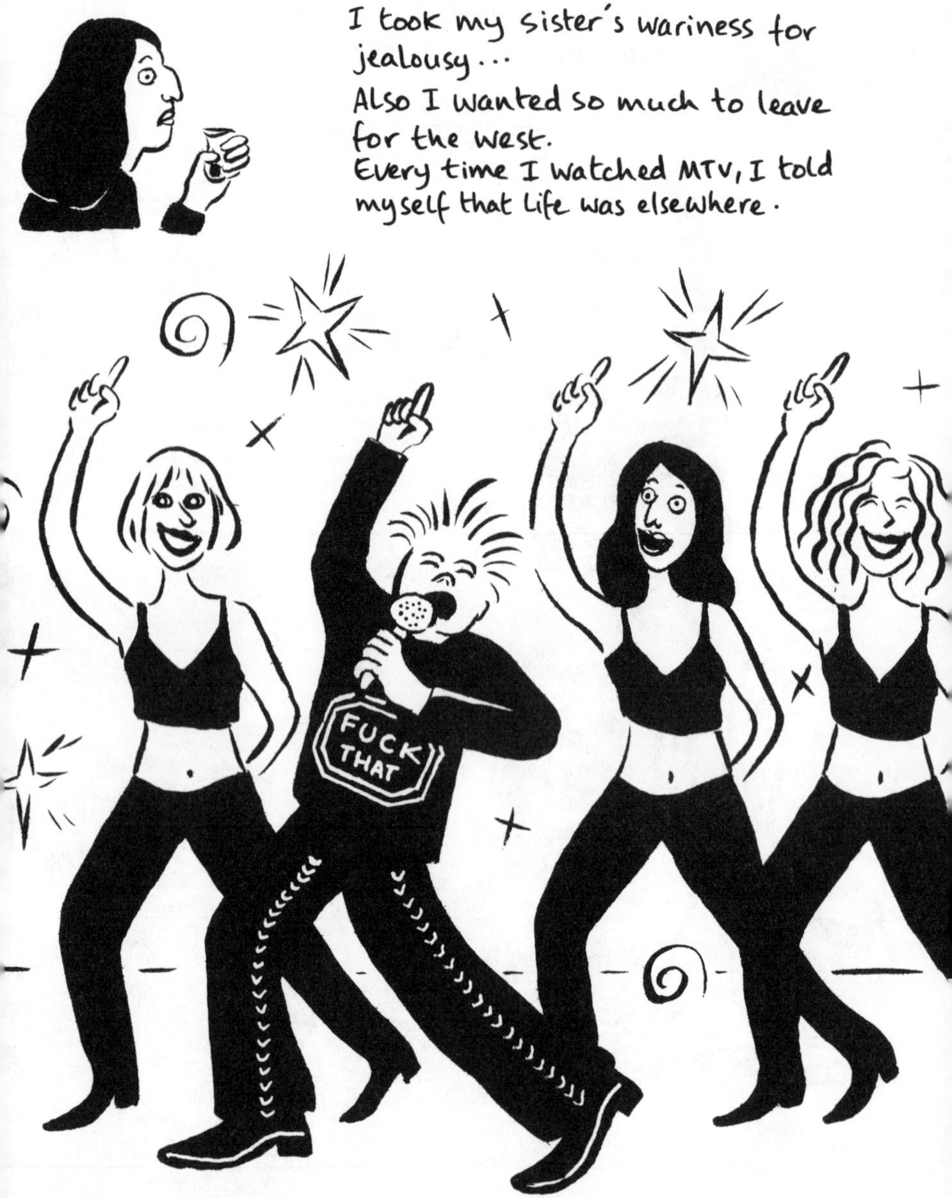
I took my sister's wariness for jealousy...
Also I wanted so much to leave for the west.
Every time I watched MTV, I told myself that life was elsewhere.
FUCK THAT

What's MTV?
You know, it's that music channel!
The one with all the assholes who sing half naked?
Yes, Grandma!
Oh, this poor Azzi is so stupid!

Finally, after thinking about it a thousand times, I told my parents that it was okay with me. So my mother called the neighbor, who right away called her brother and sister-in-law, so that they would come and officially ask for my hand. They brought me this photo of him, saying that he would be in Tehran in a month, because even if their son was handsome and intelligent and nice, I should get to know him before getting engaged! Look, this is him!

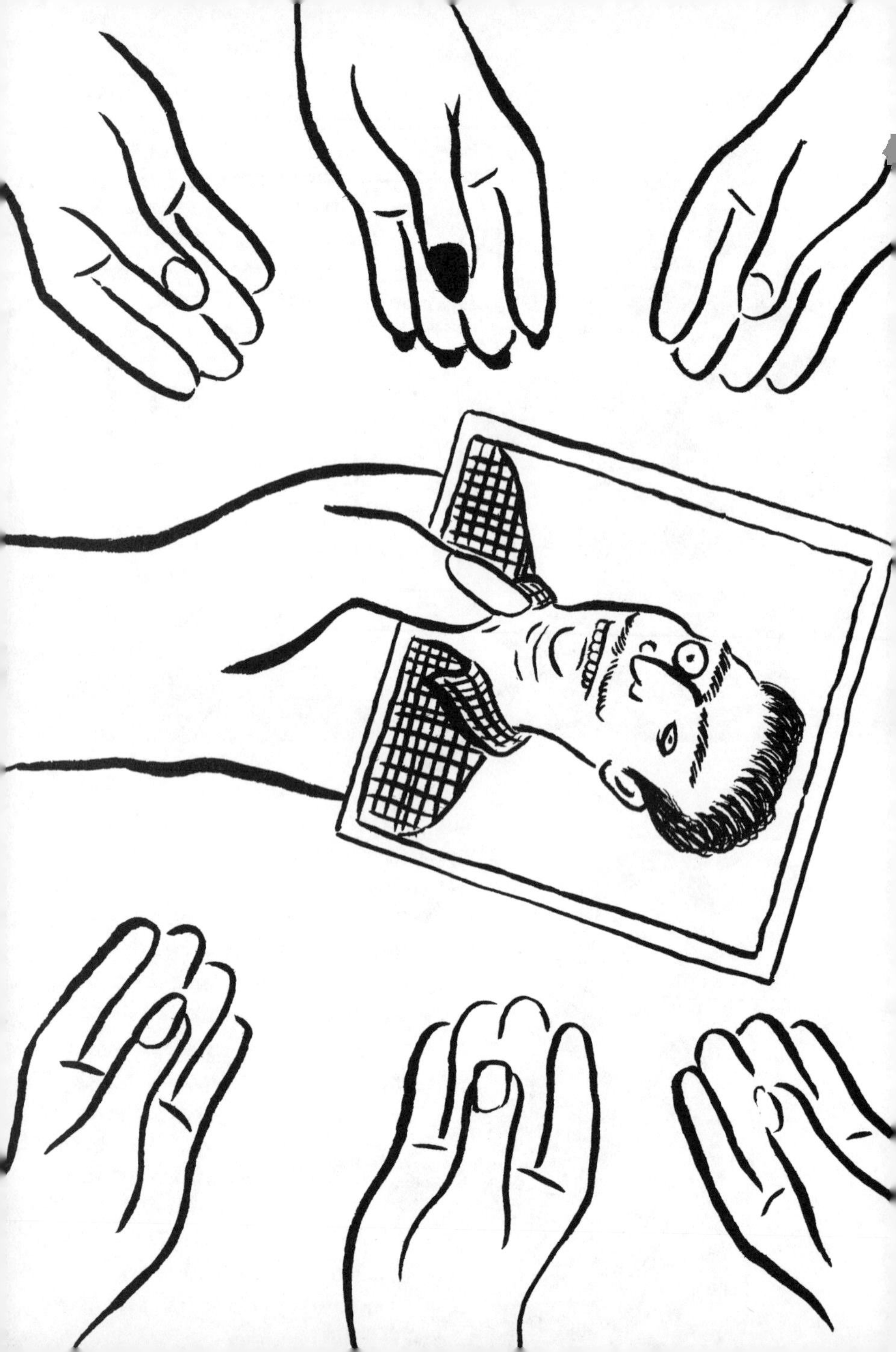

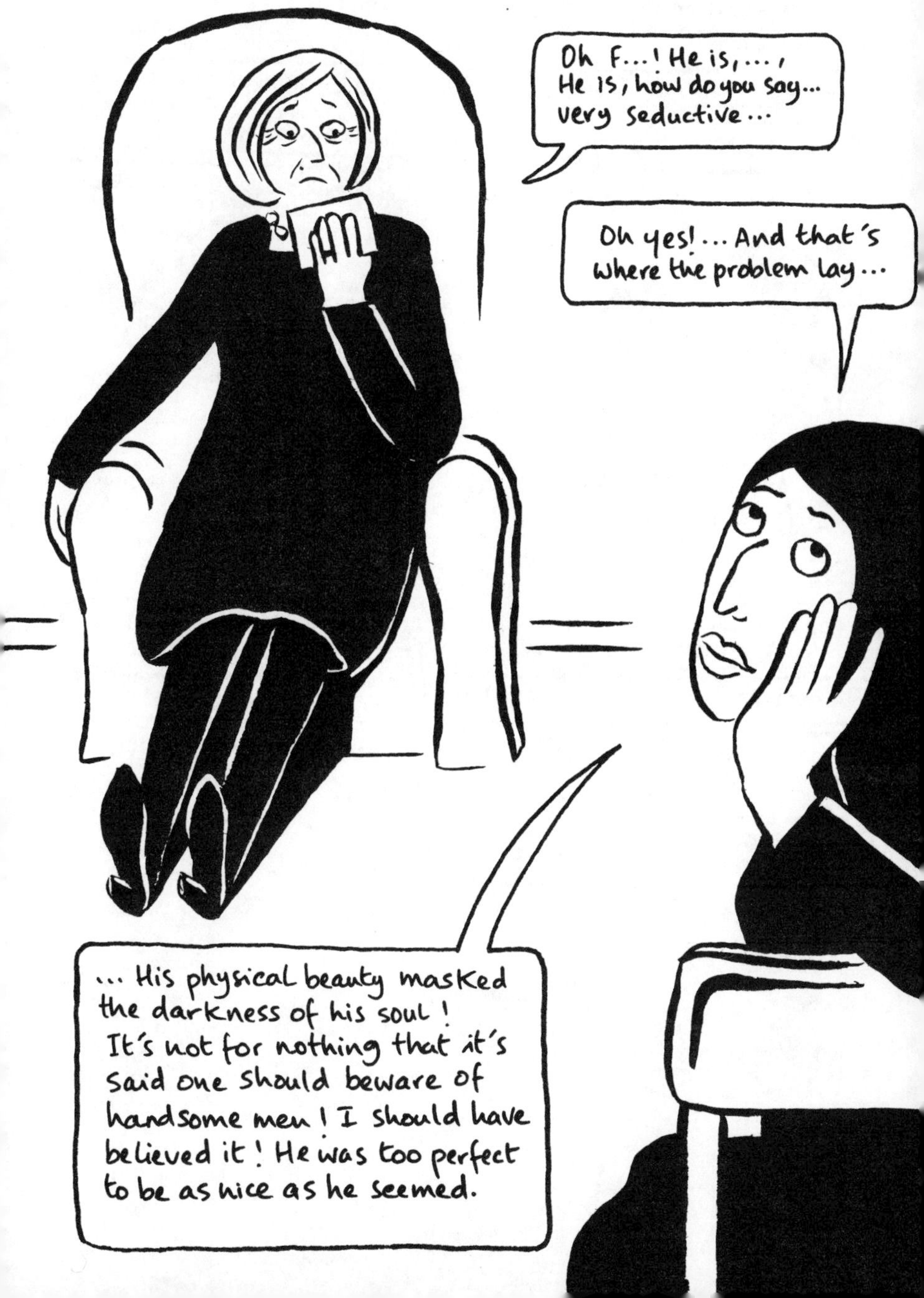
Oh F...! He is, ..., He IS, how do you say... very seductive...
Oh yes! ... And that's where the problem lay...
... His physical beauty masked the darkness of his soul! It's not for nothing that it's said one should beware of handsome men! I should have believed it! He was too perfect to be as nice as he seemed.

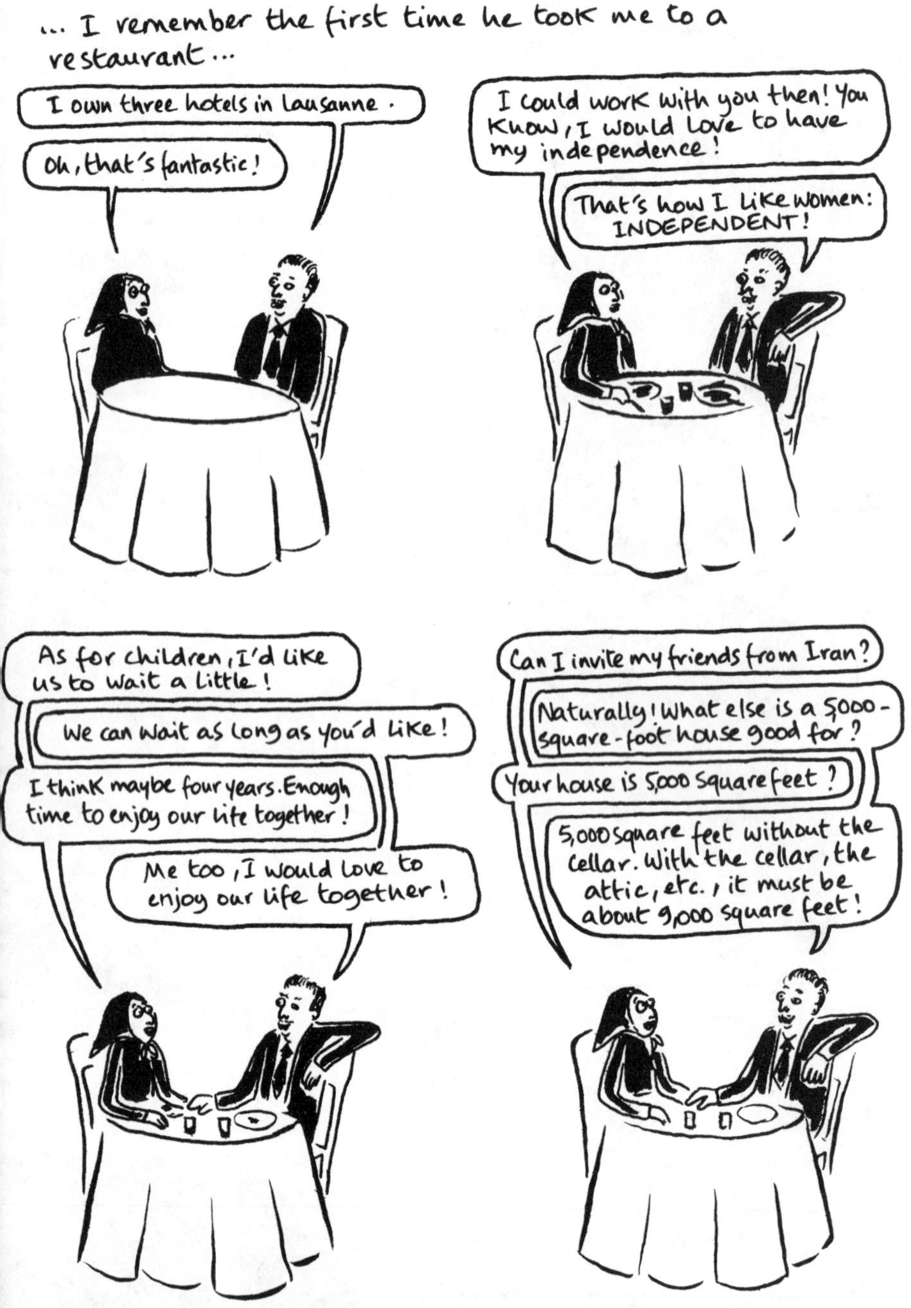
... I remember the first time he took me to a restaurant...
I own three hotels in Lausanne.
Oh, that's fantastic!
I could work with you then! You know, I would love to have my independence!
That's how I like women: INDEPENDENT!
As for children, I'd like us to wait a little!
We can wait as long as you'd like!
I think maybe four years. Enough time to enjoy our life together!
Me too, I would love to enjoy our life together!
Can I invite my friends from Iran?
Naturally! What else is a 5,000-square-foot house good for?
Your house is 5,000 square feet?
5,000 square feet without the cellar. With the cellar, the attic, etc., it must be about 9,000 square feet!

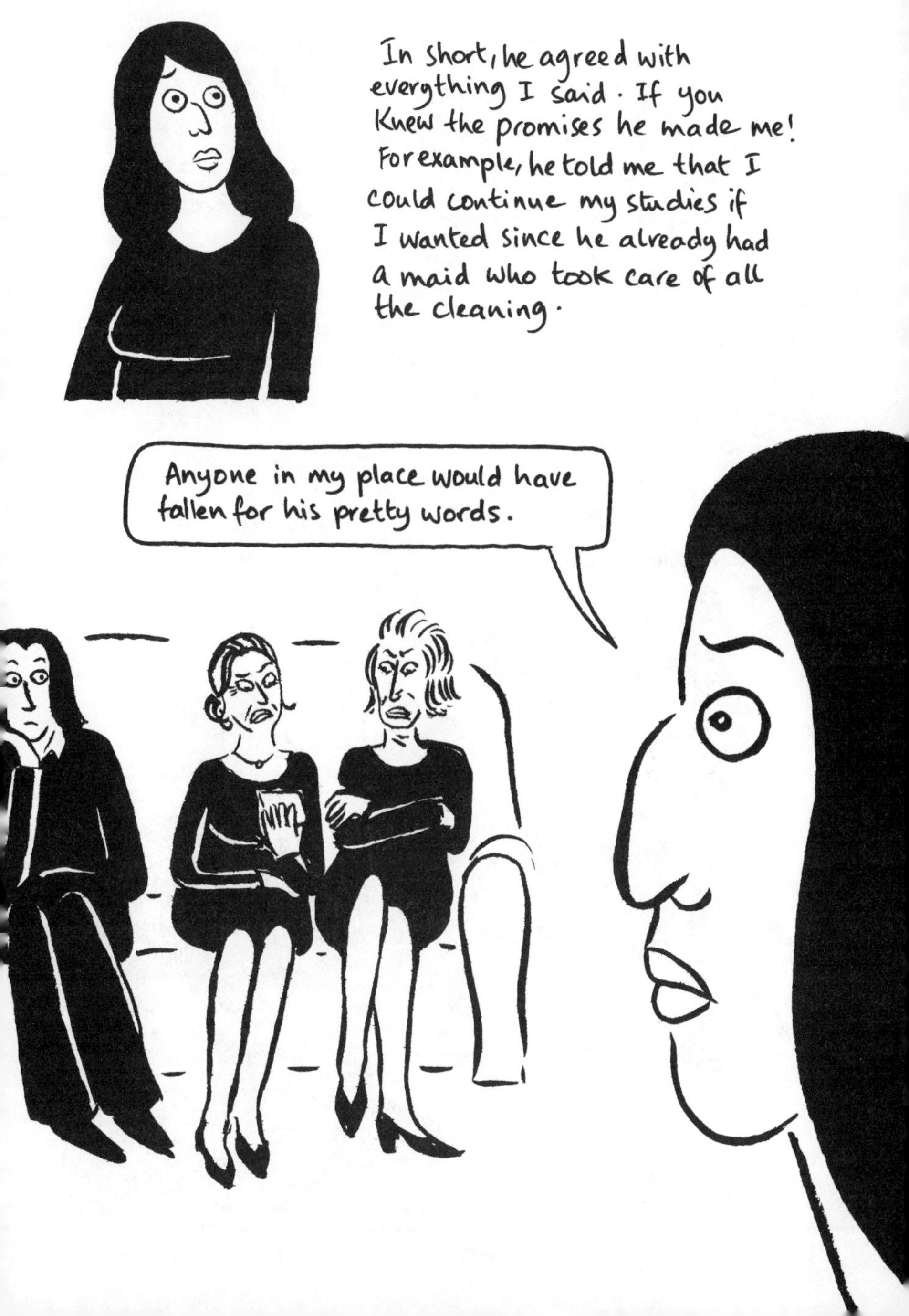
In short, he agreed with everything I said. If you Knew the promises he made me! For example, he told me that I could continue my studies if I wanted since he already had a maid who took care of all the cleaning.
Anyone in my place would have fallen for his pretty words.

... And so we were married. I went to the best hairdresser in Tehran. Ever since my dear and earliest childhood, I had wished for only one thing, and that was to see myself dressed as a bride. My dream had just come true. Even better, my dress was made by Mrs. Tabatabai, you know, the super-famous designer. We received 700 guests. I was offered so many jewels I would have needed several more fingers, arms, ears and necks to be able to wear them all. It was incredible.*

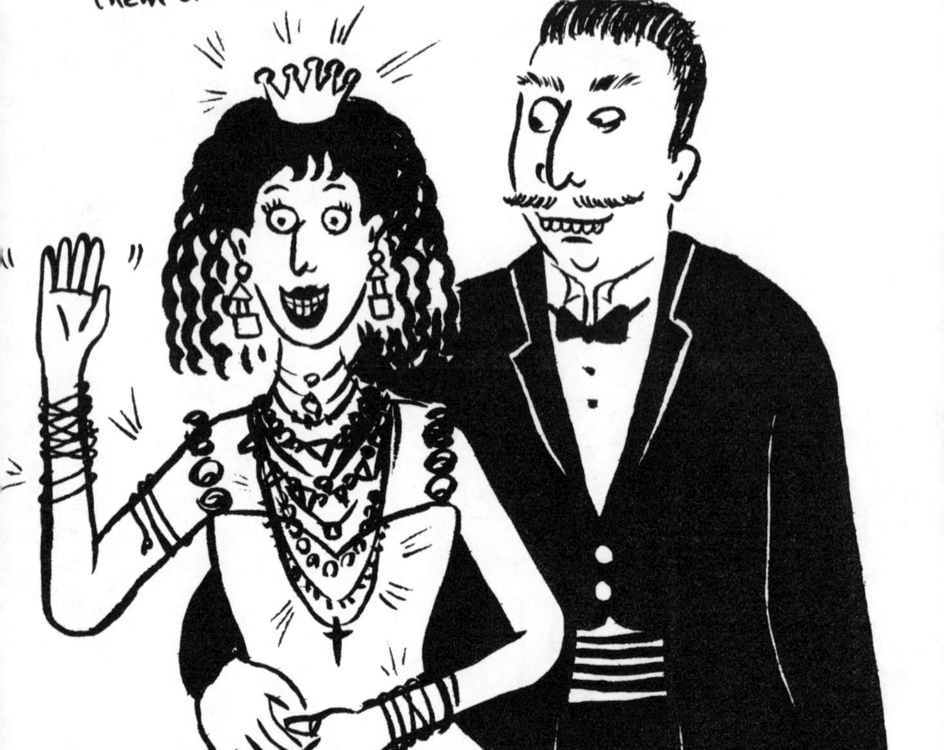

* During a wedding in Iran, almost all the gifts are for the bride.

The day after our wedding night, he began to lay the foundation for his diabolic plan.

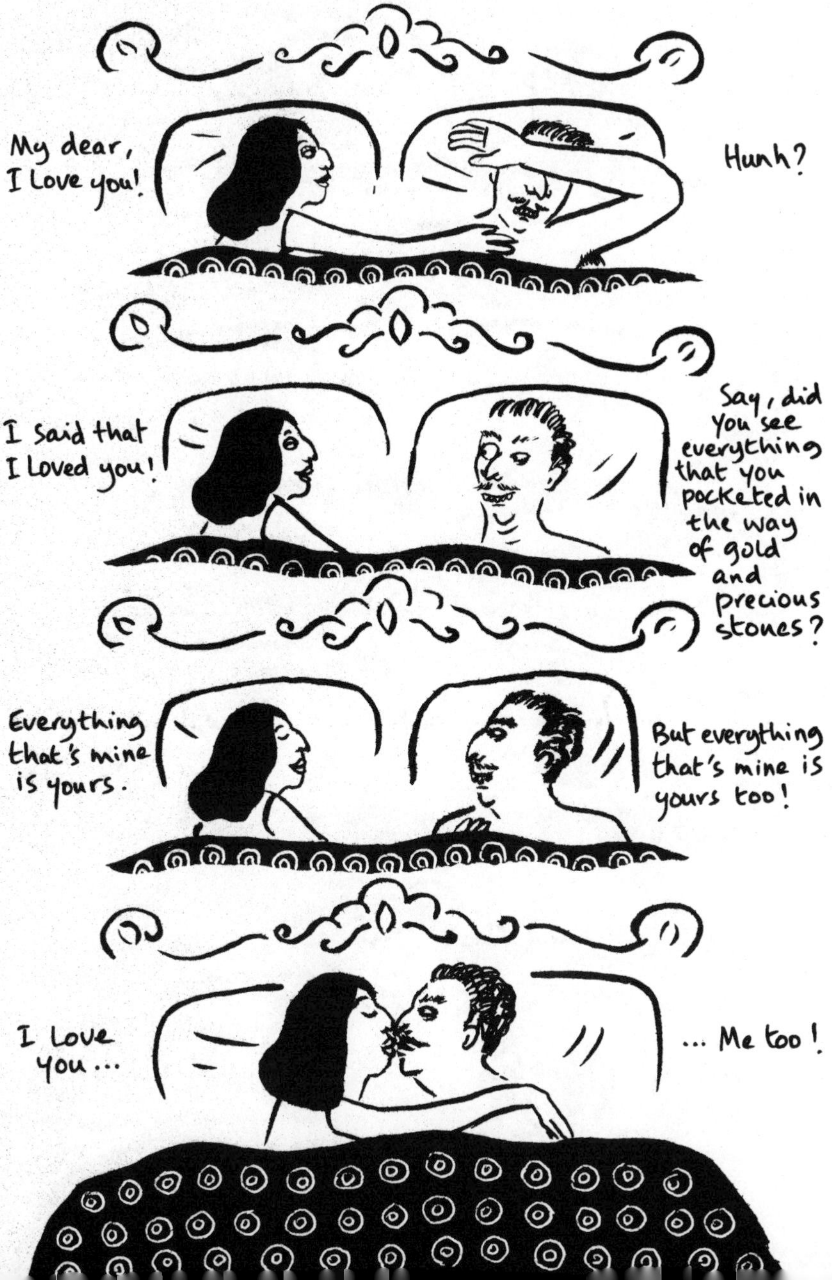
My dear, I Love you!
Hunh?
I said that I Loved you!
Say, did you see everything that you pocketed in the way of gold and precious stones?
Everything that's mine is yours.
But everything that's mine is yours too!
I Love you...
... Me too!

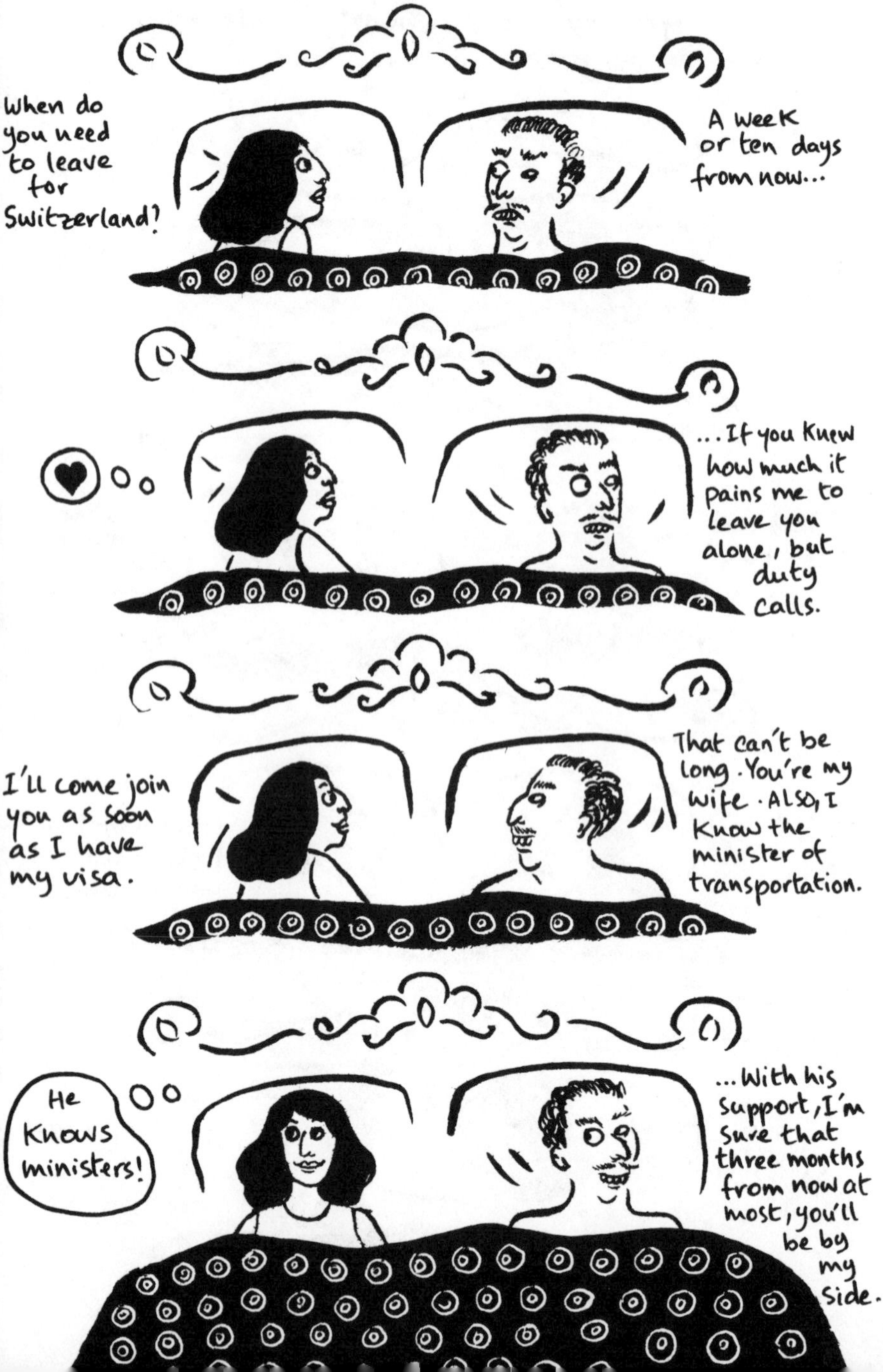

When do you need to leave for Switzerland?
A week or ten days from now...
...If you knew how much it pains me to leave you alone, but duty calls.
I'll come join you as soon as I have my visa.
That can't be long. You're my wife. ALSO, I know the minister of transportation.
He knows ministers!
...With his support, I'm sure that three months from now at most, you'll be by my side.

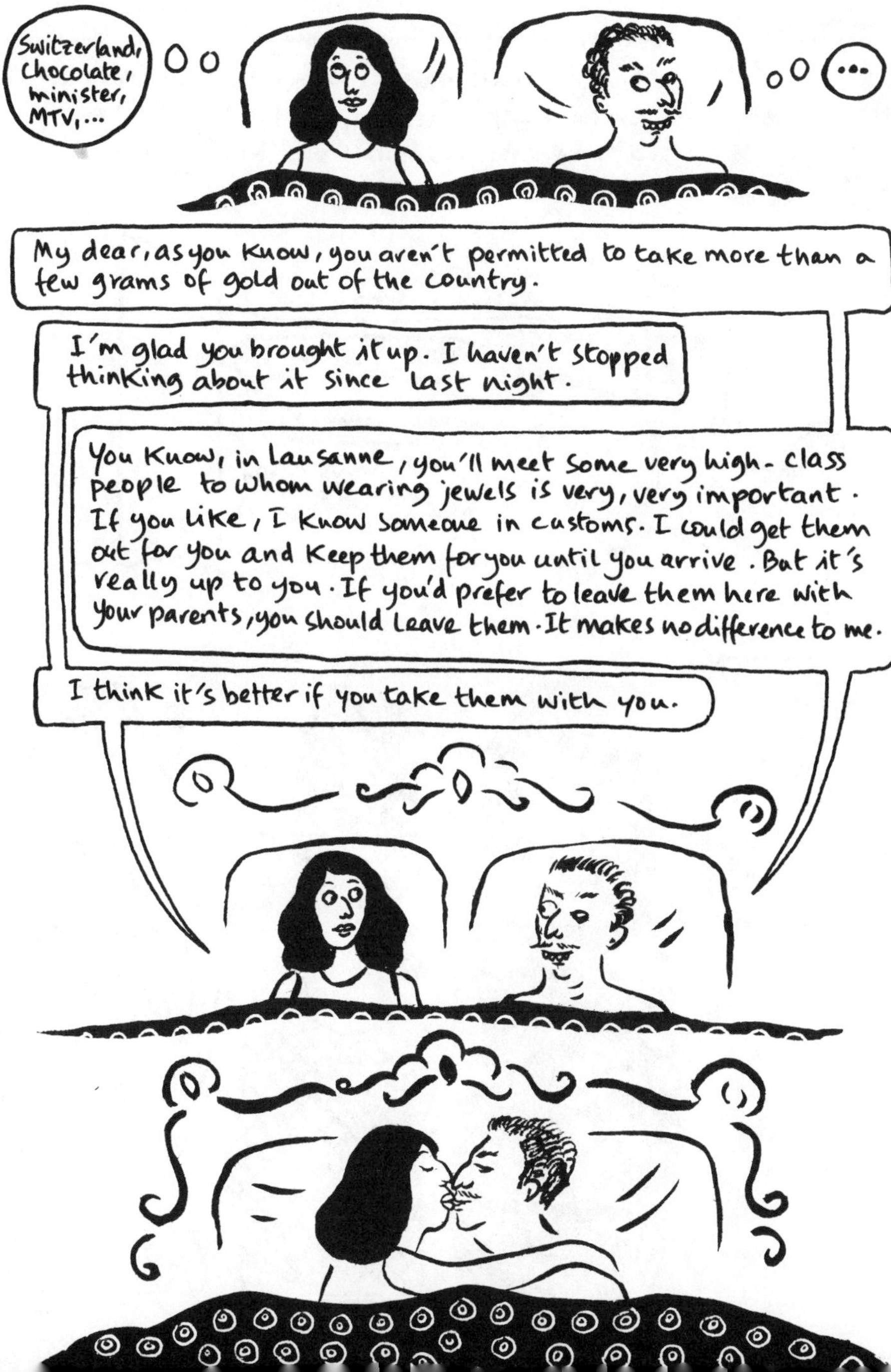

Switzerland, chocolate, minister, MTV,...
...
My dear, as you know, you aren't permitted to take more than a few grams of gold out of the country.
I'm glad you brought it up. I haven't stopped thinking about it since last night.
You know, in Lausanne, you'll meet some very high-class people to whom wearing jewels is very, very important. If you like, I know someone in customs. I could get them out for you and keep them for you until you arrive. But it's really up to you. If you'd prefer to leave them here with your parents, you should leave them. It makes no difference to me.
I think it's better if you take them with you.

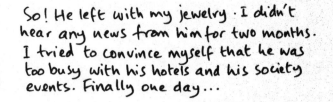

So! He left with my jewelry. I didn't hear any news from him for two months. I tried to convince myself that he was too busy with his hotels and his society events. Finally one day...

Azzi! You have a letter!

A letter? From whom?

From your husband!

God be praised!

So, so! What does he say? Is it done? Is your visa ready?

Uh, Oh

He... He wants a divorce

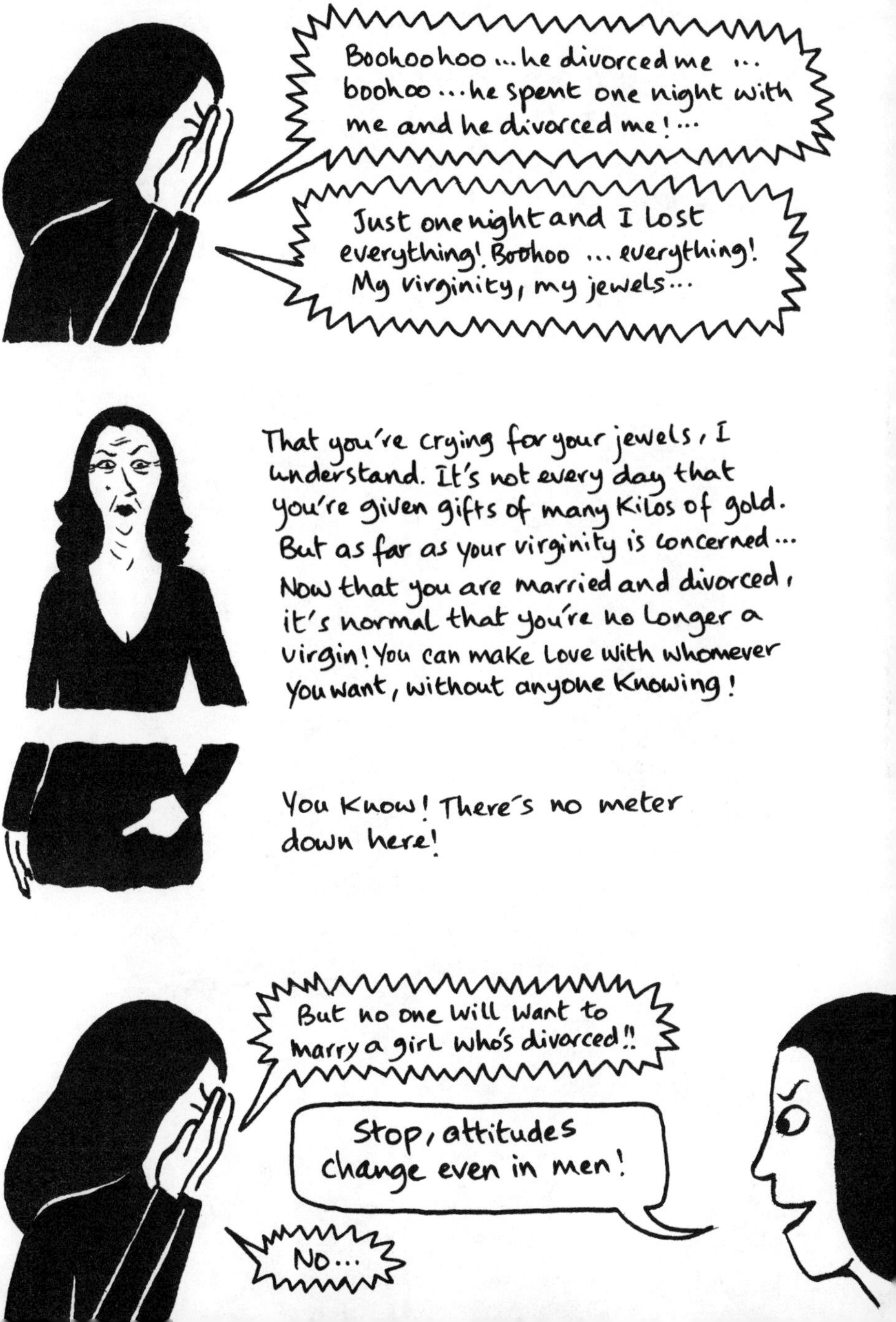
Boohoohoo ... he divorced me ... boohoo ... he spent one night with me and he divorced me! ...
Just one night and I lost everything! Boohoo ... everything! My virginity, my jewels ...
That you're crying for your jewels, I understand. It's not every day that you're given gifts of many kilos of gold. But as far as your virginity is concerned ... Now that you are married and divorced, it's normal that you're no longer a virgin! You can make love with whomever you want, without anyone knowing!
You know! There's no meter down here!
But no one will want to marry a girl who's divorced!!
Stop, attitudes change even in men!
No ...

Yes! I have a cousin who always maintained that he would only marry a virgin. The other day he called me to tell me that he had changed his mind. When I congratulated him on his enlightenment, he answered: "Marji, if I changed my mind, it's because no girls are virgins anymore." That's what he told me word for word. Do you see?

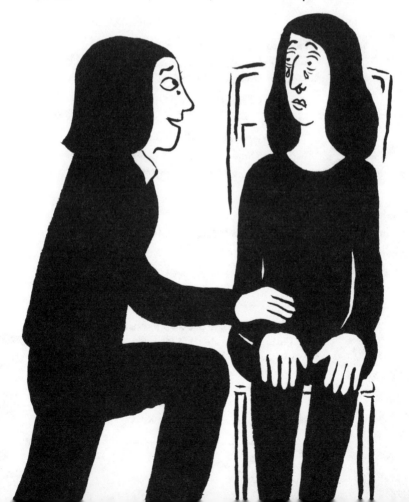

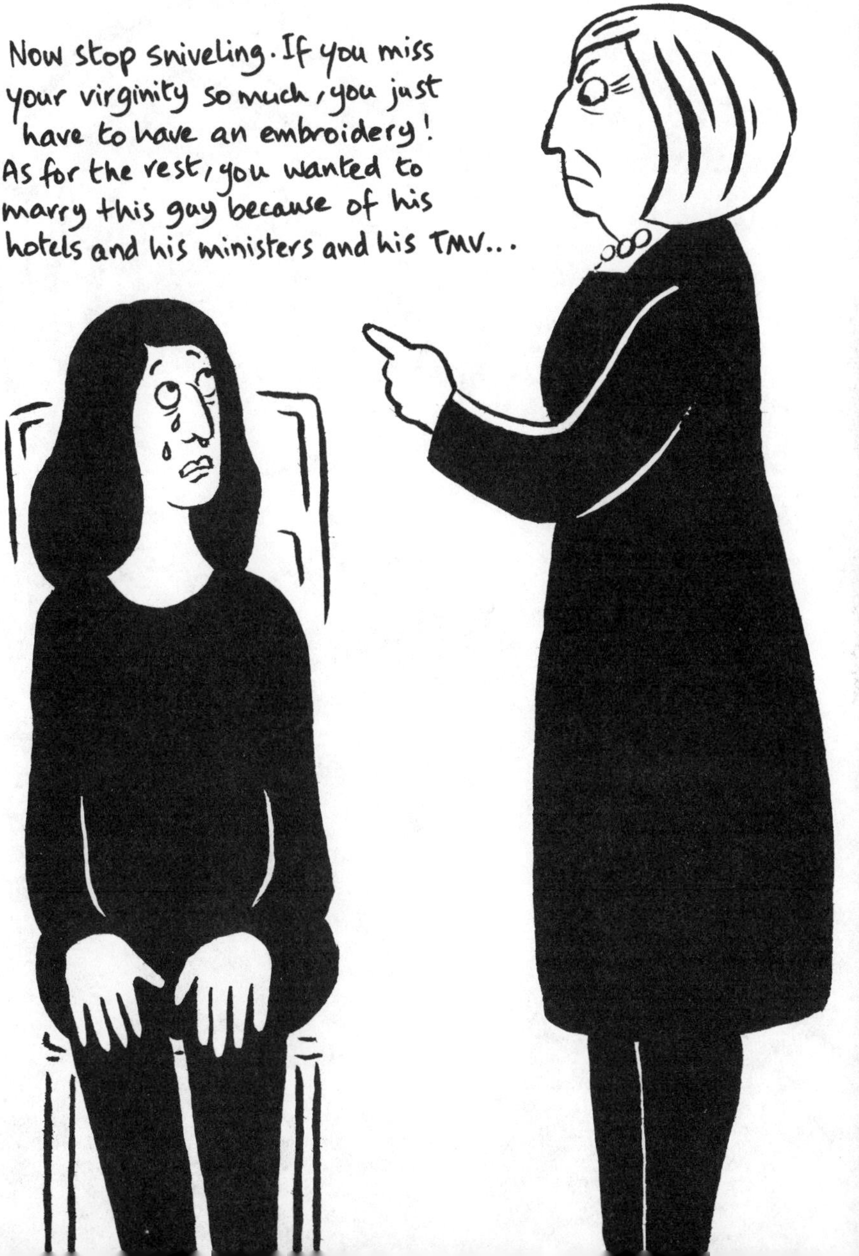
Now stop sniveling. If you miss your virginity so much, you just have to have an embroidery! As for the rest, you wanted to marry this guy because of his hotels and his ministers and his TMV...

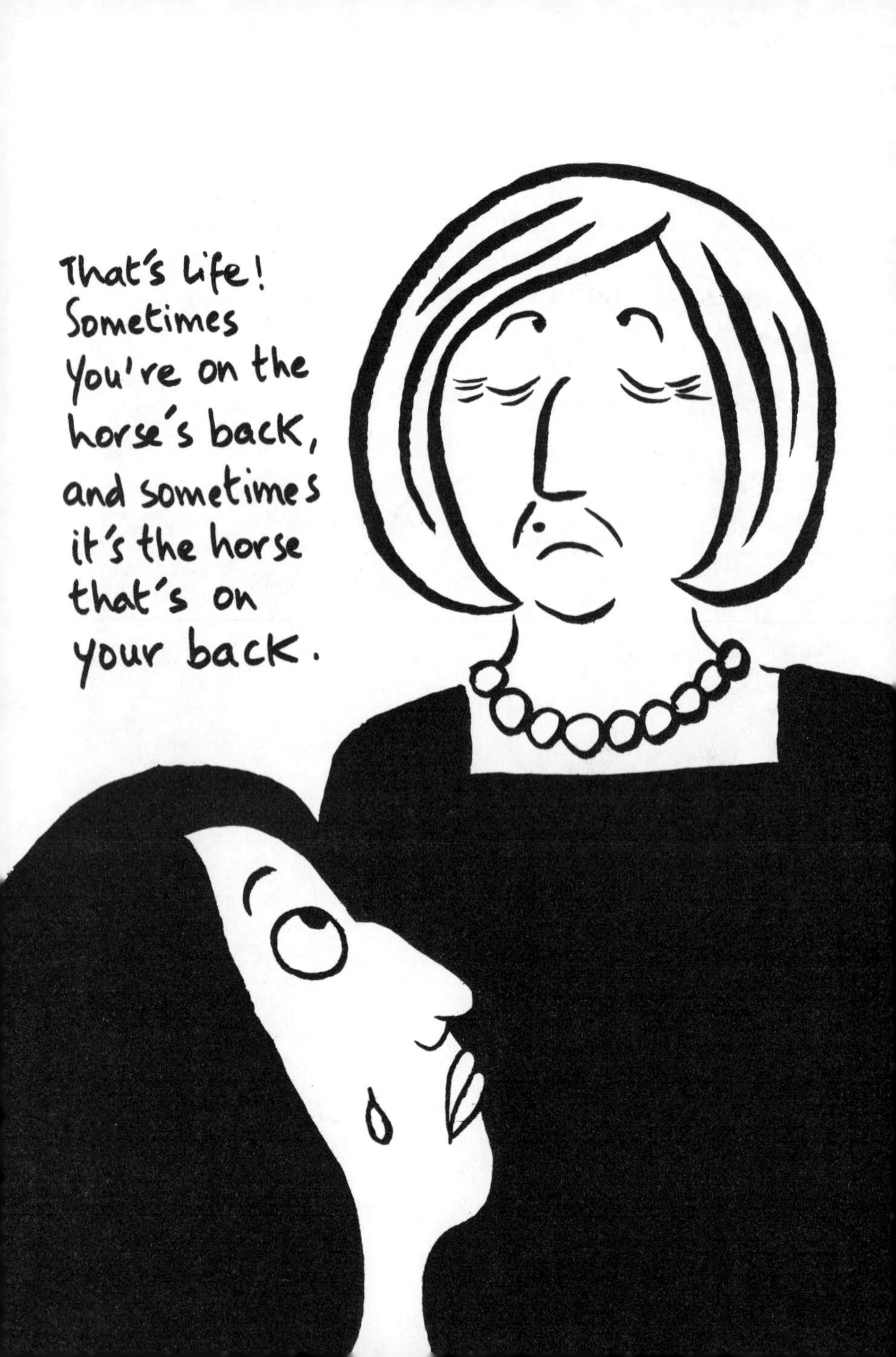
That's life! Sometimes you're on the horse's back, and sometimes it's the horse that's on your back.

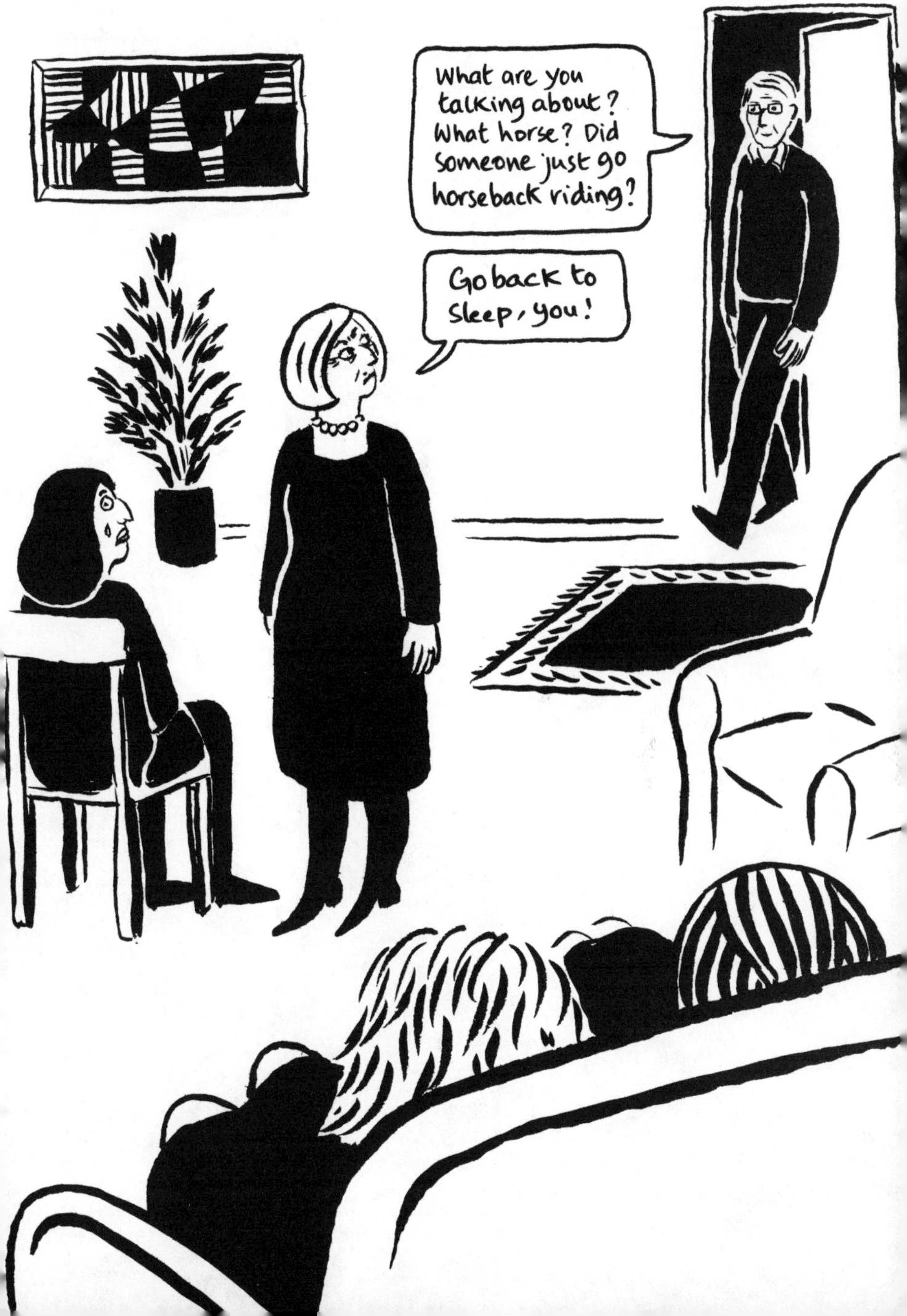
What are you talking about? What horse? Did someone just go horseback riding?
Go back to sleep, you!

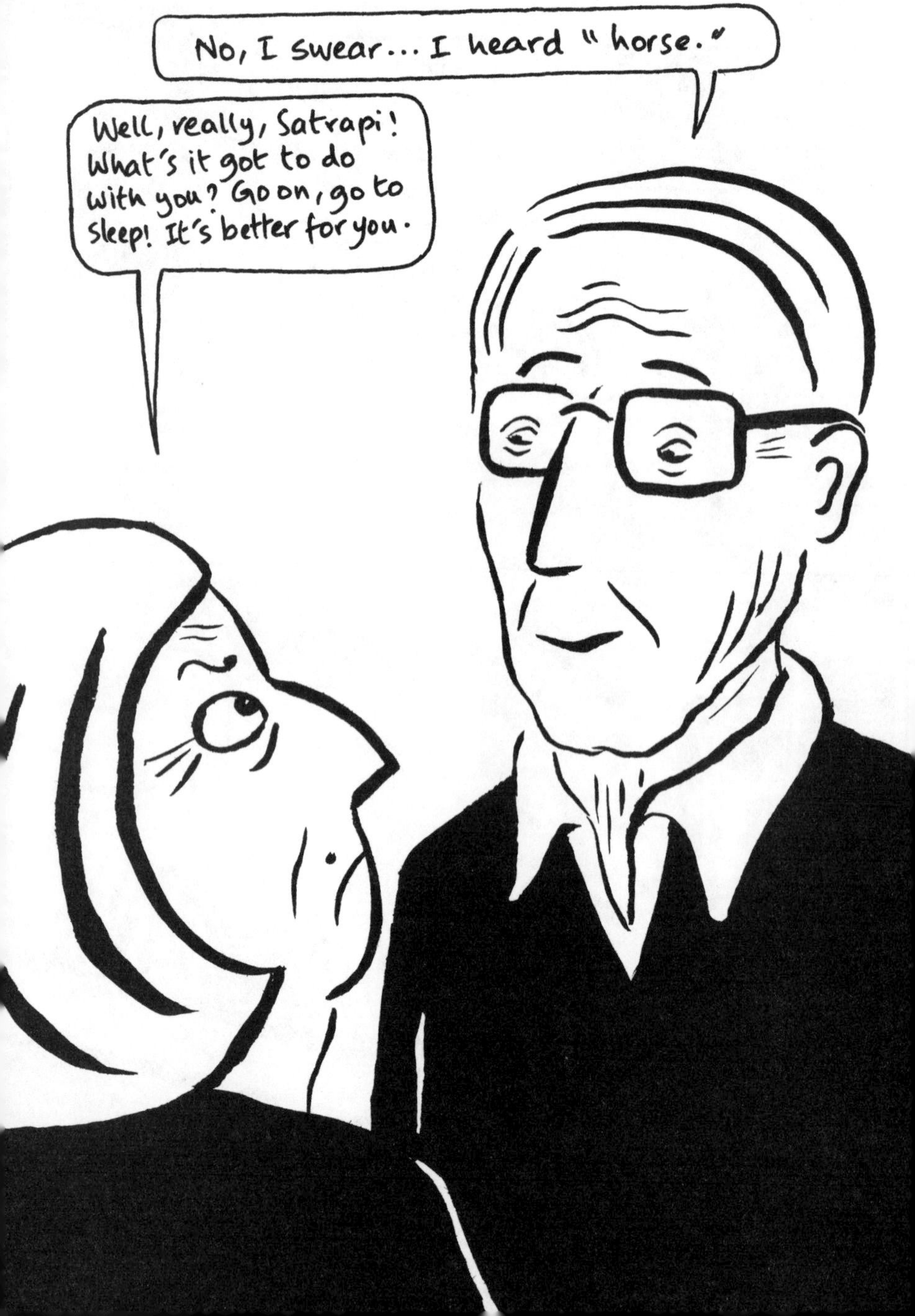
No, I swear... I heard "horse."
Well, really, Satrapi! What's it got to do with you? Go on, go to sleep! It's better for you.

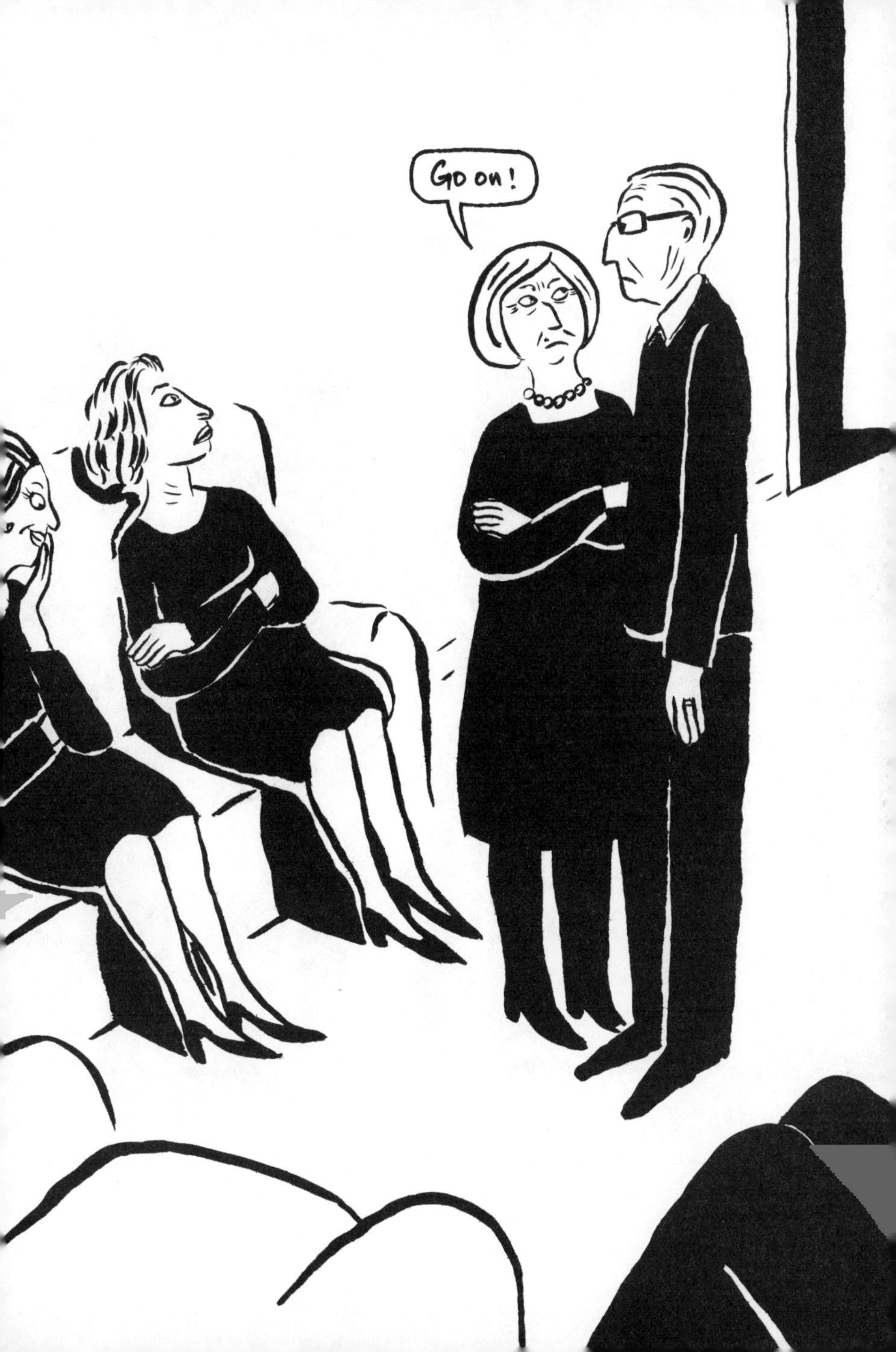
Go on!

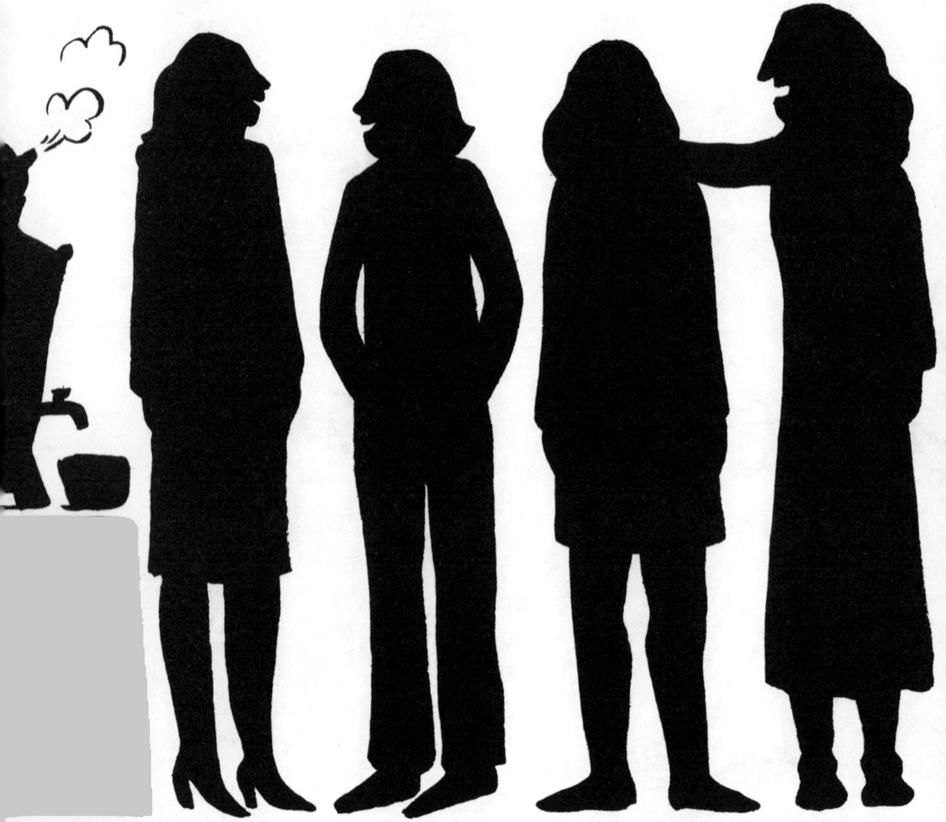

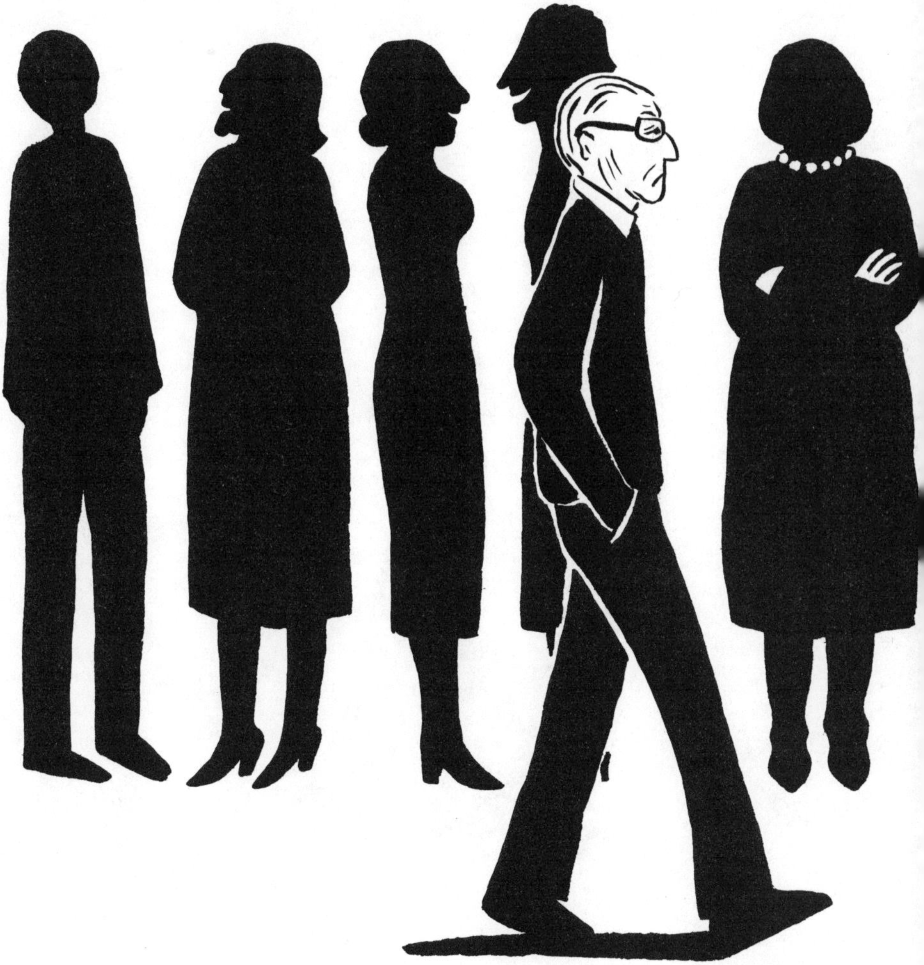

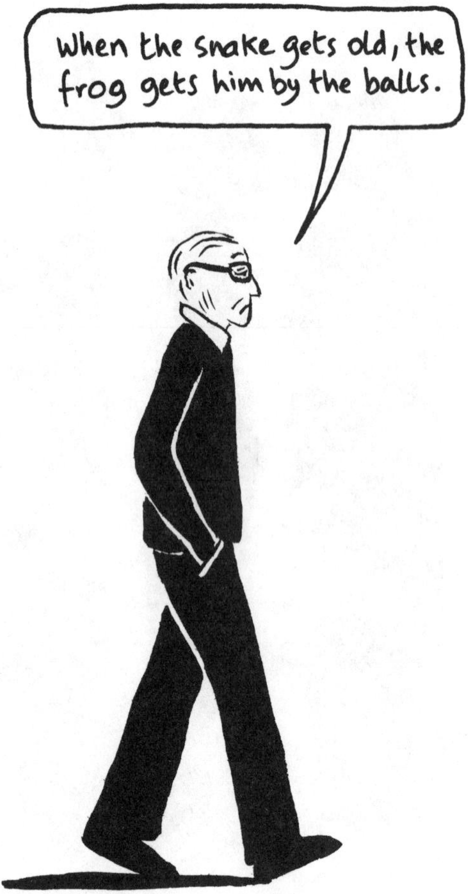
When the snake gets old, the frog gets him by the balls.